The Greatest
War Films of
All Time

D0645348

CITADEL PRESS BOOKS are published by

Kensington Publishing Corp.
850 Third Avenue
New York, NY 10022

Copyright © 2004 Andrew J. Rausch

All rights reserved. No part of this book may be reproduced in any form or by any means without the prior written consent of the publisher, excepting brief quotes used in reviews.

All Kensington titles, imprints, and distributed lines are available at special quantity discounts for bulk purchases for sales promotions, premiums, fund-raising, educational, or institutional use. Special book excerpts or customized printings can also be created to fit specific needs. For details, write or phone the office of the Kensington special sales manager: Kensington Publishing Corp., 850 Third Avenue, New York, NY 10022, attn: Special Sales Department, phone 1-800-221-2647.

CITADEL PRESS and the Citadel logo are Reg. U.S. Pat. & TM Off.

First printing: February 2004

10 9 8 7 6 5 4 3 2 1

Printed in the United States of America

Library of Congress Control Number: 2003106190

ISBN 0-8065-2470-7

In memory of
Leo and Francis Rausch.

Contents

⁓

Foreword

~

Ironically, this foreword was composed on Wednesday, March 19, 2003, as the United States was on the eve of war with Iraq. That this looming conflict is of great moral complexity and the cause of political disagreement highlights what makes war and the films about it so important and interesting.

War is life at its most extreme. Loss of life is always possible and, in war, often imminent. Choices in war have a huge and immediate impact on the life and death of individuals, ideologies, and nations. Life during war is paradoxically at its most basic in the microcosm (Survive!) and its most complicated in the "big picture" (Why fight? Who's "right"? How do we win? What do we do once we've won?). War pushes human behavior to its outer limits: War brings out the worst and the best in human beings. Fear is at its most extreme. Love is at its most passionate. Hate is at its blindest. Friendship is at its deepest. Cruelty is at its most vicious.

War films have been used as patriotic rallying cries; they have been made as antiwar statements. There are also films that depict the drama of war without taking sides or stances. One thing I ask of a war film is: Are the filmmakers honest in the way they depict warfare? I rankle at films that disingenuously make war look like a purely heroic and noble endeavor, movies that reduce the experience of war to a man going off to glory and coming home a hero. Such war movies take the blood and pain and loss out of war. If a film makes warfare look grand and glorious, fifteen-year-olds will leave the theater with a very different point of view than if they are presented with *All Quiet on the Western Front*. War is unique: Most people have had the experience of falling in love or many of the other things someone might make a film about. They can compare their own experiences to what is depicted in film and judge whether or not what they are seeing is truthful. But most modern western people haven't been to war, so what they see on film is as close to the reality as they're ever going to get. People internalize those images and begin to believe that real-life war is just as it is onscreen.

The reality is, even a "good" war is awful. World War II was absolutely morally justifiable and unavoidable, but it was still horrific. On the human level, it still boiled down to bunches of naïve young human beings—most of whom had no political say in their nation's choices and whose national allegiance was simply an accident of birth—trying not to die and trying to kill other naïve young human beings with whom they had no personal conflict.

War movies can be wildly effective short-term propaganda tools, but they often achieve that by reducing the "enemy" from a human being to an evil or cowardly caricature (often both). We make them less than us in order to bolster our spirit and confidence, but also to make killing them less difficult, less of a moral quagmire.

Another responsibility of someone making a film about war is to portray history and the ghosts of the people who lived and died for the things they believed in. Filmmakers affect society's perceptions of historical events. Whether treating the Alamo or Vietnam, they have to be careful to make sure they aren't just bending history to fit the fashion of the moment. Or telling people what they want to hear.

On the other hand, war movies can capture the strange exhilaration of war: the triumphs within misery of the prisoner escaping against all odds; the random acts of kindness in the midst of cruelties; the brilliant plans that change the course of the conflict and, with it, the future of our planet.

The drama of war is as old as society itself: Shakespeare loved war stories. The Greeks dramatized war and its issues. One can only hope that we will someday live in a world where our war films will be important as anthropological records of a time past, instead of what they are now: a mirror into the souls of the present and a warning about the possible graves of the future.

War involves tiny individuals and huge armies, primitive emotions and neat, gleaming technology. It is explosions and quiet and tears and a shared laugh and a stolen kiss before dying. It is epic and personal. What could be more cinematic?

—Keith Gordon

The Greatest War Films of All Time

Quiz No. 1:

ALL QUIET ON THE WESTERN FRONT (1930)

Screenplay by Maxwell Anderson, George Abbott, and Del Andrews (based on a novel by Erich Maria Remarque)
Directed by Lewis Milestone
Starring Louis Wolheim, Lew Ayres, and John Wray
Universal Pictures
Available on VHS, DVD

> *You think it's beautiful to die for your country. The first bombardment taught us better. When it comes to dying for country, it's better not to die at all.*
> —PAUL BAUMER

The first significant American "talkie" to deal with the subject of war, *All Quiet on the Western Front* is one of the finest films ever made. Lewis Milestone's direction is near perfect and the cinematography is stunning. Unlike King Vidor's *The Big Parade* (1925), which had been released only five years before, *All Quiet on the Western Front* shows the all-too-real horrors of modern warfare without being sidetracked by the obligatory love story subplot. More than seventy years after its initial release, the film's characters, story, and dialogue retain their relevance. Much of the credit for this belongs to novelist Erich Maria Remarque, whose beautifully crafted novel provided Milestone and company ample material with which to make a profoundly moving statement on the futility of war. By following the World War I exploits of young German foot soldiers, the film shows viewers that the horrors of war are universal.

Today, the film enjoys a well-deserved reputation as being the greatest antiwar film ever produced. In 1998, the American Film Institute named *All Quiet on the Western Front* to its "100 Years, 100 Movies" list of the one hundred finest films in the history of American cinema at number fifty-four. In addition, the film received four Academy Award nominations in the categories of Best Picture (Carl Laemmle Jr.), Best Director (Milestone), Best Screenplay (George Abbott, Maxwell Anderson, and Del Andrews), and Best Cinematography (Arthur Edelson). These nominations yielded Oscars for Best Picture and Best Director. The film was listed to the National Film Registry as a classic in 1990.

1. What does the boys' professor say "must be thrown aside"?

2. What does Katczinsky do to "calm" Kemmerich's nerves?

3. In its prologue, which is taken directly from the novel, the film is said to be neither an accusation nor what?

4. In 1937, a sequel entitled *The Road Back* was produced. In the film, Slim Summerville reprises the role of Tjaden. What legendary filmmaker directed this sequel?

5. The boys give Himmelstoss a nickname. What is this?

6. Which of the students is hesitant to enlist?

7. The film's dialogue coach became a successful filmmaker whose directorial credits include *The Philadelphia Story* (1940), *A Star Is Born* (1954), and *My Fair Lady* (1964). Who is this?

8. *All Quiet on the Western Front* was the fourth film directed by Lewis Milestone to feature actor Louis Wolheim. Can you name their three previous collaborations?

9. Why does Paul believe the dead Frenchman accuses him?

10. The hospitalized Kemmerich says, "Why didn't they tell me?" To what is he referring?

11. *All Quiet on the Western Front* was the second of three collaborations between actor John Wray and director Lewis Milestone. Can you name the other two films?

12. About what does Paul say you can't "fool anybody" for too long on the front line?

13. What does Himmelstoss say the boys must forget?

14. What legendary silent screen actress was initially cast as Mrs. Baumer, but later replaced by Beryl Mercer?

15. After winning the Oscar for Best Director with *All Quiet on the Western Front*, Lewis Milestone received another nomination the following year for another film with the word "front" in its title. What is this film?

16. What is Himmelstoss's occupation prior to the war?

17. A scene depicting the Nazis was added to the 1939 rerelease version. What are they doing?

18. One of the film's uncredited extras became a successful filmmaker whose directorial credits include the World War II films *The Seventh Cross* (1944), *The Men* (1950), and *From Here to Eternity* (1953). Who is this?

19. The hand shown reaching for the butterfly does not actually belong to actor Lew Ayres. Whose hand is it?

20. Who does Paul's mother warn him about, saying, "They're no good"?

21. What do the soldiers conclude that "every full-grown emperor" needs?

22. Which of the classmates is the first to be killed?

23. Tjaden says fresh soldiers only know how to do one thing. What is this?

24. Whose idea is it to bushwhack the drunken Himmelstoss?

25. Paul tells the dead Frenchman, "You're better off than me." What does he mean by this?

Quiz No. 2:

APOCALYPSE NOW

(1979)

Screenplay by John Milius and Francis Ford Coppola (based on a novella by
  Joseph Conrad)
Directed by Francis Ford Coppola
Starring Martin Sheen, Marlon Brando, and Robert Duvall
United Artists
Available on VHS, DVD

> *It's a way we had over here with living with ourselves. We cut 'em in
> half with a machine gun and give 'em a Band-Aid. It was a lie. And
> the more I saw of them, the more I hated lies.*
> —CAPT. BENJAMIN L. WILLARD

After being told in a screenwriting class that many extraordinarily talented screenwriters had attempted to tackle Joseph Conrad's novella *Heart of Darkness*, John Milius set his sights on adapting the work in a Vietnam War setting. This updated version of Conrad's story would depict Captain Willard (Martin Sheen) undertaking a C.I.A. "black ops" mission to "terminate" a renegade Green Beret Colonel named Kurtz (Marlon Brando). After Milius hammered out the first draft of the script he called *Apocalypse Now,* the project spent a number of years being passed from one director to the next. Finally, Francis Ford Coppola, who rewrote much of the script himself, signed on to direct the film. Coppola and company then embarked on one of the most difficult and storied shoots in the history of American cinema. The budget soon began to soar when expansive sets were destroyed by natural disaster, the lead actor was fired during filming, and actor Brando arrived on set weighing slightly less than an elephant. The film then required nearly three years to be edited into a cohesive narrative. Despite the film's copious setbacks, *Apocalypse Now* became a box-office hit and eventually recognized as a bonafide classic.

In 1998, the American Film Institute named *Apocalypse Now* to its "100 Years, 100 Movies" list of the one hundred greatest American films at number twenty-eight. In addition, the film received eight Academy Award nominations in the categories of Best Picture (Coppola, Fred Roos, Gray Frederickson, and Tom Sternberg), Best Screenplay (Milius and Coppola), Best Director (Coppola), Best Supporting Actor (Robert Duvall), Best Cinematography (Vittorio Storaro), Best Film Editing (Richard Marks, Walter Murch, Gerald B. Greenberg, and Lisa Fruchtman), Best Sound (Murch, Mark Berger, Richard Beggs, and Nathan Boxer), and Best Art Direction–Set Decoration (Dean Tavoularis, Angelo P. Graham, and George R. Nelson). These nominations resulted in six Oscars awarded for Best Picture, Best Screenplay, Best Director, Best Supporting Actor, Best Film Editing, and Best Art Direction–Set Decoration. Other honors include the prestigious Golden Palm Award at Cannes, a Writers Guild nomination for Best Screenplay, seven nominations at the World Stunt Awards when the film was rereleased in 2001, and three Golden Globe Awards for Best Director, Best Supporting Actor, and Best Original Score (Carmine Coppola and Francis Ford Coppola). The film was listed to the National Film Registry as a classic in 2000.

1. Dennis Hopper's primary reason for signing on to appear in *Apocalypse Now* was to fulfill his lifelong dream of working with Marlon Brando. How many scenes did Hopper and Brando film together?

2. While Martin Sheen was hospitalized, another actor was used in his place to shoot a number of distance shots. Then, when Sheen was unavailable to read additional dialogue for the voice-over, this same actor was again hired to deliver Sheen's dialogue. However, this actor received no screen credit for his work on the film. Who is this?

3. The character G.D. Franklin plays in the film was named after Francis Ford Coppola's mentor. Who is this?

4. What is the photojournalist's reason for assuming that Kurtz likes Willard?

5. From where does Chef hail?

6. Who makes a cameo in the film as a documentary filmmaker?

7. The actor playing the Eagle Thrust Seven chopper pilot later appears much more prominently in *Purple Hearts* (1984), *Full Metal Jacket* (1987), and *The Siege of Firebase Gloria* (1989). Who is this?

8. What is the title of the critically acclaimed 1991 film directed by Fax Bahr and George Hickenlooper that documented the making of *Apocalypse Now*?

9. When George Lucas was attached to the project as director in 1971, he and screenwriter John Milius devised a plan to shoot the film economically. However, the studio officials vetoed this idea because they felt it was too dangerous. What was this?

10. Who appears in an uncredited cameo as a television photographer?

11. Harvey Keitel was the first actor cast as Willard. After Keitel was fired, Martin Sheen was hired as his replacement. Keitel and Sheen later appear together in a film that was released the same year as *Apocalypse Now*. What is this film?

12. What does Willard say he was given for his sins?

13. Francis Ford Coppola reedited the film for a 2001 theatrical release. This version was also retitled. What is the title of Coppola's recut?

14. Who does Willard describe as having a "weird light" around him?

15. Harrison Ford's character is named after a filmmaker both he and director Coppola had worked with previously. Who is this?

16. How old was Laurence Fishburne when *Apocalypse Now* began filming in 1974?

17. Kurtz says he had a dream about a snail. What was the snail crawling along?

18. What is Tyrone Miller's nickname?

19. What, according to Willard, is "Charlie's" idea of R&R?

20. What adorn posts around Kurtz's compound?

21. Miller shoots a Vietnamese woman when she begins running. What is she running to?

22. What does Kurtz say is the "middle word" in life?

23. Francis Ford Coppola later directed a second Vietnam War picture. This film, released in 1987, was written by Ronald Bass and starred James Caan. What is this film?

24. Martin Sheen and Marlon Brando later reunite in a 1998 straight-to-video bomb directed by Yves Simoneau. What is this film?

25. The photographs in Kurtz's dossier were taken from a 1967 John Huston film in which Marlon Brando appears as an army officer. What is this film?

Quiz No. 3:

BAND OF BROTHERS

(2001)

Screenplay by Erik Jendresen, Tom Hanks, John Orloff, E. Max Frye, Graham
   Yost, Bruce C. McKenna, and Erik Bork (based on a book by Stephen
   Ambrose)
Directed by Phil Alden Robinson, Richard Loncraine, Mikael Saloman,
   David Nutter, Tom Hanks, David Leland, David Frankel, and Tony To
Starring Damian Lewis, Donnie Wahlberg, and Ron Livingston
Twentieth Century-Fox/Dream Works/HBO
Available on VHS, DVD

> *We're all scared. You hid in that ditch because you think there's still
> hope. But Blithe, the only hope you have is to accept the fact that
> you're already dead. And the sooner you accept that, the sooner you'll
> be able to function as a soldier is supposed to function. Without
> mercy. Without compassion. Without remorse. All war depends on it.*
> —LT. RONALD SPEIRS

Executive produced by Steven Spielberg and Tom Hanks for HBO, this
adaptation of historian Stephen Ambrose's book of the same title is
one of the most ambitious television miniseries ever produced. Like
Spielberg and Hanks's previous collaboration *Saving Private Ryan*
(1998), *Band of Brothers* is a gritty, uncompromising look at the
American GI during World War II. Spanning the entire war in Europe,
the film follows the exploits of an airborne infantry company. Most of
the battle scenes were shot with a handheld camera, lending the film a
feeling of authenticity, and the grayish muted colors à la *Saving Private
Ryan* gives *Band of Brothers* a feeling of yesteryear nostalgia. Interviews
with the surviving members of Easy Company also add to the effectiveness of the film, reminding the viewer that these aren't simply
characters from a novel; this really happened. Although the cast is
comprised largely of actors with which the audience is likely to be un-

familiar, there's not a phoney performance to be found here. The entire cast—from the top-billed Damian Lewis to the unseen uncredited extras—turn in remarkably convincing performances.

Band of Brothers received a whopping nineteen Emmy nominations for Outstanding Miniseries, Outstanding Direction, Outstanding Writing, Outstanding Casting, Outstanding Cinematography, Outstanding Art Direction, Outstanding Sound Editing, Outstanding Hairstyling, Outstanding Main Title Design, Outstanding Prosthetic Makeup, Outstanding Non-prosthetic Makeup, Outstanding Single-camera Picture Editing, Outstanding Stunt Coordination, and multiple nominations in the categories of Outstanding Single-camera Picture Editing, Outstanding Single-camera Sound Mixing, and Outstanding Special Visual Effects. These nominations resulted in six awards for Outstanding Miniseries, Outstanding Directing, Outstanding Casting, Outstanding Sound Editing, Outstanding Single-camera Sound Mixing, and Outstanding Single-camera Picture Editing. Other honors include the American Film Institute Award for Miniseries of the Year, an American Cinematographers Award, and the Casting Society of America's Award for Best Casting in a Television Miniseries.

1. Actor John Frank Hughes and executive producers Steven Spielberg and Tom Hanks all reunited on a film that was released in 2002. The film, which was directed by Spielberg, stars Hanks and Hughes as Federal Bureau of Investigations officers. What is this film?

2. What is Sgt. Darrell Powers's nickname?

3. The Hatfield Aerodrome in Hertford, North Carolina, the location where much of the film was shot, had been used previously for another World War II film. What is this film?

4. Perconte is shown reading a 1943 novel penned by Betty Smith. What is the title of this book?

5. Luz asks Janovek why they're fighting the war. What is Janovek's memorable response?

6. The title of both the film and Stephen Ambrose's book came from a line in a play written by William Shakespeare, "We few, we happy few, we band of brothers." From what play was this line derived?

7. What river does Muck claim to have swum across?

8. The actor who appears in the film as Col. Sink also served as the military advisor on the film. This retired marine captain also appears

in a handful of other war films including *Platoon* (1986), *Casualties of War* (1989), and *Saving Private Ryan*. Who is this?

9. What is the name of the Georgia-based camp where the men train under Lt. Sobel?

10. What does Winters advise Compton to never put himself in the position to do?

11. How many companies are in Easy Company's regiment?

12. What *Saturday Night Live* alum appears in *Band of Brothers* as Lt. George Rice?

13. Why was actor Damian Lewis worried that he might not land the role of Maj. Richard Winters?

14. One of the primary characters has a drinking problem that worsens as the film progresses. Who is this?

15. What does Nixon say any of the men would double-time Currahee to do to Lt. Sobel?

16. Which of the film's directors also helmed *Field of Dreams* (1989), *Sneakers* (1992), and *The Sum of All Fears* (2002)?

17. In a scene featuring an interview with the real-life Richard Winters, he recalls being asked by his grandson if he was a hero during the war. What was Winters' response?

18. What does Toye predict will happen if he kills Adolf Hitler?

19. Winters is wounded by a piece of shrapnel. Where on his body is the wound?

20. Throughout the film, the soldiers spread a tale involving an officer who passed out cigarettes to a group of German prisoners and then gunned them down. Who is this?

21. According to one of the film's taglines, "They depended on each other." Who does the tagline say depended on them?

22. *Band of Brothers* was the second epic HBO miniseries executive produced by Steven Spielberg and Tom Hanks. What was the first?

23. Guarnere says there are only two people you can trust in battle. Who are they?

24. What does Sobel say is slang for "bullshit"?

25. Who are the "stupid, arrogant sons of bitches" Webster yells at for "interrupting" his life?

Quiz No. 4:

BATTLEGROUND

(1949)

Screenplay by Robert Pirosh
Directed by William A. Wellman
Starring Van Johnson, John Hodiak, and Ricardo Montalban
Metro-Goldwyn-Mayer
Available on VHS

> *You know, they got a man in the army. A two-star general that all he does is fly around in a private plane looking for ugly places; flat, sandy places; no trees; no water. Then he checks up on the climate. If it's too hot in the summer for human life and too cold in winter, and if it has more rain and fog and wind and snow than any other spot he can find, then he plants the American flag and proclaims it a U.S. Army camp.*
> —WILLIAM J. HOOPER

Four years after crafting *The Story of G.I. Joe* (1945), William A. Wellman returned to World War II Europe. *Battleground,* which tells the story of one platoon fighting at the Battle of the Bulge, is very similar to the previous film. Like *The Story of G.I. Joe, Battleground* is a very gritty film—unusually gritty for the period in which it was produced—featuring flawless performances from a strong ensemble. The film examines the day-to-day life and neverending uncertainty of the American GI during the war. It has a tight script by veteran screenwriter Robert Pirosh, skillful direction by Wellman, and seamless editing by John D. Dunning. But the true star here is Paul Vogel's stunning black-and-white cinematography. Although it was a huge box-office hit in 1949, *Battleground* somehow got lost in the shuffle since then. Nevertheless, it remains one of the finest pre–*Saving Private Ryan* (1998) World War II films ever captured on celluloid.

Battleground received six Academy Award nominations for Best Picture (Dore Schary), Best Screenplay (Pirosh), Best Director (Wellman),

Best Supporting Actor (Whitmore), Best Black-and-White Cinematography (Vogel), and Best Film Editing (Dunning). These nominations resulted in two statuettes for the film's screenplay and cinematography.

1. What is the name of the French woman Holly fancies?
2. Where does Holly say he spent most of his time in Paris?
3. What was Jarvess's occupation prior to the war?
4. William A. Wellman directed actor Van Johnson in a second film two years after the release of *Battleground*. What is the title of this film?
5. What does Rodriguez say he's never seen before?
6. Jarvess repeatedly asks Abner not to use a phrase. What is this?
7. The perimeter password used in the film is a baseball term. What is this?
8. One of the soldiers steals some eggs from a henhouse in Bastogne. Who is this?
9. What telltale sign tips off Holly that the GIs they meet in the woods are German soldiers in disguise?
10. Who does Rodriguez ask to telephone his family?
11. When Abner says "There ain't nuthin' we like to talk about more," to what is he referring?
12. What nickname does the film say the soldiers earned at the Battle of the Bulge?
13. What kind of booze do the soldiers recall toting in their gas mask bags?
14. Which cast member later appears in war films such as *Attack* (1956), *The Dirty Dozen* (1967), and *The Devil's Brigade* (1968)?
15. Which of the soldiers is awaiting a dependency discharge because his wife is too ill to care for their children?
16. What does Holly say happened the last time he allowed Bettis to dig his foxhole?
17. One of the cast members later worked as pop icon James Dean's acting coach. Who is this?
18. What does Kapp claim to have lost in the forest?
19. Jarvess concludes that "things just happen." What does he then say one does afterward?
20. One of the men is wounded and trapped beneath a jeep in an area overrun with Germans. Who is this?

21. What does Jarvess conclude to be a better way to get off the line than pneumonia?

22. William A. Wellman directed another film featuring actors Ricardo Montalban, John Hodiak, and James Whitmore two years after the release of *Battleground*. What is this film?

23. What does Kinnie say must happen before the aid station will help soldiers with frostbitten feet?

24. According to regulations, a soldier must have a certain temperature before he can be removed from the line for a fever. What is this?

25. A Nazi plane drops propaganda literature on the soldiers. What do the pamphlets say?

Quiz No. 5:

THE BATTLE OF ALGIERS
(1965)

Screenplay by Gillo Pontecorvo and Franco Solinas
Directed by Gillo Pontecorvo
Starring Jean Martin, Yacef Saadi, and Brahim Haggiag
Casbah/Igor Films
Available on VHS

> *Starting a revolution is hard, and it's even harder to continue it.*
> *Winning is hardest of all. But only afterward, when we have won,*
> *will the real hardships begin.*
> —BEN M'HIDI

Commissioned by the Algerian government, Gillo Pontecorvo's *The Battle of Algiers* is one of the finest antiwar films ever produced. Shot guerilla style with handheld cameras on grainy black-and-white film, *The Battle of Algiers* presents both sides of the Algerian revolution. Fast-paced and beautifully reenacted, it's easy to forget this is a dramatization rather than actual documentary footage. *Guardian* film critic Derek Malcolm calls *The Battle of Algiers* a "model of how, without prejudice or compromise, a filmmaker can illuminate history and tell us how we repeat the same mistakes. In fact, this study of the Algerian guerilla struggle against the French colonialists in the fifties ought to be looked at not just as pure cinema but as a warning to those who seek by force to crush independence movements."

Among the film's many honors are Oscar nominations for Best Foreign Language Film, Best Director (Pontecorvo), and Best Original Screenplay (Franco Solinas and Pontecorvo). The film also took home a number of awards from various European film festivals and received the United Nations Award at the 1972 British Academy of Film and Television Awards.

1. *The Battle of Algiers* was the third film on which screenwriters Gillo Pontecorvo and Franco Solinas collaborated. On what two films had they worked together previously?

2. What is Lt. Col. Mathieu's first name?

3. The film was nominated for three Italian National Syndicate of Film Journalists Awards in the categories of Best Director, Best Producer, and Best Black-and-White Cinematography. In how many of these categories did the film win?

4. What three subjects are on the agenda for the United Nations debates?

5. What does Mathieu call an "inevitable stage in revolutionary war"?

6. What is the name of the police informer who owns the cafe at Random 40?

7. In what subject does Matheiu hold a degree?

8. What primary figure in the film's production appears in a cameo as an FLN leader?

9. Why does Kader tell Ali he opted not to have him murder the bartender as a test of his loyalties?

10. On what street is Dare Jackie killed?

11. At what time is the curfew imposed?

12. What does Ben M'Hidi say wars and revolutions are *not* won by?

13. What does FLN stand for?

14. According to Matheiu, how many Arabs reside in Casbah?

15. For how many days is the FLN's strike scheduled?

16. What operation title do Mathieu and the General decide on?

17. The condemned man and the political prisoners all chant the words *"tahia el Djez-air!"* What does this mean?

18. In 1967, *The Battle of Algiers* was nominated for an Oscar in the category of Best Foreign Language Film. However, it lost. What film won the honor?

19. According to the assistant commissioner, how many children does Lardjane Boualem have?

20. The FLN proposes "an honorable program of discussion to the French authorities" on one condition. What is the condition?

21. Omar instructs Ali to walk with a young girl carrying a basket. What is in the basket?

22. What, according to the film, occurred on July 2, 1962?
23. What is Ali la Pointe's real name?
24. Petit Omar observes that men "have two faces." What are these?
25. What are said to be the "most dangerous weapons of colonialism"?

Quiz No. 6:

BATTLE OF THE BULGE

(1965)

Screenplay by Bernard Gordon, John Melson, and Milton Sperling
Directed by Ken Annakin
Starring Henry Fonda, Robert Shaw, and Robert Ryan
Warner Bros.
Available on VHS

> *Unfortunately we did not have time to get better acquainted. But you all know my reputation. My command always suffers the highest casualties. The price of victory is never cheap. In this battle, we will be as hard as our tanks. I will reach the objectives assigned to me no matter what the cost.*
> —COL. MARTIN HESSLER

Ken Annakin's *The Battle of the Bulge* tells the story of one of World War II's most important battles. Like many other World War II films, *The Battle of the Bulge* details the movements of both the Americans and the Germans. While Col. Hessler (Robert Shaw) is merciless, just as we would expect from a Nazi officer in any Hollywood war film, he is given more dimension than the Nazis who generally inhabit Tinseltown productions. Still, there is little here that we haven't seen before. A storyline in which one American officer (Henry Fonda) suspects that the enemy is on the move but can't get anyone to listen to him is a familiar but nonetheless effective device. Other stock characters include a fresh-faced inexperienced officer (James MacArthur), an army hustler who can get anything for the right price (Telly Savalas), and smug, uninformed commanders (Robert Ryan and Dana Andrews). Despite its lavish budget, *The Battle of the Bulge* owes more to the exploitation pictures of Roger Corman than to large-scale epics such as *The Ten Commandments* (1956) or *Spartacus* (1960); rather than attempting to fashion a historically accurate film, the filmmakers opt to deliver an action-packed popcorn movie designed to entertain audiences.

Composer Benjamin Frankel and actor Telly Savalas received Golden Globe nominations in 1966 in the categories of Best Original Score and Best Supporting Actor. However, both lost in their respective bids.

1. How many sons does Conrad have?

2. What, according to Col. Pritchard, does not make a jungle?

3. What former government official quickly denounced this film as being historically inaccurate in a 1965 press conference?

4. Screenwriter Bernard Gordon, who had been blacklisted and labeled a communist in the 1950s, worked on this film under a pseudonym. What was this pseudonym?

5. What, according to Col. Hessler, "is blood"?

6. Henry Fonda appeared as Adm. Chester W. Nimitz in another war film released the same year as *Battle of the Bulge.* Can you name this film?

7. Who narrates the film?

8. The actor who appears in the film as Maj. Von Diepel also plays German soldiers in a number of other war films, including *The Great Escape* (1963), *Is Paris Burning?* (1966), *Battle of Britain* (1969), *Kelly's Heroes* (1970), and *Slaughterhouse-Five* (1972). Who is this?

9. What does Kiley say does not disqualify him from thinking?

10. What is stenciled on the side of Sgt. Guffy's tank?

11. What does Maj. Wolenski recall being strange regarding the GIs who were about to destroy the bridge?

12. Telly Savalas, who appears as Sgt. Guffy, plays another tank commander in a 1970 war film costarring Clint Eastwood. What is this film?

13. Charles Bronson, who appears as Maj. Wolenski, appears in another popular war movie two years after *Battle of the Bulge* was released. In this second film, Bronson plays a character named Joseph T. Wladislaw. What is this film?

14. Where does Hessler predict that Conrad will die?

15. What does Hessler say the Germans are the best in the world at making?

16. Remarkably, *Battle of the Bulge* was just one of three films directed by Ken Annakin that were released in 1965. What were the other two films?

17. What does Guffy say he will not be when he returns home?

18. What does Pritchard say the German prisoners "aren't even tough enough" to be classified as?

19. What is Schumacher's primary assignment?

20. What does Gen. Kohler believe Hessler has "too little faith in"?

21. What does Conrad say he's always been fortunate to have done?

22. What, according to Kiley, is sometimes more important during interrogation than what the prisoners say?

23. Gen. Kohler shows Hessler a clock that only turns in one cycle. How many hours does this cycle consist of?

24. What does Louise say Kohler admires most about Hessler?

25. What does Wolenski say is the "only action" his men are seeing?

Quiz No. 7:

BEAU GESTE

(1939)

Screenplay by Robert Carson (based on a novel by Percival Christopher Wren)
Directed by William A. Wellman
Starring Gary Cooper, Ray Milland, and Robert Preston
Paramount Pictures
Available on VHS

> *When I was a little boy, I thought soldiers always died in battle. I didn't know there were so many soldiers and so few battles.* —LT. MARTIN

More than sixty years after its initial release, *Beau Geste* remains one of the most satisfying adventure yarns ever filmed. The film, directed by the incomparable William A. Wellman, features a terrific cast that includes four future Oscar winners: Gary Cooper, Ray Milland, Broderick Crawford, and Susan Hayward, who makes her film debut here. Despite the fact that novelist Percival Christopher Wren's novel had already been adapted as a 1926 silent film starring Ronald Colman and would later be adapted several more times, Wellman's 1939 version remains the quintessential *Beau Geste*. That the film begins with Beau and his brothers as adolescents dreaming of enlististing into the Foreign Legion years before actually doing so is telling considering their later exploits feel very much like the daydreams of prepubescent boys. This is, perhaps, the reason *Beau Geste* continues to appeal to audiences—it makes us remember a simpler time when being a cowboy or a legionnaire still seemed like a reasonable occupational option.

Beau Geste received two Academy Award nominations for Best Supporting Actor (Brian Donlevy) and Best Art Direction (Hans Dreier and Robert Odell), but failed to snag an Oscar in either category.

1. Numerous versions of *Beau Geste* have been filmed. A 1977 parody directed by comic Marty Feldman was billed as the "last remake of *Beau Geste*." What is the title of this film?

2. What does the name "Beau Geste" mean?

3. What is Beau's real name?

4. The valley where the film was shot was later renamed Beau Geste Valley. What was it known as during the period in which the film was made?

5. What is the name of the cursed sapphire around which the story's plot revolves?

6. The first film version of Percival Christopher Wren's novel *Beau Geste* was released in 1926. Two years later, a sequel was produced. Interestingly, Gary Cooper—the star of this 1939 remake—stars in that film. What is the name of the 1928 sequel?

7. In whose hand does John leave Beau's "public letter"?

8. What does Sgt. Markoff say Rasinoff will receive if Beau doesn't have the sapphire?

9. Director William A. Wellman was chosen for this project because he had a special knowledge of the subject. What was this?

10. The actor who appears as Beau at age twelve had appeared in *Sons of the Legion* (1938) the year before and later came to prominence as the human lead in the *Francis the Talking Mule* films. Who is this?

11. John says there is only one thing he would ever consider stealing from Brandon Abbas. What is this?

12. Who is the first of the brothers to follow Beau into the Foreign Legion?

13. Who is the first person Sgt. Markoff and Rasinoff disarm in the attempt to put down the impending mutiny?

14. Who does Beau call the "best soldier we'll ever see"?

15. How many men does Sgt. Markoff want the Arabs to believe are defending the fort?

16. What does Sgt. Markoff demand the two returning deserters do?

17. Another legendary director was attached to *Beau Geste* before William A. Wellman was hired. Who was this?

18. Gary Cooper, Ray Milland, and Robert Preston—the three actors who appear in this film as the Geste brothers—appear in cameos in a 1947 musical directed by George Marshall. What is this film?

19. What does Beau say he knows about mutinies?

20. Why was Sgt. Markoff exiled from the Siberian penal colonies?

21. Who does Sgt. Markoff order to execute Schwartz and Renoir?

22. Renoir says Beau wouldn't feel so patriotic if he had something. What is this?

23. Gary Cooper and director William A. Wellman had already collaborated on a film about the French Foreign Legion prior to *Beau Geste*. However, this 1928 film dealt with an airborne Foreign Legion. The film also stars Fay Wray and Barry Norton. Can you name this film?

24. Who is the "cute little fellow" Beau and Digby trap behind the couch but find themselves unable to harm?

25. Who does Sgt. Markoff refer to as "scum"?

Quiz No. 8:
THE BIG PARADE
(1925)

Screenplay by Harry Behn (based on a play by Joseph Farnham)
Directed by King Vidor
Starring John Gilbert, Renne Adoree, and Hobart Bosworth
Metro-Goldwyn-Mayer
Available on VHS

> *Waiting! Orders! Mud! Blood! Stinking stiffs! What the hell do we get out of this war anyway? Cheers when we left and when we get back! But who the hell cares . . . after this?* —JAMES APPERSON

Believed to be the highest-grossing silent film ever made, King Vidor's *The Big Parade* was the first film to examine the horrors of modern warfare in a realistic manner. While the film has not aged particularly well and many of its themes were revisited to much better effect five years later in *All Quiet on the Western Front* (1930), *The Big Parade* remains a landmark cinematic achievement. It's been said that all great war films are truly antiwar films, and this one is no exception. Vidor's film, which was adapted from a play by Joseph Farnham tells the stories of three American soldiers deployed to France during World War I. *The Big Parade* begins with their pre-war loves and occupations, and then follows them to France, where they find love, death, and horror. The success of the film brought matinee idol John Gilbert stardom, and Gilbert does the finest work of his career here.

The Big Parade was awarded the Photoplay Awards' Medal of Honor in 1925. Some fifty-eight years after its initial release, the film received honorable mention for the OCIC Award at the San Sebastian International Film Festival. It was also listed in the National Film Registry as a classic in 1992.

1. *The Big Parade* was the third film King Vidor directed that featured actor John Gilbert. Can you name their two previous collaborations?

2. What is Slim's surname?

3. As Jim, Slim, and Bull crowd together in a foxhole, Bull comments that he should throw something across to where the German soldiers are. What is this?

4. How far do the soldiers march before their arrival in Champillon?

5. What is the name of the French girl Jim becomes infatuated with?

6. *The Big Parade* was one of two films directed by King Vidor that were released in 1925. What is the other film?

7. What is Bull's occupation before the war?

8. What does Bull commend Jim on "makin' this war"?

9. Bull says he joined the army to fight. What does he say he did *not* join the army to do?

10. Which of the soldiers is a construction worker prior to the war?

11. What kind of food does Justyn send Jim?

12. Which of the soldiers is the son of a wealthy mill owner?

13. What kind of creature does Jim catch at the stream while walking with the French girl?

14. What nickname is given to the German pilot who "sneaked across the line to give [the soldiers] their first welcome"?

15. What, according to Mr. Apperson, is there no room in his home for?

16. Jim is tricked into going to the French village. What does he go to obtain?

17. Who informs Jim's parents that he has enlisted?

18. What does Jim say "is Greek to me"?

19. What is the name of Jim's younger brother?

20. What does Bull label men who joined the navy as being?

21. What does Jim inform Slim that one does not "handle" girls like?

22. What does the film say came from "avenue and alley"?

23. What does Justyn imagine "fills the air" on the battlefront?

24. What does Bull sing that the soldiers should "shovel and chuck"?

25. As Bull dies, he tells Jim that he will meet him somewhere. Where is this?

Quiz No. 9:

THE BIG RED ONE

(1980)

Screenplay by Samuel Fuller
Directed by Samuel Fuller
Starring Lee Marvin, Mark Hamill, and Robert Carradine
United Artists
Available on VHS, DVD

> *Surviving is the only glory in war, if you know what I mean.*
> —THE SERGEANT

Although legendary auteur Samuel Fuller made standout films in a number of genres, he is best remembered for his war films. A World War II veteran himself, Fuller had already directed several outstanding war films—*The Steel Helmet* (1951), *Fixed Bayonets* (1951), and *Merrill's Marauders* (1962) among others—before going to work on The *Big Red One*. Fuller began writing the largely autobiographical film in the late 1960s, spending more than a decade polishing it. The film, which follows the World War II exploits of one rifle squad, features a number of excellent performances. However, these performances are overshadowed by that of Lee Marvin, who delivers what is arguably the finest work of his career in his turn as the squad's nameless sergeant. While the film's depiction of D day doesn't come close to the opening scene of *Saving Private Ryan* (1998), it is nonetheless effective.

The Big Red One was nominated for the prestigious Palme de Or at the 1980 Cannes Film Festival.

1. What is the name of the soldier Zab nicknames "Baby Face"?
2. What unhandy weapon causes Zab to remark that he'd like to meet the "asshole" who invented it?
3. What actors does Zab say will star in the adaptation of *The Dark Deadline*?

4. What was unusual regarding the casting of the Nazi concentration camp guards in *The Big Red One*?

5. At the beginning of the film, Lee Marvin's character (known only as "the sergeant") kills a German soldier in World War I. However, unbeknown to him, the Armistice has been signed. For how long has the war been over?

6. "You know how you smoke out a sniper?" Zab asks. "You send a guy out in the open and you see if he gets shot." Where does Zab conclude that this technique was devised?

7. What nickname does the sergeant use for the members of his squad?

8. Who freezes up during the brief battle with the French?

9. Where is the temporary German hospital where the sergeant is held located?

10. What does Zab conclude to be the "creepy thing about battle"?

11. A Sicilian boy agrees to lead the squad to the concealed Tiger tank in exchange for a casket for his mother that has "at least four handles." How many handles are on the casket he receives?

12. *The Big Red One* was nominated for the prestigious Golden Palm Award at the Cannes Film Festival in 1980. However, it lost. What two films won the honor that year?

13. Who is referred to as the "Hemingway of the Bronx"?

14. For how many months does the squad "hang around England" preparing for D day?

15. What four sounds does Zab say could be heard on the boat at the Algerian Beach landing?

16. Seven years after starring in *The Big Red One*, real-life marine veteran Lee Marvin was buried in Arlington National Cemetery. What is the significance of this?

17. Who are dubbed the Four Horsemen?

18. The sergeant explains, "We don't murder." What does he say they instead do?

19. What type of shop has Zab's father always dreamed of owning?

20. According to the captain, who has "as much right to go crazy in this war as men have"?

21. Thys Ockerson directed a documentary about the making of *The Big Red One* in 1979. What is the title of this film?

22. *The Big Red One* was director Samuel Fuller's first theatrical

film in ten years. Prior to this film, what had been Fuller's previous theatrical film?

23. What navy cruiser fires on the Germans in Sicily, thus saving the squad?

24. At what Algiers hotel does Shep say he found the German knife?

25. *The Big Red One* was the second film in which Samuel Fuller directed actor Lee Marvin. What was the first?

Quiz No. 10:
BLACK HAWK DOWN
(2001)

Screenplay by Ken Nolan (based on a book by Mark Bowden)
Directed by Ridley Scott
Starring Josh Hartnett, Eric Bana, and Tom Sizemore
Columbia Pictures
Available on VHS, DVD

> *You know what I think? Don't really matter what I think. Once that*
> *first bullet goes past your head, politics and all that shit just goes right*
> *out the window.* —SFC NORM HOOTEN

Black Hawk Down depicts the United States' 1993 incursion into Mogadishu, Somalia. Ridley Scott's slick $90 million film is significant because it focuses on the type of isolated military action that the film industry has generally overlooked in the past. Rather than Hollywoodize this story—taken from Mark Bowden's excellent book by the same title—Scott opted to shoot the film in a straightforward documentary-like style, utilizing vibrant colors and quick-paced cutting-edge editing. This unorthodox style allowed *Black Hawk Down* to avoid many of the clichés that plague so many war films. Unfortunately, this also provides the film's detractors with ammunition in that Scott and screenwriter Ken Nolan provide very little background or depth for their characters. But those who see this as a shortcoming miss the point: This is a true story presented exactly the way this botched raid actually occurred. The real-life U.S. Marines didn't stop during firefights to reflect on motivations or share anecdotes about their pasts. To have added such fodder would have been false. That's just not the way these things happen. Scott crafted an extraordinary film that is sure to radically alter the playing field for war films in the years to come.

Black Hawk Down received four Academy Award nominations for Best Director (Scott), Best Cinematography (Slavomir Idziak), Best

Editing (Pietro Scalia), and Best Sound (Michael Minkler, Myron Nettinga, and Chris Munro).

1. Who is *Black Hawk Down* dedicated to?
2. An Elvis Presley tune plays as Durant and Wolcott argue about their Scrabble game. What was this song?
3. What is Durant holding when he is attacked by the militia?
4. How many American soldiers does the film's postscript say were killed during the raid?
5. *Black Hawk Down* was one of two 2001 war films executive produced by Jerry Bruckheimer. The other film is *Pearl Harbor*. Five actors appear in both films. How many of them can you name?
6. Eversmann says there are two things Americans can do regarding the turmoil in Somalia. What are these?
7. One soldier is shown reading a paperback edition of a John Grisham novel. This is an error as the paperback was not released for another five months after this story takes place. What is this book?
8. What does the militia soldier say is considered negotiation in Somalia?
9. What does Hoot say he plans to tell anyone inquiring about his motivations for risking his life in the military?
10. The first director attached to *Black Hawk Down* resigned during preproduction to helm *Lara Croft: Tomb Raider* (2001). Who is this?
11. What does Nelson say he hates being?
12. What does Durant tell Wolcott is not a word?
13. What does Grimes say he made during Operation Desert Storm?
14. By what name does Grimes say Mogadishu should be referred to?
15. Joyce concludes that two things Ruiz does are bad luck. What are they?
16. What does the militia soldier say cannot exist without a victory?
17. What Oscar-winning screenwriter worked on the film's script but did not receive credit?
18. *Black Hawk Down* was the second film adapted from the writing of journalist/author Mark Bowden. The first film, which was released in 1993, was based on an article Bowden wrote entitled "The

Joey Coyle Story." The film was directed by Ramon Menendez and features John Cusack, Benicio Del Toro, and James Gandolfini. What is this film?

19. What does Corporal Smith ask Eversmann to tell his parents?

20. Steele threatens to make Pilla clean latrines for a long time if he ever undermines his authority again. What two tastes does Steele say Pilla will not be able to distinguish between when he's through?

21. *Black Hawk Down* is one of two films directed by Ridley Scott that were released in 2001. The other film stars Anthony Hopkins and Julianne Moore. What is this film?

22. How does Maj. Gen. Garrisson assess the situation?

23. Director Ridley Scott received his second straight Best Director Oscar nomination for *Black Hawk Down*. For what film had Scott been nominated the previous year?

24. Garrisson says three hundred thousand casualties is not a war. What does he say it is?

25. What does Grimes conclude to be a "bullet magnet"?

Quiz No. 11:
THE BOYS IN COMPANY C
(1977)

Screenplay by Sidney J. Furie and Rick Natkin
Directed by Sidney J. Furie
Starring Stan Shaw, Andrew Stevens, and R. Lee Ermey
Columbia Pictures
Available on VHS

> *Undoubtedly you people have set some new kind of a record today!*
> *You have fucked over these weapons so goddamn bad they'll probably*
> *never fire again!* —SGT. LOYCE

That the lower-budget *The Boys in Company C* tends to be overshadowed by *The Deer Hunter* (1978) and *Apocalypse Now* (1979) is a shame because, in many ways, it's a far better film than either of them. A clear predecessor to films like *Platoon* (1986) and *Full Metal Jacket* (1987), Sidney J. Furie's *The Boys in Company C* was one of the first films to depict the Vietnam conflict in a realistic manner. Former drill sergeant R. Lee Ermey, who later earned kudos for his turn in *Full Metal Jacket,* turns in an almost identical performance in this picture shot more than a decade before Stanley Kubrick's film. Furie and cowriter Rick Natkin's script crackles with sharp dialogue that rings with authenticity. Under the watchful eye of Furie, the cast turn in quality performances all around. Especially notable is Stan Shaw as the hard-headed squad leader Tyrone Washington. Those who haven't seen *The Boys in Company C* will walk away from this picture wondering why they haven't heard more about it.

In 1979, Andrew Stevens received a Golden Globe nomination for Best Motion Picture Acting Debut, but lost out to Brad Davis for *Midnight Express* (1978).

1. Alvin Foster says he's from Emporia, Kansas. One of the primary actors involved with this production is actually from Emporia. Who is this?

2. What, according to Sgt. Loyce, will "tear your asshole the size of a goddamn" basketball?

3. One of the actors in the film has a father who received an Oscar nomination for his turn in William A. Wellman's classic war film *Battleground* (1949). Who is this?

4. Sgt. Loyce calls a cadence that asks "Why you got that funny walk?" What is the platoon's response?

5. Who does Sgt. Loyce ask to help him prepare the platoon for Vietnam?

6. What does Washington say is the one thing sent back to the United States that is not thoroughly searched?

7. What does Capt. Collins believe to be the Vietcong's game?

8. Who does Foster call the "biggest goddamn bastard I ever knowed in my life"?

9. Rick Natkin wrote the first draft of the screenplay as an assignment in his college film class. What university did Natkin attend?

10. Who does Capt. Collins refer to as "twinkle toes"?

11. Which of the soldiers contracts a "dose of the clap" from a prostitute?

12. Washington tells the platoon that someone is going to die in Vietnam. Who is this?

13. Only half of the men are given combat duty. What are the rest of the men assigned?

14. R. Lee Ermey appeared in a second film directed by Sidney J. Furie in 1984. Like *The Boys in Company C*, this film was also written by Furie and Rick Natkin. What is this film?

15. What does Washington tell Capt. Collins he should do if he's dumb enough to pull a gun on someone?

16. What does Brisbee say he won't do with either a rifle or a radio?

17. What does Sgt. Aquilla advise the recruits to do if they want to keep their "balls"?

18. Who blows up Gen. Dearborne's trailer?

19. What is the occupational designation 0300?

20. Why does the receiving sergeant say the last man off the bus had better give his soul to Jesus?

21. What does Pike erroneously assess as a "light-weight sleeping bag"?

22. Why does Col. Buford change Fazio's orders, redirecting him to Vietnam?

23. How many men from the company does Capt. Collins theorize will die?

24. What is the only kind of paper Alvin says he could find on which to write his journal?

25. What does Pike tell his girlfriend it's "not the right time" for?

Quiz No. 12:

BRAVEHEART

(1995)

Screenplay by Randall Wallace
Directed by Mel Gibson
Starring Mel Gibson, James Robinson, and Sean Lawlor
Paramount Pictures
Available on VHS, DVD

> *Lower your flags and march straight back to England, stopping at*
> *every home to beg forgiveness for a hundred years of theft, rape, and*
> *murder. Do this and your men shall live. Do it not, and every one of*
> *you will die today.*   —WILLIAM WALLACE

While it's far from historically accurate, Mel Gibson's epic *Braveheart* is one of the most lavish, entertaining spectacles Hollywood has produced in the past twenty-five years. Taking a cue from *Spartacus* (1960), the film successfully weaves together storylines focusing on love and battlefield heroism. *Braveheart* is the story of William Wallace, a Scottish commoner who led his people in rebellion against English rule around the end of the thirteenth century. The film, with characters as big as its scope, was fashioned by Gibson around a magnificent screenplay by Randall Wallace. By and large, the cast is superb. While Gibson provides one of his strongest performances to date, supporting actors Patrick McGoohan and Angus MacFayden steal nearly every scene in which they appear. Packed with beauty, passion, brutality, tension, and comedy—with very little pretension—*Braveheart* is one of the fastest-moving three-hour films ever produced.

Braveheart received ten Oscar nominations for Best Picture (Gibson, Alan Ladd Jr., and Bruce Davey), Best Screenplay (Wallace), Best Director (Gibson), Best Cinematography (John Toll), Best Film Editing (Steven Rosenblum), Best Music (James Horner), Best Makeup (Peter Frampton, Paul Pattison, and Lois Burwell), Best Costume

Design (Charles Knode), Best Sound (Andy Nelson, Scott Millan, Anna Behlmer, and Brian Simmons), and Best Sound Effects Editing (Lon Bender and Per Hallberg), winning five statuettes for Best Picture, Best Director, Best Cinematography, Best Makeup, and Best Sound Effects Editing. Other honors include three British Academy of Film and Television Awards (of seven nominations), a Golden Globe Award for Best Director, a Directors Guild Award, and a Writers Guild Award for Best Original Screenplay.

1. Who does William Wallace believe has "far worse manners than I"?

2. How many earls of Bruce have preceded Robert the Bruce?

3. Who does the narrator say history is written by?

4. What is the name of William Wallace's father?

5. True or false: screenwriter Randall Wallace is a descendant of William Wallace?

6. What is the name of Edward's princess?

7. Before battle, Stephen tells Wallace, "The Lord tells me he can get me out of this mess." What does he then say the lord is "pretty sure" of regarding Wallace?

8. What kind of men does the leper say are easy to admire?

9. What does Stephen say an Irishman is forced to do "in order to find his equal"?

10. What is the name of Wallace's slain wife?

11. What is the name of the law that allows English nobility to take new brides the first night of their marriages?

12. *Braveheart* was the second film directed by Mel Gibson. What was the first?

13. What, according to Longshanks, is "the key to Scotland"?

14. Where does Wallace conclude that the test of a soldier is *not?*

15. What does Wallace say spears should be twice the length of?

16. Wallace says he will attack no more towns or cities if Longshanks will do something. What is this?

17. Actor Patrick McGoohan, who appears in the film as Longshanks, won two Emmys for his guest appearances in a telefilm series. What is this series?

18. What is noticeably absent from the film's depiction of the Battle of Stirling Bridge?

19. Before opting to helm the film himself, Mel Gibson offered *Braveheart* to another director. Who was this?

20. What is the name of the newly declared high counselor that Longshanks sends flying through a castle window to his death?

21. What, according to Longshanks, is "the trouble with Scotland"?

22. Why does Wallace say he could not understand his father's eulogy?

23. According to legend, how tall is Wallace said to be?

24. What does Argyle say Wallace must learn to use before learning the sword?

25. What does Wallace say he will go to England to make sure the people have?

Quiz No. 13:

BREAKER MORANT

(1980)

Screenplay by Jonathan Hardy, David Stevens, and Bruce Beresford (based
on a play by Kennth G. Ross)
Directed by Bruce Beresford
Starring Edward Woodward, Jack Thompson, and John Waters
South Australian Film Corporation
Available on VHS, DVD

> *War changes men's natures. The barbarities of war are seldom com-*
> *mitted by abnormal men. The tragedy of war is that these horrors are*
> *committed by men in abnormal situations, situations in which the*
> *ebb and flow of everyday life have departed and been replaced by a*
> *constant round of fear and anger, blood and death. Soldiers at war are*
> *not to be judged by civilian rules.* —MAJ. J. F. THOMAS

Bruce Beresford's *Breaker Morant* is an adaptation of Kenneth G.
Ross's play of the same title, but there's nothing stagey about this film.
One of the finest adapations of a stage production ever made, *Breaker
Morant* chronicles the true story of three Australian officers who were
court-martialed in 1901 for executing Dutch prisoners. The three
men—played to perfection by Edward Woodward, Bryan Brown, and
Lewis Fitzgerald—readily admit to having shot the prisoners in question. However, they insist that they were ordered to do so. As their attorney (Jack Thompson) diligently fights for their lives, it quickly
becomes apparent that the trial is little more than a legality, and that
justice may be well out of reach. While some critics have questioned
Breaker Morant's accuracy, the quality of the film cannot be disputed.
Whatever the film lacks as a historical teaching tool, it more than com-
pensates for in its artistry and entertainment value.

Breaker Morant received thirteen Australian Film Institute Award
nominations in the categories of Best Film (Matthew Carroll), Best

Screenplay (Jonathan Hardy, David Stevens, and Beresford), Best Director (Beresford), Best Actor (Woodward), Best Actor (Thompson), Best Supporting Actor (Bryan Brown), Best Supporting Actor (Fitzgerald), Best Supporting Actor (Charles Tingwell), Best Cinematography (Donald McAlpine), Best Editing (William M. Anderson), Best Costume Design (Anna Senior), Best Production Design (David Copping), and Best Sound (Gary Wilkins, William Anderson, Jeanine Chiavlo, and Phil Judd). Other honors include an Academy Award nomination for Best Adapted Screenplay, the Best Supporting Actor Award (Thompson) at the Cannes Film Festival, and a nomination for the presitigious Palme de Or.

1. What does Lord Kitchener call a "small price to pay" for peace talks?

2. Who does Hadcock call the "source of my greatest joy"?

3. How many men does Morant order to form the firing squad that executes the man captured wearing Hunt's uniform?

4. Actor Edward Woodward and director Bruce Beresford later collaborated on two more films released in 1985 and 1990. Can you name them?

5. Morant quotes Matthew 10:36. What is this verse?

6. Who does Morant refer to as a "minor" poet?

7. What does Morant call the "next best thing" to Hunt returning from the dead?

8. What does Hadcock say Drummond could not do even if he were in bed?

9. What does Hadcock say is a "good day for chasing a few tarts"?

10. How did Morant get the nickname "Breaker"?

11. What is Witton sentenced to?

12. Bruce Beresford received a Best Director Oscar nomination four years after the release of *Breaker Morant*. For what film did Beresford receive this nomination?

13. What does Morant say poets crave?

14. What does Thomas say is Witton's only crime?

15. What does Morant say is customary during a war?

16. Edward Woodward later received two Emmy nominations as the star of a television series that aired from 1985 to 1989. What is this series?

17. How many prisoners did Morant shoot prior to Hunt's death?

18. What, according to the film's tagline, happens when "they speak of heroes—of villains—of men who look for action, who choose between honor and revenge"?

19. What are Morant's last words?

20. What is the significance of the day Morant enlisted into the Bushveldt Carbineers?

21. How many court-martials does Thomas say he has defended prior to Morant's?

22. Who killed Reverand Hess?

23. Why does Morant reason that people should live each day as though it will be their last?

24. Jonathan Hardy, David Stevens, and Bruce Beresford received an Oscar nomination for Best Adapted Screenplay in 1981, but lost. Who defeated them?

25. What does Thomas say prisoners of war should not be judged by?

Quiz No. 14:

THE BRIDGE AT REMAGEN
(1969)

Screenplay by Richard Yates, William Roberts, and Roger Hirson
Directed by John Guillermin
Starring George Segal, Robert Vaughn, and Ben Gazzara
Metro-Goldwyn-Mayer
Available on VHS, DVD

> *It's a crapshoot, Major. Take that bridge and we shorten the war.*
> *We're risking a hundred men, but we may save 10,000—even 50,000!*
> *It's your chance to make history, Major! What you've got to do is*
> *throw your men across. Now, Major!* —GEN. SHINNER

The Bridge at Remagen depicts the 1945 battle between the United
States and Germany for the last German-held bridge on the Rhine
River. Unlike most war films that had preceded it, *The Bridge at
Remagen* is a gritty picture that realistically examines the tensions felt
between comrades who have spent too many days and nights together.
This isn't a jingoistic film that stresses the battlefield camaraderie of an
eager platoon; while these tired, reluctant warriors will lay down their
lives for one another, they don't always see eye to eye. The direction of
journeyman helmer John Guillermin is effective, the special effects are
well done, and the cast deliver solid performances. Ben Gazzara shines
as the duplicitous Sgt. Angelo, and George Segal's turn reminds us just
how effective an actor he was in the prime of his career. While *The
Bridge at Remagen* doesn't come close to landmark war films such as *All
Quiet on the Western Front* (1930) or *Saving Private Ryan* (1998), it's a
thoroughly engaging film that deserves a second look.

1. How many of the German soldiers are portrayed by Americans?
2. On paper, the Nazis have sixteen hundred men at their disposal.
According to Capt. Schmidt, how many men do they actually have?

3. Which soldier loots the bodies of dead German soldiers?

4. Actor Bo Hopkins, who plays Cpl. Grebs, also appeared in another 1969 film that was later named to the American Film Institute's "100 Years, 100 Movies" list of the one hundred greatest American films ever produced. What is this film?

5. The film's technical advisor had served at the actual assault on Remagen. Who is this?

6. What is the name of the "bridge at Remagen"?

7. What is the name of the officer known for referring to his men as "cutting edge"?

8. What is the name of the officer who is killed when his jeep is hit with an antitank shell?

9. Filming shut down on August 21, 1968. What event caused this shutdown?

10. What is significant regarding the German soldier Angel kills in the hotel room?

11. What does Maj. Kreuger drop when he's wounded on the bridge?

12. *The Bridge at Remagen* was filmed in Czechoslovakia. What is the significance of this?

13. What does Krueger call Germany's "most dangerous enemy"?

14. Which cast member directed the 1990 film *Beyond the Ocean*?

15. *The Bridge at Remagen* was the second collaboration between actors George Segal and Ben Gazzara. What was the first?

16. Krueger witnesses a German soldier being gunned down before a firing squad. Why is the man killed?

17. Krueger tells his commanding officer that his regrets won't save the bridge. What does he suggest might?

18. Lt. Hartman says the bridge is not a bridge at all. What does he conclude it to be?

19. Who does Maj. Barnes threaten to have court-martialed?

20. Hartman tells Angel, "If there ain't enough for everybody, there sure as hell ain't enough for you." To what is he referring?

21. *The Bridge at Remagen* director John Guillermin was later nominated for a Razzie Award in the category of Worst Director. For what 1984 bomb did Guillermin receive this dubious honor?

22. What does Maj. Krueger see when he looks through his binoculars at the tower beside the bridge?

23. While shooting *The Bridge at Remagen*, the filmmakers were ac-

cused of being Central Intelligence Agency agents and American soldiers disguised as actors and crew members. Who made these accusations?

24. The German soldiers hide to protect themselves from the impending explosion of the bridge. Where do they hide?

25. Two-thirds of the way through filming, the production had to be relocated (see question 9). Where was the filming moved to?

Quiz No. 15:

THE BRIDGE ON THE RIVER KWAI (1957)

Screenplay by Michael Wilson and Carl Foreman (based on a novel by Pierre Boulle)
Directed by David Lean
Starring William Holden, Alec Guinness, and Jack Hawkins
Columbia Pictures
Available on VHS, DVD

> *I'd say the odds against a successful escape are about one hundred to one. But may I add another word, Colonel? The odds against survival in this camp are even worse.* —MAJ. SHEARS

Like most war films of its era, *The Bridge on the River Kwai* is not historically accurate. However, it is extremely entertaining and very well constructed. The screenplay is tight and, as usual, director David Lean delivers the goods. *The Bridge on the River Kwai* tells the story of a group of English prisoners who are held in an isolated Japanese prison camp. The prisoners are led by the rigid by-the-book Col. Nicholson (Alec Guinness), and the prison camp is overseen by the barbaric Col. Saito (Sessue Hayakawa). After initially squaring off against Saito, Nicholson decides to show the Japanese what British soldiers are capable of accomplishing. When ordered to construct a railway bridge, Nicholson vows to construct the finest bridge he can. At the same time, a special unit of American soldiers are moving into position to destroy the bridge.

The Bridge on the River Kwai was named to the American Film Institute's 1998 "100 Years, 100 Films" list of the one hundred greatest American films (despite the fact that it was a British production) at number thirteen. In addition, the film received eight Academy Award nominations in the categories of Best Picture (Sam Spiegel), Best Screenplay (Pierre Boulle), Best Director (Lean), Best Actor (Alec Guinness), Best Supporting Actor (Sessue Hayakawa), Best Cinematography (Jack Hildyard), Best Film Editing (Peter Taylor), and Best Original Score (Malcolm Arnold). The film won seven Oscars, losing only in the category of Best Supporting Actor. Other honors include four British Academy of Film and Television Awards, three Golden Globes, a Directors Guild Award, four National Board of Review Awards, and three New York Film Critics Circle Awards. The film was listed to the National Film Registry as a classic in 1997.

1. Laurence Olivier was the first actor approached to play the role of Col. Nicholson. However, Olivier passed to appear in another film. What is this film?

2. What does Nicholson conclude to be the duty of a captured soldier?

3. What, according to Shears, is the "only important thing"?

4. Novelist Pierre Boulle was the only credited screenwriter when the film was initially released in 1957. However, he had absolutely nothing to do with the writing of the screenplay and could not speak a word of English. Why was he the only writer credited?

5. Who accepted the Best Adapted Screenplay Oscar for novelist Pierre Boulle?

6. What does Nicholson say he supposes he would "have to do" if he were Col. Saito?

7. Nicholson was modeled after a real-life British officer. Who was this?

8. The country where *The Bridge on the River Kwai* was filmed is now known as Sri Lanka. However, it had a different name then. What was this?

9. A sequel to *The Bridge on the River Kwai* was later produced. The film stars Timothy Bottoms, Chris Penn, and George Takei. What is this film?

10. Shears trades uniforms with a dead officer. Why?

11. Alec Guinness's name was originally misspelled in the film's credits. How was his name spelled?

12. James Donald plays Maj. Clipton, the camp's medical officer. In 1965, Donald played another physician being held in a Japanese prisoner of war camp in a film directed by Bryan Forbes. What is this film?

13. Producer Sam Spiegel, director David Lean, and actor Alec Guinness collaborated on a second film five years later. What is this film?

14. Shears is given a simulated rank while working with Force 316. What is this?

15. What does Shears say he does not want over his head?

16. How much of the twenty-eight years he's spent in the military does Nicholson believe he's spent at home?

17. Nicholson says two things happen when an officer loses respect. What are these?

18. In 1984, screenwriter Michael Wilson was finally presented his long-overdue Oscar for *The Bridge on the River Kwai*. What significant event occurred the following day?

19. Sessue Hayakawa lost in his bid for the Best Supporting Actor Oscar. Who won the award?

20. *The Bridge on the River Kwai* was the highest grossing film of 1958 in the United Kingdom. How many films outgrossed the film in the United States?

21. Alec Guinness claims that David Lean greeted him at the airport by announcing that he had wanted another actor to play Nicholson. Who was this?

22. Who does Nicholson incorrectly assess as being "quite a reasonable type"?

23. Why didn't Alec Guinness attend the Academy Awards ceremony in 1957?

24. What screenwriter performed an uncredited rewrite of the film's script?

25. Just before signing on to direct *The Bridge on the River Kwai*, David Lean had worked on another project about a Japanese prisoner of war. This project, which was to have been an adaptation of a novel by Richard Mason, was aborted. What was this project?

Quiz No. 16:

THE BRIDGES AT TOKO-RI

(1954)

Screenplay by Valentine Davies
Directed by Mark Robson
Starring William Holden, Grace Kelly, and Fredric March
Paramount Pictures
Available on VHS, DVD

> *All through history men have had to fight the wrong war in the wrong place, but that's the one they're stuck with.*
>
> —ADM. GEORGE TARRANT

The story of a Korean War fighter pilot (William Holden) struggling with fear and faced with his own mortality, *The Bridges at Toko-Ri* is one of the finest war films ever made. The film was clearly intended as a military recruitment tool. Because of this, the U.S. Navy provided the filmmakers an unprecedented degree of assistance and access to fighter planes and aircraft carriers, which lend the film a genuine feel that is uncommon for war films produced in the 1950s. Despite an uneven script that is at times overly jingoistic, the film's third act is as thrilling and suspenseful as anything Hollywood has ever produced. As always, William Holden turns in a fine performance, as does Grace Kelly, who appears as his troubled wife. Journeyman filmmaker Mark Robson also does some of his finest work here. Though underappreciated, *The Bridges at Toko-Ri* is a must-see for war movie buffs.

The Bridges at Toko-Ri received two Oscar nominations in 1956 for Best Film Editing (Alma Macrorie) and Best Special Effects, winning the latter.

1. *The Bridges at Toko-Ri* was one of two war films adapted from the writing of James Michener that were released in 1955. The second film features Van Johnson and Keenan Wynn. What is this film?

45

2. Adm. Tarrant says there are two things he hates to see a young officer do. The first is to "go over someone's head." What is the second?

3. Who does Adm. Tarrant conclude that "war is no place for"?

4. What *Gunsmoke* regular appears in a cameo as an air intelligence officer?

5. How much money does Brubaker pay the military police to cover the damages of a brawl Mike Forney started?

6. What is the name of Brubaker's wife?

7. Who was this film dedicated to?

8. Thirteen years prior to this film, director Mark Robson served as an associate editor on a film considered by many as the greatest American film ever produced. What is this film?

9. Mike Forney says you can say anything to an officer as long as you do one thing. What is this?

10. How many years has Cmdr. Wayne Lee served in the navy?

11. Where in the United States does Brubaker reside?

12. What are the names of Brubaker's two daughters?

13. How many bridges at Toko-Ri serve as the primary target?

14. What is the name of Mike Forney's sidekick?

15. Of what item does Brubaker remark "not that I've ever used it"?

16. What is the name of Adm. Tarrant's son who was killed at the Battle of Midway?

17. What is the final line of the film?

18. Why doesn't Brubaker use his life raft when his plane ditches in the ocean?

19. *The Bridges at Toko-Ri* is one of two films released in 1955 starring William Holden and Grace Kelly. What is the second film?

20. Why does Adm. Tarrant say he doesn't drink alcohol?

21. What does Mike Forney believe ditched pilots who are seconds away from death take comfort in seeing as he rescues them?

22. What does Lee advise Brubaker to dive into after crash landing?

23. What is Brubaker's civilian occupation?

24. The admiral receives a dispatch regarding Brubaker just before his plane ditches. What does it say?

25. *The Bridges at Toko-Ri* is one of two films released in 1955 starring William Holden and Fredric March. What is the second film?

Quiz No. 17:
A BRIDGE TOO FAR
(1977)

Screenplay by William Goldman (based on a novel by Cornelius Ryan)
Directed by Richard Attenborough
Starring James Caan, Michael Caine, and Sean Connery
United Artists
Available on VHS, DVD

> *Hancock, I've got lunatics laughing at me from the woods. My original plan has been scuppered now that the jeeps haven't arrived. My communications are completely broken down. Do you really believe any of that can be helped by a cup of tea?*
> —MAJ. GEN. ROY URQUHART

There's an old joke in the army that the motto of the American military is "Hurry up and wait," and this is exactly what *A Bridge Too Far* is about. The film chronicles a poorly executed 1944 Allied mission in which thirty-five thousand men were dropped behind enemy lines to hold bridges for British forces moving into the area. Once there, these soldiers found themselves in the wrong locations with the wrong supplies. Superbly crafted by director Richard Attenborough, this epic film features one of the most impressive casts ever assembled for a single project. While the film is a bit long at 175 minutes, it's entertaining and amazingly well acted.

Despite being completely snubbed by the Academy of Motion Picture Arts and Sciences, *A Bridge Too Far* received eight British Academy of Film and Television Awards nominations in the categories of Best Film, Best Direction (Attenborough), Best Supporting Actor (Edward Fox), Best Cinematography (Geoffrey Unsworth), Best Film Editing (Antony Gibbs), Best Sound (Peter Horrocks, Gerry Humphreys, Simon Kaye, Robin O'Donoghue, and Les Wiggins), Best Original Score (John Addison), and Best Production Design–Art Direction (Terence

Marsh). Of these nominations, the film scored four statuettes for Best Supporting Actor, Best Cinematography, Best Original Score, and Best Sound. Other honors include a National Society of Film Critics Award for Best Supporting Actor (Fox) and a British Society of Cinematographers Award.

1. When the Germans offer to surrender, what is Lt. Gen. Frost's response?

2. Lt. Col. Vandeleur asks Col. Stout if he's ever been liberated. What is Stout's humorous response?

3. What does Field Marshal Model say all of his generals want to destroy?

4. Maj. Gen. Urquhart and his men find a group of people wandering through the woods laughing maniacally. Who are they?

5. One of the British paratroopers is gunned down attempting to retrieve a supply drop. After he is killed, the package comes open. What is in the parcel?

6. What is the name of the Allied operation chronicled in this film?

7. What does Capt. Bestebreurtie say he knew no "Jerry" would carry?

8. What nationality is Gene Hackman's character?

9. Who narrates the film?

10. Although it appears that there are many Sherman tanks in the film, many of them are actually plastic molds placed on top of automobiles. How many real Sherman tanks did the producers obtain for the film?

11. *A Bridge Too Far* was the fifth film written by William Goldman in which Robert Redford appeared. What were their four previous collaborations?

12. What does Maj. Cook advise his men to use in lieu of oars?

13. *A Bridge Too Far* was the first of three William Goldman screenplays directed by Richard Attenborough. What are the two projects that followed?

14. In what country does Stout say he was born?

15. Why does Model reason that paratroops cannot fight for long?

16. What type of sickness does Urquhart say he's prone to?

17. Who does Cook jokingly say he intends to cross the river like?

18. Dr. Spaander says winning and losing are not his concern. What does he say is his concern?

19. One actor who appears in *A Bridge Too Far* later became a regular on the television sitcom *Cheers.* Who is this?

20. What does Model believe the Allied forces who have landed near Arnhem have come to do?

21. What does Gen. Sosabowski say just before jumping from his plane?

22. *A Bridge Too Far* is one of five films directed by Richard Attenborough in which Anthony Hopkins appears. Can you name the other four films?

23. How many miles from Arnhem is the Allied drop zone?

24. This was one of two films released in 1977 in which Maximilian Schell played a Nazi officer. The other film was directed by Sam Peckinpah. What is this film?

25. Why are the VHF sets useless to Urquhart's men?

Quiz No. 18:

THE CAINE MUTINY

(1954)

Screenplay by Stanley Roberts and Michael Blankfort (based on a novel by
   Herman Wouk)
Directed by Edward Dmytryk
Starring Humphrey Bogart, Jose Ferrer, and Van Johnson
Columbia Pictures
Available on VHS, DVD

> *There is no escape from the* Caine *save death. We are all doing
> penance; sentenced to an outcast ship manned by outcasts and named
> after the greatest outcast of them all.*   —LT. TOM KEEFER

The Caine Mutiny is a brilliant examination of the effects that the pressures of both war and military leadership can have on a man. Unlike
most of the other films in this book, the war itself takes a backseat in
this story. However, it's never far beneath the surface considering that
Capt. Queeg's (Humphrey Bogart) meltdown takes place after two years
of intense sea duty. Bogart gave the performance of his life, and Stanley
Kramer's choice of veteran helmer Dmytryk to direct was inspired.
The screenplay—based on Herman Wouk's Pulitzer Prize–winning
novel by the same title—snaps with clever dialogue. Fred MacMurray
is also impressive here as the cowardly Lt. Tom Keefer. *The Caine Mutiny*
isn't simply one of the greatest war films of all time, it's one of the
greatest films ever produced in any genre.

   The film received seven Academy Award nominations for Best Picture
(Kramer), Best Screenplay (Stanley Roberts and Michael Blankfort),
Best Actor (Bogart), Best Supporting Actor (Tom Tully), Best Film
Editing (William A. Lyon and Henry Batista), Best Original Score (Max
Steiner), and Best Sound Recording (John P. Livadary). Sadly, the film
did not win a single Oscar. In addition, *The Caine Mutiny* received

British Academy of Film and Television Awards nominations for Best Film and Best Foreign Actor (Jose Ferrer).

1. How big, according to film's tagline, is *The Caine Mutiny*?
2. Who are the three men who leave the *Caine* to meet with Adm. Halsey?
3. Who does Lt. Keefer refer to as the *Caine*'s "fireball"?
4. Capt. Queeg says there are four ways to do things. What are they?
5. When Keith remarks that Queeg is "certainly navy," what is Keefer's memorable response?
6. What gift does the "fouled-up crew" of the *Caine* give Capt. DeVriess?
7. What is the name of the song Keefer writes about Queeg?
8. The studio wanted another actor cast as Queeg. Who was this?
9. What does Keefer say is the first thing Keith and Harding need to learn about the *Caine*?
10. *The Caine Mutiny* was remade by director Robert Altman in 1988. What actor plays Capt. Queeg in this remake?
11. Who is referred to as the *Caine*'s favorite author?
12. Keith graduated from an Ivy League school in 1941. What school was this?
13. Actress Donna Lee Hickey appears in the film as May Wynn. What is the significance of this?
14. May believes herself to be the second-ranking woman in Keith's life. Who does she believe to be the first-ranking woman?
15. Queeg's insanity comes to light when he accuses the men of stealing fruit. What kind of fruit?
16. *The Caine Mutiny* lost in its bid for the Best Picture Oscar. What film won the statuette?
17. What, according to a message at the beginning of the film, has never happened?
18. What does Keefer refer to as "those monstrous papers that transform ex-civilians into men without minds"?
19. Who does Greenwald say doesn't have one-tenth of the guts Queeg has?
20. *The Caine Mutiny* is one of two films directed by Edward Dmytryk that were released in 1954. The other film was a Western starring Spencer Tracy and Robert Wagner. What is this film?

21. With what does Keefer say Queeg crawls?

22. What does Queeg call "one of the nice things" about being captain?

23. What percent of things done in the engine room does Keefer say requires creative intelligence?

24. By what name is Claude Aikins's character known?

25. The *Caine* is initially described as a minesweeper that has never been asked to do something. What is this?

Quiz No. 19:

CASUALTIES OF WAR

(1989)

Screenplay by David Rabe (based on a book by Daniel Lang)
Directed by Brian De Palma
Starring Michael J. Fox, Sean Penn, and Don Harvey
Columbia Pictures
Available on VHS, DVD

> *Ye though I walk through the valley of evil, I shall fear no death . . .
> 'cause I'm the baddest motherfucker in the valley.*
> —SGT. TONY MESERVE

Based on a true story, *Casualties of War* begins with Pvt. Eriksson's (Michael J. Fox) arrival in Vietnam. Soon Eriksson is faced with a moral dilemma when his fellow platoon members kidnap, rape, and eventually murder a young Vietnamese woman; while everyone—including his superiors—instruct him to look the other way, Eriksson cannot. An entertaining but dispensable film, *Casualties of War* falls short despite a first-rate ensemble, a script written by playwright David Rabe, a score by Ennio Morricone, and direction by Brian De Palma. Beyond the poor casting of lead Michael J. Fox, who plays Eriksson like *Family Ties*'s Alex P. Keaton gone to war, the film suffers from its many clichés. True, all Vietnam War films are going to cover much of the same ground; there's no getting around that. The problem is that so much of this was done far better three years earlier in Oliver Stone's *Platoon* (1986). Another critical problem is that the film's message is at times heavyhanded, which brings the action to a standstill.

Composer Ennio Morricone received a Golden Globe nomination for Best Original Score for his work on *Casualties of War*. In addition, Maurice Schell was nominated by the Motion Picture Sound Editors in the category of Best Sound Editing in a Feature Film.

1. What is Chaplain Kirk's religious denomination?

2. Who is the first person Meserve orders to "waste" Oahn?

3. This story was first reported in a 1969 article by Daniel Lang. In what publication did this story appear?

4. When Eriksson falls into an enemy tunnel, who pulls him out?

5. Meserve says he is "short." What does this term mean?

6. What does Meserve say he plans to "requisition" for "some portable R&R"?

7. What does the term "R&R" mean?

8. The other soldiers refer to Eriksson by a derogatory term signifying that he's still green. What is this?

9. When Eriksson tries to assist Oahn in her escape, who catches him?

10. Quentin Tarantino, a huge fan of this film, borrowed the line of dialogue in which a man says to his dying comrade, "Look into my eyes. You ain't gonna die" for a 1992 film he directed. What is this film?

11. Where does Lt. Reilly say he was born?

12. What is Meserve's age?

13. What does Brown say Eriksson is without Meserve?

14. What does Eriksson say to Oahn's mother?

15. Actor John Leguizamo appeared in another film directed by Brian De Palma four years after *Casualties of War*. What is this film?

16. How many days does Brown have left to serve in Vietnam when he is killed?

17. Who does Hatcher believe is "just like Ghengis Khan"?

18. Sean Penn and John C. Reilly appear together in another war film released nine years after *Casualties of War*. What is this film?

19. What is Clark's rank?

20. Who says, "I ain't gonna rape nobody"?

21. What sound does Oahn make, causing Clark to fear she will give away their position?

22. Who attempts to kill Eriksson by tossing a grenade into the latrine?

23. What is Brown's nickname?

24. Brown concludes that soldiers don't know anything in their first thirty days in Vietnam. What does he conclude regarding the final thirty days in the bush?

25. Who strikes Clark with a shovel?

Quiz No. 20:
CATCH-22
(1970)

Screenplay by Buck Henry (based on a novel by Joseph Heller)
Directed by Mike Nichols
Starring Alan Arkin, Martin Balsam, and Richard Benjamin
Paramount Pictures
Available on VHS, DVD

> *Let me see if I've got this straight: in order to be grounded, I've got to be crazy, and I must be crazy to keep flying. But if I ask to be grounded, that means I'm not crazy anymore and I have to keep flying.*
> —CAPT. JOHN YOSSARIAN

When *Catch-22* was released in 1970, it confused literal-minded audiences and quickly fell to the wayside when the less challenging *M*A*S*H* (1970) was released and became one of the highest grossing films of the year. Nevertheless, *Catch-22* isn't the dreadful film so many mainstream viewers would have you believe. Despite choosing to adapt what is largely an unfilmable novel, Mike Nichols and screenwriter Buck Henry managed to create a stylish Kafkaesque black comedy. Reminiscent of Orson Welles's 1962 Franz Kafka adaptation *The Trial* (given a nod here through the casting of director Welles and star Anthony Perkins), Nichols succeeds in capturing the eerily disconnected dreamlike atmosphere needed to realize this story. Perhaps the film is best summed up by *DVD Savant* critic Glenn Erickson, "*Catch-22* is nobody's favorite film, but it's still an impressive show—funny, bizarre, and remote at the same time."

Catch-22 received two British Academy of Film and Television Awards nominations in the categories of Best Cinematography (Dean Watkin) and the coveted United Nations Award, losing for both. Other honors include a Writers Guild Award nomination for Best Adapted

Screenplay (Henry) and a Laurel Awards nomination for Best Actor (Alan Arkin).

1. What does Col. Cathcart believe should be illegal?
2. What is the name of the man McWatt decapitates with the propellers of his plane?
3. Yossarian speaks to a "dead man" after being stabbed. Who is this?
4. Nately informs Yossarian that Dobbs is planning to kill someone. Who?
5. Where does Minderbinder say he obtained the egg?
6. Where does Danby say Orr's raft washed ashore?
7. When Yossarian says he's tried but "can't seem to get one," of what is he speaking?
8. What is the name of Minderbinder's business?
9. What is Yossarian's response when asked why he is wearing no clothes to accept his medal?
10. *Catch-22* is one of three films written by Buck Henry and directed by Mike Nichols. What are the other two films?
11. There is one thing Cathcart and Col. Korn say Yossarian must do in exchange for his being sent home. What is this?
12. What type of episodes does Korn believe should be kept at a minimum?
13. What actor was first offered the role of Cathcart, but turned it down, saying he had already played a similar role in *Dr. Strangelove* (1964)?
14. Who does Minderbinder call a victim of economic pressures?
15. Minderbinder gives Yossarian a confection as they sit in the tree during a funeral. What is this unusual confection?
16. What is Minderbinder's first name?
17. Novelist Joseph Heller served as a screenwriter on a film released the same year as this adaptation of his novel *Catch-22*. The film was directed by Burt Kennedy and stars Frank Sinatra and George Kennedy. What is this film?
18. After throwing a girl out of her window, Aardvark then says she has no right to be in the street. Why is this?
19. For what offense does Gen. Dreedle order Danby to be shot?
20. Which of the men fall in love with a prostitute?

21. Second unit John Jordan was killed during the filming of *Catch-22*. How was he killed?

22. What does Nately say is better than living on one's knees?

23. Bob Newhart, who appears in *Catch-22* as Maj. Major, made his film debut in a 1962 war film directed by Don Siegel. What is this film?

24. Why does Luciana say Yossarian cannot marry her?

25. Who does Yossarian call a "one man disaster area"?

Quiz No. 21:

THE CHARGE OF THE
LIGHT BRIGADE
(1936)

Screenplay by Michael Jacoby and Rowland Leigh (based on a poem by
   Alfred Lord Tennyson)
Directed by Michael Curtiz
Starring Errol Flynn, Olivia de Havilland, and Patric Knowles
Warner Bros.
Available on VHS

> *Here in this one room you can see everything that makes the world go
> around: riches, intrigue, and all the seeds of mutiny, war, and hatred.*
> —MAJ. GEOFFREY VICKERS

Loosely based on Lord Alfred Tennyson's poem of the same title, *The
Charge of the Light Brigade* depicts the now-infamous charge of the
Light Brigade during the Crimean War. Detractors are quick to point
out the film's glaring historical inaccuracies—here, for instance, the
conflict is relocated to India. More important, the charge, which historians now believe was a mistake, is depicted in the film as a noble act of
heroism. Yet, despite these flaws, the film is incredibly entertaining,
and the artistic liberties taken by screenwriters Michael Jacoby and
Rowland Leigh actually serve to make the film more exciting. Despite
the fact that his filmography is brimming with classic films, Michael
Curtiz's direction was rarely better than it is here. The battle sequences
are well choreographed and film editor George Amy handles them
well. Frequent screen team Errol Flynn and Olivia de Havilland—both
in their heyday here—do excellent work, and Sol Polito's cinematography is spectacular.

The Charge of the Light Brigade received three Academy Award
nominations in the categories of Best Original Score (Max Steiner),

Best Sound (Nathan Levinson), and Best Assistant Director (Jack Sullivan). These nominations resulted in a sole Oscar for Best Assistant Director.

1. What special qualification for war films did actor David Niven have?
2. What does Sir Charles say brothers "rarely avoid"?
3. What is Sir Benjamin Warrenton's nickname?
4. What does Geoffrey say he doesn't think he could lose with grace?
5. What does Sir Warrenton say life with his wife is always?
6. *The Charge of the Light Brigade* was one of two films released in 1936 that were directed by Michael Curtiz and star Olivia de Havilland. The other film, which was codirected by Mervyn LeRoy, also stars Fredric March. What is the other film?
7. Despite her engagement to Geoffrey, Elsa falls in love with someone else. Who?
8. What, according to Sir Warrenton, are his wife's two obsessions?
9. Perry says he's always looked up to his brother. What does he say he now sees Geoffrey to be?
10. Who does Sir Charles say people do not wage war against?
11. What, according to Geoffrey, are the worst years on the frontier?
12. What does the film refer to as the "livid scar never to heal"?
13. *The Charge of the Light Brigade* was the first of four films featuring both Errol Flynn and Patric Knowles. The other three films were all released in 1938. Can you name them?
14. What does Sir Charles say it's often difficult to tell the difference between during "this treacherous life"?
15. Geoffrey tells Khan he's not fighting a single outpost. What does he say he is instead fighting against?
16. David Niven later titled his 1974 autobiography after a phrase used by director Michael Curtiz throughout the production. What is this?
17. *The Charge of the Light Brigade* star Errol Flynn and actor Trevor Howard, who stars in the 1968 remake, appear together in one film. What is this film?
18. Who rewrites the orders sent from general headquarters to the light brigade?

19. Surat Khan is saved just as he is about to be killed by a leopard. Who saves him?

20. What does Sir Charles say every British soldier would give to avenge the Chukoti massacre?

21. What does Sir Charles say he cannot meet with until after he's had a drink?

22. Two years after appearing in *The Charge of the Light Brigade* together, Errol Flynn and David Niven collaborated on their second and final film. This second film, directed by Edmund Goulding, is also a war movie. What is this film?

23. What does Khan say signifies the "completion of a bargain between two gentlemen"?

24. What is Col. Campbell's response when Lady Warrenton asks what his favorite quality in a woman is?

25. What does Geoffrey call the "luck of the army"?

Quiz No. 22:

CROSS OF IRON

(1977)

Screenplay by Julius J. Epstein, James Hamilton, and Walter Kelly
Directed by Sam Peckinpah
Starring James Coburn, Maximilian Schell, and James Mason
Rapid Films/EMI Films Ltd.
Available on VHS, DVD

> *The German soldier no longer has any ideals. He is not fighting for the culture of the West, not for this one form of government that he wants, not for the stinking party. He's fighting for his life, God bless him.*
> —COL. BRANDT

Cross of Iron—director Sam Peckinpah's only true war film—is everything one might expect and hope for in such a project. In many ways, *Cross of Iron* stands in opposition to the traditional war film in much the same way Peckinpah's *The Wild Bunch* (1969) thumbed its nose at the Western genre. This gritty picture focuses on German soldiers fighting on the Russian front in 1943. This film feels true; its characters, performances, dialogue, and storyline all feel authentic, as though *Cross of Iron* might be newly discovered documentary footage of German footsoldiers on the front. This film does not glorify war, nor does it blatantly hit the viewer over the head with antiwar messages. It simply turns the camera on what could have been any German platoon during World War II and films the events that transpire. The performances are all exceptional, but the strength of the film is James Coburn's brilliant turn as a burned-out, disinterested sergeant. Most war film buffs haven't seen *Cross of Iron,* and that's truly a shame. The film is Peckinpah's forgotten masterpiece, easily on par with his most-revered works.

    Cross of Iron is an abrasively unflinching film that never once panders to its audience. It is perhaps for this reason that it was completely overlooked by the Academy. The film did, however, receive Germany's Golden Screen Award in 1977.

1. What is Sgt. Steiner's response when Capt. Stransky orders him to shoot the young Russian boy?

2. Stransky informs Triebig, "If you are caught, you will be hanged." What "crime" is he referring to?

3. What percentage of soldiers at the field hospital does the general order to be returned to active duty within three days?

4. What myth does Stransky say it's time to destroy?

5. What actor took over James Coburn's role for the inferior 1978 sequel *Sergeant Steiner*?

6. What are Marga's final words to Steiner as he leaves the hospital?

7. Col. Brandt announces that transfer orders have arrived for Stransky. Where is Stransky being sent?

8. Of what action does Brandt say he can think of "nothing more contemptible"?

9. Prior to his turn as Col. Brandt in *Cross of Iron,* James Mason had portrayed German Field Marshal Erwin Rommel in two films. Can you name them?

10. What noted filmmaker called *Cross of Iron* the finest antiwar film since *All Quiet on the Western Front* (1930)?

11. What two soldiers are asked to attest that Stransky led the counterattack against the Russians?

12. What does Kruger say the combination of natural body oils and dirt make a soldier?

13. Stransky says he cannot face his family should he return from the war without something. What is this?

14. What does Dietz believe it's bad luck to step on?

15. What does Steiner say he believes about God?

16. What is the password to gain entry into the camp?

17. What does Capt. Kiesel believe to be a myth that is "dangerous"?

18. Steiner asks Marga to hold his alcohol bottle so he can hold something else. What is this?

19. How many weeks has Dietz been a soldier?

20. The Russian boy gives something to Steiner just before being gunned down. What is this?

21. What does Kiesel say is "not worth drinking for"?

22. Both director Sam Peckinpah and screenwriter Julius J. Epstein are responsible for films listed to the American Film Institute's 1998 list of the one hundred greatest American films ever produced. Peckinpah's contribution was *The Wild Bunch* (1969), which he directed. On what top one-hundred film did Epstein serve as a screenwriter?

23. Brandt asks Kiesel what they will do after losing the war. What is Kiesel's memorable response?

24. Marga asks Steiner if he fears what he will become without something. What is this?

25. Brandt says, "We are not retreating." What does he say they are doing?

Quiz No. 23:

DAS BOOT

(1981)

Screenplay by Wolfgang Petersen (based on a novel by Lothar G. Buchheim)
Directed by Wolfgang Petersen
Starring Jürgen Prochnow, Herbert Gronemeyer, and Klaus Wenneman
Bavaria Film
Available on VHS, DVD

> *Quiet in this whorehouse! A toast to our wonderful abstaining ...*
> *womanless ... Fuhrer. Who rose gloriously from apprentice painter*
> *to become the world's greatest battle strategist. What? Isn't it true?*
> *He's the great naval expert who took it upon himself... in his wis-*
> *dom ... How's it go again?* —CAPT. PHILLIP THOMSEN

A number of fine films that take place onboard submarines have been made through the years (*Crimson Tide* [1995], *U-571* [2000], *Run Silent Run Deep* [1958], and so on), but none approach the effectiveness and sheer artistry of Wolfgang Petersen's modern classic *Das Boot*. Initially filmed as a television miniseries, *Das Boot* was released theatrically at 149 minutes. In 1996, a longer "director's cut" was released, weighing in at a hefty 216 minutes.

Despite its length, there are few films of any genre that match its brilliance, and even fewer that deal specifically with the subject of warfare. Because of Petersen's insistence that the film be shot inside the closed confines of an ultrarealistic life-sized model of a German u-boat, the film has a feeling of genuine claustrophobia that places the viewer inside the submarine and in the center of the conflict. If ever there was a film that was meant to be viewed in a widescreen format with surround sound, it is this one. Few films approach the level of perfection Petersen achieved with *Das Boot*.

Das Boot received six Academy Award nominations in the categories of Best Adapted Screenplay (Petersen), Best Director (Petersen),

Best Cinematography (Jost Vacano), Best Film Editing (Hannes Nikel), Best Sound (Milan Bor, Trevor Pike, and Mike Le Mare), and Best Sound Effects Editing (Le Mare). However, the film failed to snag a single Oscar. Other honors include the prestigious Golden Screen Award, prizes for Outstanding Individual Achievement in Sound and Outstanding Feature Film at the German Film Awards, and nominations from the Brtish Academy of Film and Television Awards and the Golden Globes for Best Foreign Language Film.

1. The film informs us that forty thousand German sailors served on u-boats during World War II. How many of those sailors does the film say never returned?

2. One crew member suffers a nervous breakdown, nearly causing Lehmann-Willenbrock to shoot him. Who is this?

3. An American filmmaker who served as montage director on *Casablanca* (1942) before directing films such as *Hell Is for Heroes* (1962), *The Killers* (1964), and *The Shootist* (1976) was allegedly attached to direct this film at one time. Who is this?

4. The submarine is destroyed at the end of the film. How?

5. Who does Lehmann-Willenbrock say Adolf Hitler refers to as a "drunkard" and a "paralytic"?

6. How many meters beneath the sea is the submarine when it sinks to the bottom?

7. Jürgen Prochnow appeared in four films directed by Wolfgang Petersen prior to their collaborating on *Das Boot*. Since that project, they have made only one film together. What is this 1997 film?

8. What does Lehmann-Willenbrock believe the crew needs the way infantrymen need alcohol?

9. All of the crew members are shown at a celebration party at the beginning of the film. What are they celebrating?

10. What does the chief conclude that Lehmann-Willenbrock knew the moment he received the radiogram in Vigo?

11. How many meters beneath the sea is the sub when its bolts begin to burst from the pressure?

12. *Das Boot* producers Mark Damon and Gunter Rohrback later reunite on another noted World War II film. This 1993 film stars Dominique Horwitz and was directed by Joseph Vilsmaier. What is this film?

13. Director Wolfgang Petersen later returns to the sea with a 2000 film about a fishing boat. What is this film?

14. What belief does Thomsen say can be seen in the eyes of the young sailors?

15. Which crew member is referred to as the "Ghost"?

16. Which of the men has a sick wife at home?

17. Just before shipping out, Lehmann-Willenbrock informs the crew that there is a guest onboard. Who is this?

18. A dubbed version of *Das Boot* was released in the United States in 1982. What is the title of this version?

19. What is the nationality of Ullman's girlfriend?

20. What regarding the appearance of the sailors does Lehmann-Willenbrock say will be different when the crew returns home?

21. The first lieutenant says the crew members did something to him while he was on his way to the party. What was this?

22. Where does Lehmann-Willenbrock say the British sailors are celebrating the sinking of the submarine?

23. What does Lehmann-Willenbrock say there is nothing as beautiful as?

24. What is the name of the German merchant ship the submarine is supposed to locate at Vigo?

25. How many toilets are there on the u-boat?

Quiz No. 24:

THE DEVIL'S BRIGADE

(1968)

Screenplay by William Roberts
Directed by Andrew V. McLaglen
Starring William Holden, Cliff Robertson, and Vince Edwards
Metro-Goldwyn-Mayer
Available on VHS, DVD

> *Those high muckety-muck generals. . . . You know, Jesus Christ was satisfied with just one star. Some of those brainy brass hats gotta have four. You know how they get 'em? By screwin' things up!*
> —PVT. ROCKWELL ROCKMAN

The Devil's Brigade is a fictionalized account of the First Special Service Force and its World War II exploits. Lt. Col. Robert T. Frederick (William Holden) is assigned this new unit comprised of the Canadian military's finest soldiers and U.S. Army troublemakers culled from various military prisons, and given four months to mold them into an elite fighting unit. The Canadian and U.S. soldiers initially find themselves at odds with one another, but eventually unite in battle. While it never succeeds in being quite as effective as the similarly themed *The Dirty Dozen* (1967), which was released the year before, *The Devil's Brigade* is an outstanding film. The film, which features a solid cast, is one of noted war helmer Andrew V. McLaglen's finest efforts. As usual, leading man William Holden turns in a wonderful performance. Equally impressive is Claude Akins, who provides comic relief. The true star here, however, is William H. Clothier, who provides scene after scene of sharp, gorgeous cinematography. Sadly, *The Devil's Brigade* is one of the lesser-known inclusions in this book. War movie aficionados be advised: If you haven't seen this gem, you're missing out.

1. *The Devil's Brigade* marked the second and final collaboration between actors William Holden and Cliff Robertson. What was the first film in which they appeared together?

2. Richard Dawson and William Holden appear together in this film. Dawson later appears as a regular on a television series loosely based on a film starring Holden. What is this series and film?

3. After taking the German-held town, one soldier asks, "Now what do we do with it?" What is Lt. Col. Frederick's response?

4. How many lumberjacks are injured in the barfight?

5. Two versions of this film exist. The differences between the two versions concern the dialogue of the German soldiers. What are these differences?

6. What does Maj. Bricker say he collects?

7. What does Frederick observe on Pvt. Theodore Ransom's wrists?

8. Cliff Robertson won the Oscar for Best Actor for another film released the same year as *The Devil's Brigade*. What film was this?

9. Who does Sgt. Maj. O'Neill call a "monstrous tub of lard"?

10. From where did the filmmakers cast the three hundred extras used in the Wasatch Mountain battle scenes?

11. What, according to Rockman, is "fraternizing with the Canadians" considered to be?

12. Maj. Crown says the "most memorable" compliment to the unit came from the German commanding officer he was interrogating. What did the German call the unit?

13. What lesson does Crown say he learned at Dunkirk?

14. What is the name of the deserted base where the unit trains?

15. What, according to Frederick, does the unit have "in excess"?

16. What musical instrument does Ransom play?

17. Who does Lt. Gen. Clark call an "insolent bastard"?

18. How many pounds of rocks are contained in the soldiers' ruck sacks for the thirty-mile road march?

19. To how many camps has Bricker been assigned?

20. How long does Rockman conclude it would take the United States to defeat Canada in a war?

21. The thirty-mile road march becomes a race. What is the name of the soldier who wins?

22. What does Frederick order Bricker to do when addressing him?

23. To whom is this film dedicated?

24. Who agrees to become Pvt. Greco's escape partner?

25. What is the name of the officer Ransom was charged with striking?

Quiz No. 25:
THE DIRTY DOZEN
(1967)

Screenplay by Nunnally Johnson and Lukas Heller (based on a novel by E.M.
Nathanson)
Directed by Robert Aldrich
Starring Lee Marvin, Ernest Borgnine, John Cassavetes, and Charles Bronson
Metro-Goldwyn-Mayer
Available on VHS, DVD

> *You've seen a general inspecting troops before, haven't you? Just walk*
> *slow, act dumb, and look stupid.*   —MAJ. JOHN REISMAN

From the film's very first scene in which a military prisoner is executed, *The Dirty Dozen* is an intense action-packed yarn. Although its
formula was hardly a new one—a stern officer is handed a group of
screw-ups and ordered to transform them into an elite military unit—
its level of violence and its rebellious antiestablishment attitude were
groundbreaking at the time in which it was produced. The film's dialogue is razor sharp, and the cast handles it expertly. Although the ensemble is comprised largely of actors who are generally effective but
hardly deserve the distinction of being labeled great—Charles Bronson,
Jim Brown, and Telly Savalas—all of them turn in terrific performances.
John Cassavetes is, by and large, the most talented thespian in the film,
and it shows. In a film filled with excellent performances, Cassavetes
still manages to shine the brightest. More than thirty-five years after its
initial release, *The Dirty Dozen* remains a fun, action-packed film.

The Dirty Dozen received four Academy Award nominations for
Best Supporting Actor (Cassavetes), Best Film Editing (Michael Luciano),
Best Sound Effects (John Poyner), and Best Sound (Poyner). The film's
sole Oscar was awarded for Best Sound Effects. Other honors include a
gold medal at the Photoplay Awards, a Golden Globe nomination for
Best Supporting Actor (Cassavetes), and four Laurel Award nomina-

tions in the categories of Best Action-Drama, Best Action Performance (Lee Marvin), Best Supporting Actor (Jim Brown), and Best Supporting Actor (Cassavetes), resulting in one win for Marvin, a runner-up prize for Brown, and a third-place prize for Best Action-Drama.

1. Telly Savalas and Donald Sutherland appear together in only two films, both of which are war movies. One of them is *The Dirty Dozen*. What is the other film?

2. What quality does Gen. Worden say Reisman is "very short on"?

3. Which of the men believes he's doing God's work?

4. Lee Marvin, Ernest Borgnine, and Richard Jaeckel all reprised their roles in a 1985 made-for-television sequel (the first of three) directed by Andrew V. McLaglen. What is the title of this telefilm?

5. What does Franco say condemned men don't do?

6. Two of the men beat Franco after catching him attempting to escape. Who are they?

7. What is the name of the operation that frees each of the men from the stockade?

8. While posing as German officers, Reisman and Wladislaw spill something on the guestbook. What?

9. A popular rap group dubbed itself the Dirty Dozen. However, it was advised to change its name since the title was copyrighted. By what name did the group release its 2001 debut album *Devil's Night*?

10. What does Reisman say Franco should learn to do if he's going to "act tough"?

11. What is the name of the act that gives Worden permission to change the decision of a court-martial?

12. Who was the first actor approached to play the role of Reisman?

13. Wladislaw says the squad has enough grenades to blow something up. What is this?

14. *The Dirty Dozen* was the second Robert Aldrich–helmed war film to feature Lee Marvin. What was the first?

15. Which member of the squad is the first to be killed?

16. How many years is Pinkley sentenced to prior to his being freed for the mission?

17. What does Franco say he will not shave with?

18. What is Reisman's advice to Wladislaw in regard to acting like a German soldier?

19. Which member of the squad speaks German?

20. John Cassavetes received his first Oscar nomination in 1968 for his turn in *The Dirty Dozen*. The following year, he received another Oscar nomination for Best Original Screenplay. For what film was he nominated?

21. What is the name of the prison from which Reisman selects the men?

22. Reisman says Wladislaw only made one mistake when committing murder. What was this?

23. Which of the men sabotages the mission and begins shooting his comrades?

24. The film begins with Pvt. Gardner's execution. How is he killed?

25. What is A. J. Maggot's first name?

Quiz No. 26:
ENEMY AT THE GATES
(2001)

Screenplay by Jean-Jacques Annaud and Alain Godard
Directed by Jean-Jacques Annaud
Starring Jude Law, Ed Harris, and Rachel Weisz
Paramount Pictures
Available on VHS, DVD

> *All these men here know they're going to die. So, each night when they make it back, it's a bonus. So, every cup of tea, every cigarette is like a little celebration. You just have to accept that.* —VASSILI ZAITSEV

Enemy at the Gates is a solid, gritty film loosely based on the true story of famed Russian sniper Vassili Zaitsev (Jude Law) at Stalingrad. After propaganda journalist Commisar Danilov (Joseph Fiennes) writes tale after tale about his exploits, Zaitsev becomes a national hero. Realizing they must eliminate Zaitsev, the Germans send their top sniper, Major Konig (Ed Harris), to track him down and kill him. As the two snipers hunt each other, it becomes a dangerous two-way game of cat and mouse. Celebrated French filmmaker and 1990 François Truffaut Award winner Jean-Jacques Annaud deftly handles the film's direction, and he and cowriter Alain Godard's screenplay is quite impressive. The film is only hampered by the unneeded love triangle between Zaitsev, Danilov, and female sniper Tania Chernova (Rachel Weisz), which adds little to the film. *Enemy at the Gates*'s elaborate battle scenes are well crafted. Their goriness coupled with Annaud's decision to use muted colors makes them somewhat reminiscent of *Saving Private Ryan* (1998).

Enemy at the Gates received a Motion Picture Sound Editors Award nomination for Best Sound Editing, a British Society of Cinematographers Award nomination for Best Cinematography, and a nomination for the Harry Award, but failed to win in any of these competitions.

1. Khruschev says that vodka and caviar are luxuries the Russians have. What does he say is not?
2. When Zaitsev is pinned down without his weapon, Chernova uses something to momentarily blind Konig. What is this?
3. The title of the film is derived from a 1973 book by William Craig. What is the full title of this book?
4. What piece of clothing does Khruschev believe makes Zaitsev look "more heroic"?
5. When asked how he plans to find Zaitsev, what is Konig's memorable response?
6. Khruschev says the Germans sending Konig to track down Zaitsev is a sign of something. What is this?
7. Who does Chernova say she believes loves Zaitsev more than she does?
8. What kind of animal is the young Zaitsev firing at when the film opens?
9. When Zaitsev playfully swats at him, Danilov tells him he's lucky he cannot fight back. Why does he say he cannot fight back?
10. Konig wears a war merit cross that was awarded posthumously to an officer who was killed at Stalingrad. Who was this?
11. Khruschev says he wants the Russian soldiers to start acting like they have something. What is this?
12. What, according to the film's tagline, are "some men born to be"?
13. Sacha says his mother makes one dish that is the "best in town." What is this?
14. Who does Koulikov say chooses the hunting ground?
15. Why does Konig say he knows Zaitsev isn't dead?
16. What happens when Ludmilla tries to flee the old department store during the bombing?
17. Who, according to Nazi propaganda broadcast throughout the city, is the true enemy of the Russian soldier?
18. Actors Bob Hoskins and Ed Harris had previously appeared together in a 1995 film directed by Oliver Stone. What is this film?
19. Who trained Koulikov to be a sniper?
20. Where does Zaitsev recall his grandfather once taking him?

21. What subject did Chernova study at the University of Moscow?

22. Ed Harris received his third Oscar nomination the year *Enemy at the Gates* was released. For what film was he nominated?

23. *Enemy at the Gates* was the second film to feature both Joseph Fiennes and Rachel Weisz. What was the first?

24. Danilov tells Chernova that she has a duty. What is this?

25. Who does Khruschev say enjoys "good hunting stories"?

Quiz No. 27:

THE FIGHTING SEABEES

(1944)

Screenplay by Borden Chase and Aeneas MacKenzie
Directed by Edward Ludwig
Starring John Wayne, Susan Hayward, and Dennis O'Keefe
Republic Pictures Corporation
Available on VHS, DVD

> *Training to fight? You might as well start training them to drink! I'm offering you construction crews, not white-collar hats. They know what it is to fight. Every rock tunnel they drill costs a man a mile. Every steel span they bridge costs another. They know that when they take the jobs. All they want is something in their hands when the trouble starts.*
> —CMDR. WEDGE DONOVAN

If you're looking for an exciting, action-packed John Wayne vehicle, *The Fighting Seabees* fits the bill. However, if you're looking for a historically accurate account of the legendary "Seabees" without the trappings of the average 1940s war film (predictable love story, flag-waving jingoism, and so on), one should be advised to steer clear of the film. Loosely based on true events (loosely being the key word here), *The Fighting Seabees* depicts the formation of the Construction Battalion (CBs, or "Seabees"), which built bridges and fought in the Pacific during World War II. Would-be viewers should also be advised of the film's racist attitude toward the Japanese, which is somewhat understandable considering the film was produced during the war; the Japanese are referred to by virtually every anti-Asian racial slur imaginable and Japanese pilots are shown grinning maniacally as they swoop in for the kill. Despite workmanlike directon by Edward Ludwig and run-of-the-mill, wooden performances from much of the cast, *The Fighting Seabees* manages to provide consistent entertainment.

   The Fighting Seabees received one Oscar nomination in 1945 for Best Original Score (Walter Scharf and Roy Webb). However, the film lost to Max Steiner's memorable scoring for *Since You Went Away* (1944).

   1. What are Donovan's last words to Connie before she loses consciousness?
   2. Donovan says the construction workers will take care of their own food. However, he says there is one thing the navy must supply. What is this?
   3. Who is this film dedicated to?
   4. What does Donovan say Connie caused him to forget momentarily?
   5. How many contracts does Donovan say he has in the Pacific?
   6. What, according to Connie, is Donovan "innately"?
   7. Who does Connie joke that Donovan might be captured by?
   8. After being shot, Connie asks Donovan if she looks bad. What is his response?
   9. Who does Connie call a "hot-headed ape with a hair-trigger temper"?
   10. What is Eddie Powers' nickname?
   11. Which of the film's cast members would later become a regular on the television sitcom *I Love Lucy*?
   12. What three things does Connie say "time puts behind us"?
   13. How does Eddie define a "state of physical embarrassment"?
   14. John Wayne and Susan Hayward appear in three films together. One of them is *The Fighting Seabees.* Can you name the other two?
   15. From which borough of New York City does Donovan hail?
   16. What chances of survival does the doctor give Connie?
   17. *The Fighting Seabees* is one of three films in which Edward Ludwig directed John Wayne. What are the other two?
   18. What, according to Eddie, would be an unnatural working condition for Donovan?
   19. What is the name of the dead construction worker Donovan asks for when the ship arrives at the beginning of the film?
   20. How many years does Donovan suggest it will take the Dodgers to win the World Series?
   21. Lt. Cmdr. Yallow says the navy is not fighting men. What does he say it's fighting?

22. When Sawyer remarks that it's "silly the way they pack these things," to what is he referring?

23. What does Donovan say a good blaster must have done?

24. What does Donovan say he's not built for?

25. How does Connie define the word "sesquipedalian"?

Quiz No. 28:
FLYING TIGERS
(1942)

Screenplay by Kenneth Gamet and Barry Trivers
Directed by David Miller
Starring John Wayne, John Carroll, and Anna Lee
Republic Pictures Corporation
Available on VHS, DVD

> *It's good to know that every check you cash in, a Jap's cashed in, too!*
> —McINTOSH

Flying Tigers is a thoroughly engaging account of the American pilots who volunteered to assist China in its fight against Japan just before the United States entered World War II. Although the film was initially designed as a propaganda tool to encourage young men to enlist, *Flying Tigers* still has a lot to offer audiences six decades later. John Wayne, as usual, delivers an effective performance as squadron leader Jim Gordon. Charismatic actor John Carroll, doing his best Clark Gable impression, is also memorable in his turn as an arrogant hot-shot. The film's only flaws reflect the era in which it was produced more than the film itself: obviously integrated stock footage is at times distracting and Chinese characters are presented in an offensively stereotypical manner. While *Flying Tigers* may not be Wayne's finest war film, it's a solid piece of filmmaking.

In 1943, *Flying Tigers* received three Oscar nominations for Best Special Effects (Howard Lydecker and Daniel J. Bloomberg), Best Musical Score (Victor Young), and Best Sound (Bloomberg). However, these nominations did not yield a single Oscar.

1. How much are pilots paid for each Japanese plane they shoot down?

2. What does Jim jokingly say caused the five bullet holes in his plane?

3. A young Chinese girl brings Woody a "tribute." What is this?

4. Jim dryly remarks that he has "quite a collection" in his desk drawer. To what is he referring?

5. What does Jim discover after Dale's landing?

6. *Flying Tigers* was one of two films released in 1942 starring John Wayne and cowritten by Kenneth Gamet. What is the other film?

7. Who calls Woody a "one-man team"?

8. By what nickname does Woody refer to Jim?

9. Where does McIntosh jokingly say he's from?

10. Who does Jim say "paid the check" for Woody and Brooke's dinner?

11. Who's supposed to replace Hap as Jim's number-two pilot?

12. What type of ranch does Hap say he's considering purchasing?

13. What card game does Brooke play with Hap?

14. What is Brooke's insulting response the first time Woody asks her out for dinner?

15. How many enemy planes does Woody shoot down the first time he flies as a member of the Flying Tigers?

16. What does Woody observe to look like the "Taj Mahal with a hangover"?

17. Nine years after collaborating on *Flying Tigers*, John Wayne played a fighter pilot in another film written by screenwriter Kenneth Gamet. What is this film?

18. At what Rangoon hotel does Jim stay?

19. What does Jim advise the pilots to do if their parachute doesn't open?

20. What is Blackie's surname?

21. What does Blackie's wife call a "living death"?

22. What is the significance of the day on which Hap is killed?

23. Who does the physician say Hap should outlive?

24. What day of the week does Jim joke about being a good day for sleep?

25. What is Woody's surname?

Quiz No. 29:

FULL METAL JACKET

(1987)

Screenplay by Michael Herr, Gustav Hasford, and Stanley Kubrick (based on
   a novel by Gustav Hasford)
Directed by Stanley Kubrick
Starring Matthew Modine, R. Lee Ermey, and Vincent D' Onofrio
Warner Bros.
Available on VHS, DVD

> *If your killer instincts are not clean and strong, you will hesitate at the
> moment of truth. You will not kill. You will become dead marines, and
> then you will be in a world of shit because marines are not allowed to
> die without permission.* —GUNNERY SGT. HARTMAN

As with his earlier efforts like *2001: A Space Odyssey* (1968) and *A
Clockwork Orange* (1971), director Stanley Kubrick's *Full Metal Jacket*
can be clearly divided into separate films. The first of those films—
marine basic training at Parris Island—is a brilliant film that is easily
on par with anything Kubrick ever directed. No other film depicts the
experience of military boot camp so honestly. The second film—the
war itself—is lackluster and plodding, and its setting, which was
filmed in England, does not look even remotely like Vietnam. Perhaps
due in part to Kubrick's own reclusiveness, his view of the war in
Vietnam is as out of touch with reality as John Wayne's in the notori-
ously wrongheaded *The Green Berets* (1968). Noted film critic Roger
Ebert hit the nail on the head with this assessment, "The crucial last
passages of the film too often look and feel like World War II films
from Hollywood studios. We see the same sets from so many different
angles that after the movie we could find our own way around
Kubrick's Vietnam." So, in the end, the resulting film is uneven.
Because the first half of the film is so powerful and so well done, *Full
Metal Jacket* offers more good than bad.

Full Metal Jacket received one Academy Award nomination for Best Adapted Screenplay (Michael Herr, Gustav Hasford, and Kubrick), but did not win the Oscar. Other honors include two British Academy of Film and Television Awards nominations for Best Sound and Best Special Effects, Best Director and Best Supporting Actor (R. Lee Ermey), prizes from the Boston Society of Film Critics, the Best Producer Award at the David di Donatello Awards, a Writers Guild Award nomination, and Director of the Year honors from the London Critics Circle Film Awards.

1. What is Pvt. Joker's real name?
2. What is the title of the 1979 Gustav Hasford novel from which *Full Metal Jacket* was adapted?
3. Elements of the film were taken from Michael Herr's 1978 novel. What is the title of this novel?
4. The first actor cast as Joker was fired because of conflicts with the director. Who was this?
5. What does Sgt. Hartman refer to as the "magic show"?
6. Hartman says the only people with Leonard's surname are "faggots and sailors." What is Leonard's surname?
7. From what state does Pvt. Cowboy hail?
8. Who appears in a cameo as the camera operator at the mass grave?
9. R. Lee Ermey made his film debut as a drill instructor in a 1978 war film. What is this film?
10. Three years after his appearance in *Full Metal Jacket*, Matthew Modine starred in another war film. This film, directed by Michael Caton-Jones, tells the story of a World War II bomber crew. What is this film?
11. What word does Hartman say should be the first and last words from the mouths of his recruits?
12. What is the contraband Hartman discovers inside Leonard's footlocker?
13. After firing Pvt. Brown from his position as squad leader, with whom does Hartman replace him?
14. What does Crazy Earl conclude the marines are "gonna miss not having around" once they get back to the United States?
15. What is Brown's nickname?
16. Vincent D'Onofrio and R. Lee Ermey appeared in a second film

together fifteen years after the release of *Full Metal Jacket*. What is the title of this film directed by D. J. Caruso?

17. Joker says the dead know only one thing. What is this?

18. What, according to Hartman, is the "deadliest weapon in the world"?

19. Why does Hartman conclude that God "has a hard-on for marines"?

20. Hartman orders Leonard to pick up his "cover." What is this?

21. The Vietnamese prostitute's dialogue appears in a hit song performed by The 2 Live Crew. What is this song?

22. How long does Hartman say he will give Leonard to stop grinning before punishing him?

23. Just after the release of *Full Metal Jacket,* the Sacramento Police Department issued a warrant for the arrest of screenwriter Gustav Hasford. What were the allegations?

24. According to the film's tagline, "the wind in Vietnam doesn't blow." What does it do?

25. A song featuring a cadence by R. Lee Ermey, which is not in the film, appears on the motion picture soundtrack. This song, produced by Vivian Kubrick and Nigel Goulding, reached the number-two spot on the British pop charts. What is the name of this tune?

Quiz No. 30:

GALLIPOLI

(1981)

Screenplay by Peter Weir and David Williamson
Directed by Peter Weir
Starring Mel Gibson, Mark Lee, and Bill Kerr
South Australian Film Corporation
Available on VHS, DVD

> *Look, Dad, I am not gonna fight for the British Empire. I'm gonna keep my head down, learn a trick or two, and come back an officer maybe.*
> —FRANK DUNNE

Gallipoli is a moving account of Australian soldiers who served during World War I. An international hit when released in 1981, *Gallipoli* quickly brought acclaim to Aussie actor Mel Gibson and filmmaker Peter Weir, who later directed a number of standout Hollywood features including *Witness* (1985) and *Dead Poets Society* (1989). Despite being one of the finest antiwar films ever made, *Gallipoli* failed to receive the attention it deserves (although it is growing in stature, little by little). Screenwriters Weir and David Williamson deftly combine humor, irony, and action, maintaining a script that is historically accurate while avoiding the myriad of clichés that find their way into so many war films. The film features stellar performances from Gibson and the rest of the cast, but Russell Boyd's breathtaking cinematography is the film's true star. With *Gallipoli*, director Weir crafted an epic of which David Lean would have been proud. "This is not a story of thrills or heroics," writes *DVD Town* critic John J. Puccio. "Its precedent is Erich Maria Remarque's epic novel *All Quiet on the Western Front*, wherein the author writes that this is to be 'least of all an adventure.' *Gallipoli* is a very personal glimpse of the devastating effects a mindless war can have on the lives of ordinary people."

Gallipoli received twelve American Film Institute nominations, winning eight awards including Best Picture, Best Original Screenplay, Best Director, Best Achievement in Cinematography, Best Actor, and Best Supporting Actor. The film also received a Golden Globe nomination for Best Foreign Film. Despite these successes, the film was snubbed by the Academy and received no Oscar nominations.

1. What does Archy say "no Turk in his right mind" would do?
2. Director Peter Weir, screenwriter David Williamson, and actor Mel Gibson all reunite on a second project after *Gallipoli*. What is this film?
3. What does Frank say is "the same in most foreign places"?
4. How old is Archy when he enlists?
5. Archy enlists under the pseudonym LaSalles. What is his real surname?
6. Col. Robinson radios Maj. Barton because the attack is behind schedule. By how many minutes is the attack late?
7. What does Snowy say is bad luck?
8. Frank bets on himself in his race against Archy. How much does he wager?
9. Mel Gibson appeared in a World War II film released one year after *Gallipoli*. In that film, Gibson plays an Australian commando. Can you name the film?
10. Les observes that "girls run." What does Les say men do?
11. What is the name of the physician who discusses the "male reproductive organ" with the soldiers?
12. Frank receives a parcel from the women's auxiliary. Inside the parcel, Frank finds a book. What kind of book is this?
13. What does Frank say he "can't stand" about Archy?
14. What does Billy refer to as "man's first attempt to beat death"?
15. What book does Uncle Jack read to Archy's siblings?
16. What is the name of the military branch Frank says he was a member of for five years?
17. Frank says that Archy's declaration that he would be ashamed not to fight proves only one thing. What is this?
18. What animal does Archy say he'll run as fast as?
19. Mel Gibson appeared in a hit film directed by George Miller that was released the same year as *Gallipoli*. Can you name this film?
20. Cinematographer Russell Boyd and Mel Gibson had worked together prior to *Gallipoli* on a 1980 film directed by Ian Barry. In this

film about a leak at a nuclear waste storage facility, Gibson makes an uncredited appearance as a mechanic. What is this film?

21. When, according to Frank, does the Lord turn a blind eye?

22. How fast did Harry LaSalles run the one-hundred-yard dash when he was the world champion in 1899?

23. What does Snowy ask Frank to give his parents?

24. What is said to be the one thing not covered by military insurance?

25. With what phrase does Frank bid farewell throughout the film?

Quiz No. 31:

THE GENERAL

(1927)

Screenplay by Buster Keaton, Al Boasberg, Clyde Bruckman, and Charlie
  Smith
Directed by Buster Keaton and Clyde Bruckman
Starring Buster Keaton, Charles Smith, and Richard Allen
United Artists
Available on VHS, DVD

> *If you lose this war don't blame me!*   —JOHNNIE GRAY

Buster Keaton's *The General* chronicles a real incident during the Civil
War in which Union spies crossed enemy lines and stole a locomotive
engine with the plans of demolishing communication lines and
bridges along the way back to the North. The locomotive's engineer,
Johnnie Gray (Keaton)—rejected from military service at the outset of
the war—finds a way to serve the Confederacy by stealing back his engine, rescuing a damsel in distress, and delivering a crushing blow to
the Union. Filled with clever gags, most of which were improvised
during filming, *The General* is Keaton's finest effort. A testament to
Keaton's genius, the silent film still holds up well more than seven
decades later. While Keaton's work is often overshadowed today by
that of his contemporary, Charles Chaplin, *The General* serves as a reminder that, when at his best, Keaton was at least as funny as Chaplin,
if not better.

  The General was listed to the National Film Registry in 1989 as a
classic.

  1. Buster Keaton wanted to shoot this film in the locations where
the incidents actually occurred. However, he could find only one state
that still had narrow-gauge rails, so he was forced to film there. Which
state was this?

2. At what time are supply trains scheduled to meet Gen. Parker's army?

3. Who labels Johnnie a "disgrace to the South"?

4. As Johnnie returns home, a Confederate soldier shoots at him. Why?

5. What is the name of the bridge Johnnie destroys?

6. Although the filmmakers did not credit him, the film is loosely based on a memoir by William Pittenger. What is the title of this book?

7. Johnnie knocks the guard outside Annabelle's room unconscious. With what does he strike him?

8. At what town do Capt. Anderson and his men hijack the train?

9. How many men does Capt. Anderson take on his mission to steal the train?

10. According to the film, Johnnie has two loves in his life. What are they?

11. What legendary stuntman performed all of Buster Keaton's stunts for the film?

12. In what car is Annabelle when the train is stolen?

13. Johnnie runs to catch the Confederate troops, but trips and falls down in the street. What does he trip over?

14. Johnnie gives Annabelle a photograph as a gift. What is the photograph of?

15. The film's tagline promises three things that begin with the letter *L*. What are these?

16. To avoid being shot by his own cannon, Johnnie scrambles to the top of the train. However, his leg gets caught. On what is his leg caught?

17. Who is Capt. Anderson's commanding officer?

18. Johnnie returns to the recruiter's desk and offers a false name. What is this name?

19. From where did Keaton and company cast the extras that appear as the marching troops?

20. Johnnie stops the engine and ties something to the back of it with rope. What is this?

21. Both Johnnie and Anabelle injure their legs escaping. How do they sustain these injuries?

22. The Union general is played by Joe Keaton. What is Joe Keaton's relation to Buster Keaton?

23. In how many films do Buster Keaton and Marion Mack appear together?

24. Johnnie overhears the Union officers discussing their plans as he hides beneath the table. How many Union officers are there?

25. Why do the recruiters decline to accept Johnnie into the military?

Quiz No. 32:

GETTYSBURG

(1993)

Screenplay by Ronald F. Maxwell (based on a novel by Michael Shaara)
Directed by Ronald F. Maxwell
Starring Tom Berenger, Martin Sheen, and Jeff Daniels
Turner Pictures
Available on VHS, DVD

> *Tell me, Professor, can you recall a story from antiquity where two men who are the best of friends—almost brothers—by a trick of fate find themselves on opposing sides in a great war, and then on a given day find themselves facing each other on the same battlefield?*
> —COL. JOSHUA CHAMBERLAIN

Screenwriter/director Ronald F. Maxwell went to incredible lengths to make sure *Gettysburg* was historically accurate, and that hard work is evident in the resulting film. Boasting an impressive cast that includes Tom Berenger, Martin Sheen, Jeff Daniels, Sam Elliott, and C. Thomas Howell, this sprawling epic was produced as a TNT miniseries but was then picked up by New Line Cinema and given theatrical release. This film was truly a labor of love for Maxwell, and that passion can be seen in every single frame of the picture. While the film is, as its title suggests, about the Battle of Gettysburg, it's about something more than the physical conflict of war: *Gettysburg* is about humanity; it profiles the men behind the attacks and examines their motives and personal relationships. While the film is, at times, a bit preachy, it is a thoroughly entertaining film, even at its staggering 254-minute length.

Perhaps because it's neither fish nor fowl—it's not a true feature film, nor is it a television miniseries—*Gettysburg* didn't win a single award.

1. Brig. Gen. Armistead attempts to explain something that Maj. Gen. Pickett dismisses as "heathen blasphemy." What is this?

2. Who does Maj. Gen. Trimble call a disgrace?

3. Who does Armistead refer to as "Old Winnie Boy"?

4. Martin Sheen portrays Gen. Robert E. Lee in the film. Robert Duvall takes over the role in the prequel *Gods and Generals* (2003). In what 1979 Vietnam war film do both Sheen and Duvall appear together?

5. The documentarian responsible for *The Civil War* (1990) makes a cameo appearance in the film as Hancock's aide. Who is this?

6. Henry T. Harrison is Lt. Gen. Longstreet's top scout. What was his occupation prior to the war?

7. What was the film's working title?

8. What does Col. Chamberlain continually ask his brother not to call him?

9. What, according to Brig. Gen. Buford, can one find by following the cigar smoke?

10. What does Longstreet say he's always believed the Confederate army's strategy was?

11. Who does Armistead say is the most beautiful woman he's ever seen?

12. The term "John Henry" is used in the film. What does this term mean?

13. What does Gen. Lee say is no longer an option?

14. A billionaire and media mogul makes a cameo appearance in the film. Who is this?

15. What does Longstreet say he will not have time to read on the day of the battle?

16. Which member of the cast played James Bond in *On Her Majesty's Secret Service* (1969)?

17. What does Buster say you cannot judge?

18. What was Col. Chamberlain's occupation before the war?

19. From what state are the 120 mutineers who are delivered to Chamberlain?

20. What does Longstreet say is his only cause?

21. Of whom does Gen. Lee say "there is no one I trust more"?

22. Tom Berenger and Sam Elliott later appear together in a 1997 war film directed by John Milius. What is this film?

23. What does Gen. Lee say he has never concerned himself with?

24. Buster says only one thing matters. What is this?

25. What is the "soldier's farewell"?

Quiz No. 33:

GLORY

(1989)

Screenplay by Kevin Jarre (based on books by Lincoln Kirstein and Peter
    Burchard and letters by Robert Gould Shaw)
Directed by Edward Zwick
Starring Matthew Broderick, Denzel Washington, and Cary Elwes
TriStar Pictures
Available on VHS, DVD

> *And who are you? So full of hate that you have to fight everybody be-*
> *cause you've been whipped and chased by hounds. Well, that might*
> *not be living, but it sure as hell ain't dying. And dying's what these*
> *white boys have been doing for going on three years now, dying by the*
> *thousands, dying for you, fool.*   —SGT. MAJ. JOHN RAWLINS

In detailing the struggle of black soldiers who served and fought in the
Civil War, *Glory* provides a look at an important aspect of American
history that Hollywood had previously ignored. Screenwriter Kevin
Jarre and director Edward Zwick are clearly at the top of their game
here, and the cast is magnificent. Especially effective are Andre
Braugher and Denzel Washington, who gives his finest performance
yet in a career filled with brilliance. (If the look on Washington's face
as his character is lashed doesn't bring a tear to your eye, nothing ever
will.) Equally effective are the efforts of composer James Horner, cinematographer Freddie Francis, and production designers Keith Pain
and Dan Webster. One of the most realistic examinations of the Civil
War ever filmed, *Glory*'s battle scenes are wonderfully choreographed
and incredibly realistic. Thankfully, the filmmakers give this material
the respect it truly deserves.

   Glory received five Academy Award nominations in the categories
of Best Supporting Actor (Washington), Best Cinematography (Francis),
Best Film Editing (Steven Rosenblum), Best Art Direction–Set Deco-

ration (Norman Garwood and Garrett Lewis), and Best Sound (Donald O. Mitchell, Gregg Rudloff, Elliot Tyson, and Russell Williams). These nominations resulted in three Oscars for Best Supporting Actor, Best Cinematography, and Best Sound. Other honors include five Golden Globe nominations, a Grammy win for Horner, two Image Awards, a Writers Guild Award nomination, and an American Cinema Editors Award for Best Edited Feature Film.

1. Who is the first black man to volunteer for the Fifty-fourth Massachusetts Infantry?

2. For what reason does Rawlins say Trip went AWOL?

3. Thirteen dollars per month is the normal army wage. How much are black soldiers paid per month?

4. Which of the men calls the Fifty-fourth his only family?

5. Who does Shaw refer to as a "piece of rat filth"?

6. Who saves Trip's life in battle?

7. Who discovers Shaw lying injured after the Battle of Antietam Creek?

8. Denzel Washington appears in another war film directed by Edward Zwick seven years later. What is this film?

9. Who appears in a cameo as the white soldier who says "Give 'em hell, fifty-four"?

10. Of whom does Mulcahey say Shaw should "let him grow up some more"?

11. What is the name of the fort against which Shaw's men lead the attack at the end of the film?

12. Who does Shaw ask to be his flagbearer?

13. From what state does Col. Montgomery hail?

14. What is Pvt. Sharts's first name?

15. What does one white corporal observe as being like "tits on a bull"?

16. What does the wounded Searles make Shaw promise him?

17. A documentary about the Fifty-fourth Infantry was produced the year after *Glory* was released. This documentary, directed by Ben Burtt, was narrated by Morgan Freeman. What is the title of this documentary?

18. Who does Lt. Forbes say are "not noted for their fondness of the coloreds"?

19. Which member of the cast began his career as a regular on *The Electric Company?*

20. How many members of the Fifty-fourth are based on real people?

21. What is Trip's punishment for going AWOL?

22. What does Montgomery say it's impossible to envision Boston having?

23. Just before battle, Shaw asks the men who will carry the colors forward should the flagbearer fall. Who steps forward?

24. What nickname does Trip give Searles?

25. What does Shaw say many of the men in his regiment had never seen prior to the war?

Quiz No. 34:

GOOD MORNING, VIETNAM

(1987)

Screenplay by Mitch Markowitz
Directed by Barry Levinson
Starring Robin Williams, Forest Whitaker, and Tung Thanh Tran
Touchstone Pictures
Available on VHS, DVD

> *This is the country where they grow rattan love seats. God, is it hot!*
> *What a country. Heat, humidity, terrorism. . . . Still, it's better than*
> *New York in the summer.* —ADRIAN CRONAUER

Good Morning, Vietnam is an example of a film in which the lead character is so perfectly cast that it's nearly impossible to imagine another actor in the role. In his portrayal of Vietnam Armed Forces radio disc jockey Adrian Cronauer, Robin Williams deftly walks the thinnest of lines between over-the-top comedy and solemnly serious drama. While the dramatic moments of writer Mitch Markowitz's script are, at times, a bit heavyhanded, Williams lights up the screen with some of the funniest scenes ever filmed. *Chicago Sun-Times* critic Roger Ebert observes, "*Good Morning, Vietnam* works as straight comedy and as a Vietnam-era *M*A*S*H,* and even the movie's love story has its own bittersweet integrity. But they used to tell us in writing class that if we wanted to know what a story was really about, we should look for what changed between the beginning and the end. In this movie, Cronauer changes. War wipes the grin off of his face. His humor becomes a humanitarian tool, not simply a way to keep him talking and us listening."

Good Morning, Vietnam received one Oscar nomination in 1988 for Robin Williams' outstanding performance. Unfortunately, Williams lost. He did, however, receive top honors from the American Comedy Awards and the Golden Globe Awards. The film also received British Academy of Film and Television Awards nominations in the categories of Best Actor (Williams) and Best Sound (Bill Phillips, Clive Winter, and Terry Porter), losing in both.

1. What uncredited writer actually wrote all of Adrian Cronauer's broadcasts in the film?
2. Screenwriter Mark Frost wrote an unproduced sequel to *Good Morning, Vietnam*. What is the title of this screenplay?
3. What movie does Adrian take Trinh to see on their date?
4. What does Adrian say "sounds like bird droppings"?
5. According to Adrian, condoms are made in three sizes. What are these?
6. What word does Adrian define as "tall thin men who like show-tunes"?
7. What magazine, according to Lieutenant Hauk, is considering publishing two of his jokes?
8. What is the name of the chaplain who hosts a radio show?
9. Who does Adrian refer to as "Mr. Excitement"?
10. In trailers for the film, Adrian is shown broadcasting in his military fatigues. However, he wears his civilian clothes throughout the film. Why is this?
11. What actor does Jimmy Wah want to obtain nude photos of?
12. Adrian jokes that Tuan's English sounds as though he learned it from a fictitious character. Who is this?
13. What branch of the U.S. military is Adrian a member of?
14. What musician does Adrian sarcastically refer to as a "misunderstood genius"?
15. Hauk suggests playing "certain ballads" from a well-known crooner. Who is this?
16. From what state does Marty Lee Dreiwitz have cleaning supplies shipped?
17. Where does Garlick say he believes Sgt. Maj. Dickerson was wounded?
18. Adrian quips that a dictionary listing for the word "asshole" would say "see him." To whom is he referring?
19. What day does Adrian jokingly refer to as Malaria Day?
20. Adrian jokes about there being a new line of Vatican-related cleaning products. What does he say will be the first product released?
21. What, according to Gen. Taylor, is Adrian the first man in the history of Armed Forces radio to do?

22. Which *Good Morning, Vietnam* cast member directed *Waiting to Exhale* (1995) and *Hope Floats* (1998)?

23. Who, according to Adrian, sounds like Mr. Ed?

24. Who does Adrian say the women in Crete looked like?

25. What does Adrian teach his English class to say "if someone is not telling the truth"?

Quiz No. 35:

GRAND ILLUSION

(1937)

Screenplay by Jean Renoir and Charles Spaak
Directed by Jean Renoir
Starring Jean Gabin, Pierre Fresnay, and Erich von Stroheim
RAC
Available on VHS, DVD

> *For me it's simple. A golf course is for golf. A tennis court for tennis. A*
> *prison camp is for escaping.* —CAPT. BOLDIEU

Jean Renoir's *Grand Illusion* was miles ahead of its time. Ranking on many film historians' top-ten films lists, it is one of the finest films on the subject of war ever produced. Captured Frenchman Capt. Boldieu (Pierre Fresnay) tells his captor, "Neither you nor I can stop the march of time," but this film seems to have done just that; despite being produced more than sixty-five years ago, *Grand Illusion* remains endlessly enjoyable and undated, virtually untouched by the hands of time. The film, which follows a group of British officers held in a German prison camp during World War I, later influenced films as diverse as *The Great Escape* (1963) and *The Shawshank Redemption* (1994). The film was so effective that the German government banned it and later sought to destroy all copies of it during the German occupation of France.

Grand Illusion received one Oscar nomination for Best Picture (Frank Rollmer and Albert Pinkovitch), but did not win. Other honors include Best Foreign Language Film Awards, from both the New York Film Critics Circle and the National Board of Review. In addition, the film was nominated for the Mussolini Cup and won the award for Best Overall Artistic Contribution at the Venice Film Festival.

1. What does Lt. Marechal say might happen if he looks back at Elsa?

2. Marechal jokingly says he plans to purchase four things at the canteen. What are these?

3. What does Capt. Boldieu call a "fine exercise"?

4. What is the name of the girl both Boldieu and Capt. von Rauffenstein say they knew at the Maxim?

5. Boldieu says the children outside like to play soldier. What does he conclude happens inside the barracks?

6. What instrument do the prisoners play for their five o'clock "concert"?

7. How many planes has von Rauffenstein downed with Marechal's?

8. What is the significance of *Grand Illusion*'s being nominated for the Best Picture Oscar?

9. Why does Marechal say he dislikes fur coats?

10. Where do the prisoners hide their rope during the barracks inspection?

11. Prisoners sing a message to Marechal and the other new arrivals. What do they advise them to do?

12. *Grand Illusion* was the second film Jean Renoir directed starring Jean Gabin. What was the first?

13. What does Marechal say his cell smells of?

14. Who does Cartier refer to as "Mr. Monocle"?

15. Rosenthal asks Marechal if he believes Boldieu is dead. What is Marechal's response?

16. A can on a rope is used as an alarm when a prisoner is digging. What does the ringing alarm signify?

17. Why does von Rauffenstein wear gloves all the time?

18. Which member of the cast directed *Greed* (1925), *The Wedding March* (1928), and *Queen Kelly* (1929)?

19. What two things do the prisoners conclude that women back home now wear short?

20. What trait does Rosenthal say Jehovah gave his family an "overdose" of?

21. What type of liquor is sent to the prisoners in mouthwash bottles?

22. What does von Rauffenstein say he has applied "so as not to be accused of German barbarism"?

23. What two sicknesses does Boldieu say are "not working-class diseases"?

24. What does Boldieu say there's no room for in war?

25. Who shoots Boldieu?

Quiz No. 36:

THE GREAT ESCAPE

(1963)

Screenplay by James Clavell and W. R. Burnett (based on a book by Paul
  Brickhill)
Directed by John Sturges
Starring Steve McQueen, James Garner, and Richard Attenborough
United Artists
Available on VHS, DVD

> *Col. von Luger, it is the sworn duty of all officers to try to escape. If
> they can't, it is their sworn duty to cause the enemy to use an inordi-
> nate number of troops to guard them. And our sworn duty to harrass
> the enemy to the best of their ability.* —CAPT. RUPERT RAMSEY

Despite being based on a true story of a mass escape from a German
prison camp in 1944, *The Great Escape* takes significant liberties with
history (due in part to demands made by actor Steve McQueen). Nevertheless, *The Great Escape* is a magnificent film. John Sturges's direction
is nearly flawless and the casting is exceptional. Sturges mines terrific,
naturalistic performances from the cast, which includes McQueen,
James Garner, Richard Attenborough, Charles Bronson, James Coburn,
Donald Pleasance, and David McCallum. Written by novelist James
Clavell, a former prisoner of war himself, the screenplay is well crafted
and nourishes the film's talented cast with an abundance of sharp,
witty dialogue.

The Great Escape received only one Academy Award nomination for
Best Film Editing (Ferris Webster), but failed to snag the Oscar. Other
honors include a Golden Globe nomination for Best Dramatic Motion
Picture, three Laurel Award nominations, a Writers Guild Award nomination, and the award for Best Actor (McQueen) at the Moscow International Film Festival.

1. Two years after *The Great Escape,* a novel by screenwriter James Clavell was adapted into a film. Like *The Great Escape,* this film was about soldiers in a World War II prison camp. The film was directed by Bryan Forbes and stars George Segal. What is this film?

2. Who is appointed the "Big X"?

3. A horrid made-for-television sequel was produced in 1988. What is this film?

4. *The Great Escape* was the second film directed by John Sturges that featured Steve McQueen, James Coburn, and Charles Bronson. What was the first?

5. Hilts says the guards in the towers will be watching the compound. What does he say they will not be watching?

6. Donald Pleasance had some knowledge of the subject prior to his being cast. What was this?

7. Who is the "Tunnel King"?

8. What was Hilts's major in college?

9. Which of the escapees steals a bicycle?

10. Which of the escapees steals a motorcycle?

11. What are the names Bartlett gives the three tunnels?

12. How many Americans were involved in the real-life escape on which the film is based?

13. A real-life "tunnel king" served as an advisor on this film. What is his name?

14. In what 1975 Walter Hill–directed film did Charles Bronson and James Coburn reunite as characters named Chaney and Speed?

15. Who is referred to as the "Scrounger"?

16. To what country does Sedgewick escape?

17. What nickname does Hilts earn for his time in the cooler?

18. John Sturges directed an adaptation of a novel by screenwriter James Clavell two years after making *The Great Escape.* This film stars George Maharis, Richard Basehart, and Anne Francis. What is this film?

19. What does Blythe call tea without milk?

20. Which cast member directed *A Bridge Too Far* (1977), *Gandhi* (1982), and *Chaplin* (1992)?

21. Why does Willinski suggest the furnace be kept lit at all times?

22. Who performed the stunt where the German soldier rides a motorcycle into a trip wire?

23. Which two escapees steal a plane?

24. How many of the escapees are executed by the Gestapo?

25. Why does Sedgewick say he's watching Willenski shower?

Quiz No. 37:

GUADALCANAL DIARY

(1943)

Screenplay by Lamar Trotti and Jerome Cady (based on a book by Richard
Tregaskis)
Directed by Lewis Seiler
Starring William Bendix, Richard Conte, and Anthony Quinn
Twentieth Century-Fox
Available on VHS, DVD

> *Now most of you guys have never had any experience in the jungle
> and the Japs have. Plenty. So let me give you a word of advice: keep
> your mouths shut. Stop yellin' your head off. We can beat 'em at their
> own game of silence if we try, but, well, you know how marines are.
> Some dope'll yell, "Hey, Mack, is that C Company over there?" No, it
> isn't funny. Don't laugh. The minute you guys start runnin' over to see
> if C Company is over there, what kind of chow C Company's havin',
> you're liable to end up chow yourselves.*
> —GUNNERY SGT. HOOK MALONE

Lewis Seiler's *Guadalcanal Diary* is a realistic film about a platoon of
U.S. Marines fighting in the South Pacific. However, the film is not
without flaws. First, the soldiers are too happy. In Terrence Malick's
The Thin Red Line (1998), which is a very different film about the same
battle, Nick Nolte's Lt. Col. Tall comments that you know a GI is dead
when he stops "bitching." Well, if that's the case, then all of these happy
warriors are dead because they never complain once throughout the
film. But then, such propaganda is understandable considering that
the film was produced in 1943 while the war was still raging. Second,
there are many clichés to be found here. The film's third flaw—the offensively racist attitude toward the Japanese—is, again, blatant propaganda that is somewhat understandable considering the period in
which it was made. Racial slurs such as "little monkeys" are abundant,
and the Japanese are depicted as being cruel, cowardly, and unintelli-

gent. Despite these shortcomings, *Guadalcanal Diary* is an entertaining film that is well directed and features a number of impressive performances.

1. What is Pvt. Johnny Anderson's nickname?
2. What are Japanese cigarettes said to consist of?
3. Father Donnelly was a football player. What position did he play?
4. Alvarez is asked "Conchita or Lolita?" What is his response?
5. What is Taxi's real name?
6. Anthony Quinn and Preston Foster appear together in a second film one year after collaborating on *Guadalcanal Diary*. In this film, Foster plays a gangster named Roger Touhy. What is this film?
7. A reference is made to a 1941 war film starring Gary Cooper. What is this film?
8. When the squad is ambushed, there is one survivor. Who is this?
9. What does the cook search for at the start of every battle?
10. What does Mr. Weatherbee describe as being "good stuff for the Japs to hide in"?
11. What does Capt. Cross keep inside his helmet liner?
12. Which cast member also appears in the war films *Sands of Iwo Jima* (1949), *The Dirty Dozen* (1967), and *The Devil's Brigade* (1968)?
13. Who does the narrator say is a "persistent fool"?
14. How did Davis and Cross know each other before the war?
15. What are referred to as "pineapples"?
16. Where is Taxi from?
17. What does the narrator say is visible in the eyes of the soldiers after their first battle?
18. What was Taxi's occupation prior to the war?
19. Anthony Quinn also appeared in a classic William A. Wellman film starring Henry Fonda that was released the same year as *Guadalcanal Diary*. Can you name this film?
20. What, according to the narrator, is the soldiers' "favorite occupation"?
21. Anderson is shot going after a souvenir. What is this?
22. Actors Lionel Stander and Anthony Quinn had appeared together in one film prior to *Guadalcanal Diary*. The film was a 1936 Harold Lloyd comedy directed by Leo McCarey. In the film, which was

one of Quinn's first, he appeared as an uncredited extra. What is the name of this film?

23. Who narrates the film?

24. What does Taxi point out on Anderson's face?

25. Anderson is asked when he started smoking. What is his response?

Quiz No. 38:

THE GUNS OF NAVARONE

(1961)

Screenplay by Carl Foreman (based on a novel by Alistair MacLean)
Directed by J. Lee Thompson
Starring Gregory Peck, David Niven, and Anthony Quinn
Columbia Pictures
Available on VHS, DVD

> *Anything can happen in a war. Slapped in the middle of insanity, people pull out the most extraordinary resources—ingenuity, courage, and self-sacrifice. Pity we can't beat the problems of peace the same way, isn't it? It would be so much cheaper for everybody.*
> —COMM. JAMES JENSEN

Director J. Lee Thompson's riveting World War II adventure film laid the groundwork for an entire subgenre of war films about squads of unlikely comrades from different nations that combine their talents for an "impossible" mission. *The Guns of Navarone* not only set the standard for films such as *The Dirty Dozen* (1967), *The Devil's Brigade* (1968), and *Where Eagles Dare* (1968), but also influenced many non-war actioners. Sure, the film's plot—an Allied commando squad is sent behind enemy lines to penetrate and destroy a German fortress—is silly, completely unrealistic, and historically inaccurate, but who cares? As pure escapist entertainment, *The Guns of Navarone* remains as captivating today as it was when it was released forty years ago. And while the cast is obviously better than the breezy material they're working with, they make the best of it without ever once coming across as condescending.

The Guns of Navarone received seven Academy Award nominations for Best Picture (Carl Foreman), Best Director (Thompson), Best Adapted Screenplay (Foreman), Best Film Editing (Alan Obiston), Best Original Score (Dimitri Tiomkin), Best Sound (John Cox), and

Best Special Effects (Bill Warrington and Chris Greenham), snagging a sole Oscar for its special effects. Other honors include two Golden Globe Awards for Best Dramatic Motion Picture and Best Original Score, Laurel Awards in the categories of Top Drama and Top Male Dramatic Performance (Gregory Peck), and a single British Academy of Film and Television Awards nomination for Best British Screenplay.

    1. What "third choice" does Col. Andrea Stavros suggest regarding the injured Maj. Roy Franklin?

    2. What is the title of the hackeneyed 1978 sequel starring Robert Shaw and Harrison Ford?

    3. Who is the film's narrator?

    4. Who does Stavros believe is responsible for the death of his wife and children?

    5. One of the cast members suffered an infection during filming that nearly killed him. Who was this?

    6. What is Pvt. Brown's nickname?

    7. *The Guns of Navarone* lost in its bid for the Best Picture Oscar to a film directed by the filmmaker responsible for the war films *The Desert Rats* (1953) and *Run Silent Run Deep* (1958). What is this film and who is its director?

    8. When Franklin says he hasn't lost his sense of smell, to what is he referring?

    9. What is the "one thing" Mallory tells Franklin he cannot reveal to the Germans?

    10. The squad is held at gunpoint by a woman in St. Alexis. Who is this?

    11. What does Miller say he wasn't born to be?

    12. David Niven and Gregory Peck later appear together in a 1980 war film directed by Andrew V. McLaglen. What is this film?

    13. What was Mallory's nickname as a mountain climber?

    14. Which of the men is nicknamed "Lucy"?

    15. Whose "bystanding days" does Mallory say are behind him?

    16. What does Mallory quip that he likes nothing better than?

    17. Why does the German officer say the squad members must be considered spies?

    18. Which member of the squad tries to convince the Germans that he's a fisherman?

19. The actors spent a lot of time in a cold water tank during filming. What was administered to keep them warm?

20. Who does Mallory refer to as "a man who still has to prove to himself that he's a hero"?

21. How many of the one hundred missions he's been on does Miller believe have altered the course of the war?

22. Miller discovers that there is a traitor among them. Who is this?

23. Which member of the squad cannot swim?

24. Which member of the cast also appears in the war films *The Charge of the Light Brigade* (1936), *The Dawn Patrol* (1938), and *Escape to Athena* (1979)?

25. Which member of the team does Comm. Jensen call a "born killer"?

Quiz No. 39:

HAMBURGER HILL

(1987)

Screenplay by James Carabatsos
Directed by John Irvin
Starring Dylan McDermott, Steven Weber, and Don Cheadle
RKO Pictures
Available on VHS, DVD

> *All right, listen up. You people will not die on me in combat. You fuckin' new guys'll do everything to prove me wrong. You walk on trails, kick cans, sleep on guard, smoke dope, and diddly-bop through the bush like you were back on the block. Or on guard at night you'll write letters, play with your organ, and think of your girl back home. Forget her. Some hair head has her on her back right now and is telling her to fuck for peace.* —SGT. FRANTZ

Despite screenwriter James Carabatsos's being a Vietnam War veteran and also having done substantial research on the subject, *Hamburger Hill* fails to capture the essence and atmosphere of Oliver Stone's *Platoon* (1986). However, this is not Carabatsos's fault. Blame director John Irvin, the cinematographer, the production designer, the special effects department, and the casting director. The film's low-production values hurt the picture, making it feel like an extended-length episode of the television series *Tour of Duty*. While *Hamburger Hill*'s flaws are numerous, the film's cast is its most problematic area. With a few notable exceptions—particularly Don Cheadle and Courtney B. Vance, who turns in a terrific performance here—the ensemble is comprised largely of "name" actors with minimal talent and television stars who cannot overcome the temptation to overact. The actors seem to be going through the motions as though they were searching for direction. Screenwriter Carabatsos laces the script with grunt slang and technical jargon that, had they been delivered by better actors, could have given the film the feeling of the authenticity it needs. In the mouths of actors like Dylan McDermott, who sounds ridiculously uncomfortable saying "unass my AO," these lines sound unnatural and forced. This is not to say, however, that Carabatsos is exempt of blame. Carabatsos's screenplay is filled with heavyhanded jingoistic rhetoric that is, at times, so laughable that it makes it difficult for one to take the film seriously. So, in the end, *Hamburger Hill* is a film that has a considerable following and, while it is far from being the best Vietnam War film, it's not the worst, either.

1. How many assaults on Hill 937 does the film say the Americans made in ten days?

2. The term "AO" is used in the film. What does this mean?

3. What does Doc say the "bastards" back home cannot take away from him?

4. The term "FNG" is used throughout the film. What does this abbreviation mean?

5. Who, according to Sgt. Worcester, are the only people the hippies don't love?

6. Who is Doc assisting when he's shot?

7. What does Sgt. Frantz tell Worcester he's going to do if he gets out of the valley?

8. What does Frantz tell Beletsky to do if he smokes at night?

9. Which of the men is killed by falling into a pit filled with spikes?

10. Director John Irvin returns to the battlefield in 1998 with another war film. This film, which stars Ron Eldard, is about World War II. What is this film?

11. What does the term "mudrollers" refer to?

12. A poem appears at the end of the film. Who is the poem written by?

13. Screenwriter James Carabatsos wrote a screenplay for another war film that was produced one year prior to *Hamburger Hill*. This film was directed by Clint Eastwood. What is this film?

14. By what nickname does Frantz refer to Languilli?

15. On what date does the film's postscript say the hill was taken?

16. Worcester says he found something inside his bathroom when he returned home. What was this?

17. The term "round-eye" is used throughout the film. What does this mean?

18. In whose arms does Languilli die?

19. Worcester talks about an overly cautious soldier who still got killed. What kind of undergarment does he say the GI wore?

20. What does Doc say they "don't take" at headquarters?

21. At the end of the battle, there is a makeshift sign hanging from a tree by a knife. What does the sign read?

22. What is the name of Languilli's girlfriend?

23. Courtney B. Vance appears in a 1995 World War II film directed by Robert Markowitz. In the film, Vance plays a character named Lt. Glenn. What is this film?

24. Washburn says he won't eat anything unless you can do something to it. What is this?

25. Doc says he's just what the world needs. What is this?

Quiz No. 40:

HEARTBREAK RIDGE

(1986)

Screenplay by James Carabatsos
Directed by Clint Eastwood
Starring Clint Eastwood, Marsha Mason, and Everett McGill
Warner Bros.
Available on VHS, DVD

> *Be advised that I'm mean, nasty, and tired. I eat concertina wire and*
> *piss napalm, and I can put a round through a flea's ass at two hundred*
> *meters. So you go hump somebody else's leg, muttface, before I push*
> *yours in.* —GUNNERY SGT. TOM HIGHWAY

While perhaps not a classic film, *Heartbreak Ridge* is an extremely entertaining picture. And although the episodes of the Stitch Jones (Mario Van Peebles) character haven't aged especially well, Clint Eastwood's performance as the tough-as-nails gunnery sergeant remains as inspired today as it was when the film was first released. Eastwood's aging warrior, Tom Highway, is second (and a close second at that) only to R. Lee Ermey's Sgt. Hartman in *Full Metal Jacket* (1987) as cinema's meanest, nastiest U.S. Marine Corps gunnery sergeant. But, unlike Hartman, Highway has a visible humanity. Although the film deals with the Grenada conflict, Eastwood says he was most interested in Highway's life away from the battleground, "[W]hat warriors do when they haven't got a war has always interested me, and I thought, here's a character, let's see how he interacts with people, especially women. It was an interesting story, also about a soldier who hasn't ever done anything but fight wars, and he discovers that he's reached the end of his career, and has nothing to look back on and nothing at all he can concentrate on now."

Heartbreak Ridge received one Academy Award nomination in the category of Best Sound (Les Fresholtz, Richard Alexander, Vern Poore, and Bill Nelson), but failed to win the Oscar. In addition, Mario Van Peebles won an Image Award for Outstanding Supporting Actor in a Motion Picture.

1. What does Stitch Jones say is "twelve inches and white"?
2. Sgt. Maj. Choozoo says Highway is carrying so much shrapnel he can't do something. What is this?
3. What is Swede's surname?
4. A rather memorable cadence is called saying "Model A Ford and a tank full of gas." What is the next line?
5. What is the name of the bar where Highway's ex-wife Aggie is working?
6. What concerning the taking of the university medical school is historically inaccurate?
7. What does Highway identify as being the "preferred weapon of your enemy"?
8. What is the ribbon on Highway's uniform that Choozoo says causes officers to stare in awe?
9. Which cast member later directed *New Jack City* (1991), *Posse* (1993), and *Panther* (1995)?
10. Highway says Sgt. Webster is only capable of making one thing. What is this?
11. Why does Choozoo say Maj. Powers reads the marine manual before he "mounts his old lady"?
12. Highway immediately breaks something after his introduction to his platoon. What is this?
13. Highway is asked for an assessment of the alert. What is his response?
14. A screenwriter Clint Eastwood had worked with previously on *Sudden Impact* (1983) and *City Heat* (1984) polished the script but did not receive credit. Who is this?
15. Which cast member also appears in the war films *Inglorious Bastards* (1977), *The Delta Force* (1986), and *The Dirty Dozen: The Deadly Mission* (1987)?
16. What does Choozoo say Highway is too ugly to do?
17. Jones refers to himself as the "Ayatollah of Rock and Rolla." This phrase originated in a 1981 film starring Mel Gibson. What is this film?

18. How many survivors does Choozoo say there were at Heartbreak Ridge?

19. Where does Highway say he went to college?

20. Jones says he's an expert on two subjects. What are these?

21. Where do we find Highway at the start of the film?

22. What nickname does Highway give Corporal Fragatti?

23. Fowlers says Highway should be sealed in a glass case with a sign on the outside of it. What does he say the sign should read?

24. What does Highway say is not compatible with the U.S. Marine Corps?

25. What does Highway catch Jones attempting to steal the first time they meet?

Quiz No. 41:

HELL IN THE PACIFIC

(1968)

Screenplay by Alexander Jacobs, Eric Bercovici, and Reuben Bercovitch
Directed by John Boorman
Starring Lee Marvin and Toshiro Mifune
American Broadcasting Company/Selmur Productions
Available on VHS, DVD

> *Oh! For a second I thought you were a Jap!* —AMERICAN PILOT

This American-Japanese production imagines a downed American pilot (Lee Marvin) and a Japanese officer (Toshiro Mifune) stranded together on a deserted island during World War II. Despite the film's cast consisting of only two actors, veteran actors Marvin and Mifune offer more than enough star power. When making a film with only two characters and very little dialogue, casting capable actors becomes extremely important. Having limited dialogue is certainly no problem here as the two actors manage to convey their thoughts and reactions through extremely realistic and subtle facial expressions and body language. To give the audience a feeling of the confusion and frustration the two characters are experiencing due to the language barrier, the filmmakers wisely opt not to provide subtitles—a strategy that works effectively when the film is screened in either country. *Hell in the Pacific* is a truly underappreciated gem. While other films from director John Boorman's catalogue are more popular, *Hell in the Pacific* is his finest effort.

1. The Japanese and American versions of the film feature different endings. While the American version features a contrived and abrupt ending, the Japanese print includes director John Boorman's intended ending. What is this?

2. When they first meet, the Japanese officer possesses something the American pilot wants. What is this?

3. What does the Japanese officer spot that indicates he's not alone?

4. The plot from *Hell in the Pacific* was later reworked by writers Barry Longyear and Edward Khmara as a 1985 science fiction film starring Dennis Quaid and Louis Gossett Jr. What is the title of this film?

5. At different points in the film, each man holds the other captive. Which of the two men is the first to be captured?

6. When the two men arrive together on the new island, they discover a deserted military outpost. What country's outpost was this?

7. Why does the Japanese officer blindfold the American pilot?

8. In the film's final scene, the drunken American pilot asks the Japanese officer why he does not believe in something. What is this?

9. What does the American pilot toss into the Japanese officer's campfire?

10. How does the Japanese officer learn that the American is a pilot?

11. The Japanese officer has a vision of the American pilot killing him. What weapon does the American use to do this?

12. What does the American soldier jokingly salute in the forest?

13. The American pilot tries to make the Japanese officer pretend he's an animal. What type of animal?

14. The Japanese officer finds several sealed bottles of liquor. What is this alcoholic beverage?

15. The American finds a magazine. What is this magazine?

16. On what islands was *Hell in the Pacific* filmed?

17. What does the American's military handbook suggest a soldier in his position do with prisoners?

18. The American pilot pulls something from the ocean and destroys it, angering the Japanese officer. What is this?

19. The American pilot bangs on his canteen to annoy the Japanese officer. What does he bang against it?

20. What musical instrument does the Japanese officer play in the film?

21. What does the Japanese soldier jokingly say in English when he sees the American pilot holding the liquor bottle?

22. In the film's final scene, the Japanese officer becomes angry when he sees something. What is this?

23. The American pilot sings a song about a girl as the two men float on the raft. What U.S. state does he sing about taking the girl to?

24. What is the Japanese officer doing when the American escapes?

25. After diving from the sound of gunfire, the Japanese officer feels something wet falling on his back. What is this?

Quiz No. 42:
HELL IS FOR HEROES
(1962)

Screenplay by Richard Carr and Robert Pirosh
Directed by Don Siegel
Starring Steve McQueen, Bobby Darin, and James Coburn
Paramount Pictures
Available on VHS, DVD

> *Up here this gun is your life. It's like when you were a civilian, see. It's
> what you own that makes you who you are.* —PVT. DAVE CORBY

Like *Battleground* (1949), which was also written by screenwriter
Robert Pirosh, *Hell Is for Heroes* offers a gritty, realistic look at the day-
to-day life of American GIs serving in World War II. Although the
low-budget film's cast consisted mostly of unknowns at the time the
film was produced, many of these talented actors later became stars.
Made during a period when most battle films glorified war, Don
Siegel's film exposes the grim, ugly face of combat as it really is. Siegel
and company accomplish this without giving the characters preachy
dialogue but, rather, through mood and atmosphere.

The film depicts a raggedy, depleted platoon attempting to hold the
Ziegfried Line. The ensuing battle looks to be hopeless and morale is
low. Siegel, a B-movie veteran, knew well that keeping a monster off-
screen and in the shadows is far more effective in building tension, and
he does precisely that here; as the soldiers wonder just how many
German soldiers are out there, the film keeps them off the screen, in
effect putting the audience in the position of the American soldiers.
Despite going on to helm bigger budget films such as *Dirty Harry*
(1971) and *The Shootist* (1976), Siegel's considerable gifts as a filmmaker were rarely showcased better than they are here.

1. What is Corby's nickname?

2. Sgt. Pike and Pvt. Reese have served together before. Where?

3. The challenge to enter the perimeter is "apple." What is the password?

4. *Hell Is for Heroes* is one of three films featuring both Steve McQueen and James Coburn. Can you name the other two films?

5. How many men does Reese take with him on his initial attack of the German pill box?

6. Driscoll says the company has seen the same film five nights in a row. What is this film?

7. The platoon wakes up to discover that most of the company has left. How many men does Cpl. Henshaw believe were in the camp before he went to sleep?

8. Which cast member makes his debut here and eventually stars in four different television series that feature his name in their titles?

9. How much does Corby sell ink pens "with ink" for?

10. Reese is late reporting to his new company. How many days late is he?

11. What, according to Henshaw, should every man *not* follow?

12. What is Driscoll's first name?

13. Actor L.Q. Jones, who appears in the film as Sgt. Frazer, was born Justus E. McQueen. However, he opted to change his name to L.Q. Jones, which was the name of a character he played in a 1955 war film. What is this film?

14. Why does Corby say he should be sent home by plane?

15. What does Sgt. Larkin remark as being the "best thing" he has to look forward to after the war?

16. Who does Corby teach to fire a rifle?

17. Reese says if the company was full strength, it would send out a patrol. How many men would the patrol consist of?

18. What, according to Driscoll, is the only thing he's ever done in the military?

19. How long does Henshaw predict it will take him to get some wire and gasoline?

20. Reese goes to the local tavern and requests a bottle of booze. What kind of alcohol does he order?

21. What does Reese say makes a good soldier?

22. What does Reese promise he'll do if Homer shows up on the front line?

23. Which cast member overdubbed some of the dialogue in *Giant* (1956) after James Dean's death?

24. What does Reese say the "whole world" is full of?

25. What does Reese say he'll do the next time Larkin waves his finger in his face?

Quiz No. 43:

THE HORSE SOLDIERS

(1959)

Screenplay by Harold Sinclair, John Lee Mahin, and Martin Rackin
Directed by John Ford
Starring John Wayne, William Holden, and Constance Towers
United Artists
Available on VHS, DVD

> *War isn't exactly a civilized business.*   —COL. JOHN MARLOWE

The Horse Soldiers may be one of the lesser collaborations between master filmmaker John Ford and screen icon John Wayne, but it's still significant because it's the director's only full-length Civil War film and because, well, it's a collaborative effort between Ford and the Duke. Loosely based on true events, *The Horse Soldiers* tells the story of a Union brigade that travels deep into Confederate territory to destroy a railway used to transport enemy supplies. The operation is led by Col. John Marlowe (Wayne). Along the way, Marlowe battles military physician Maj. Hank Kendall (William Holden), a beautiful southern belle (Constance Towers), and enemy troops. It's no secret that Ford was never completely satisfied with the screenplay, and his lack of confidence is apparent in the final film. Wayne and Holden both seem uncomfortable, and the lack of chemistry between Wayne and Towers leaves one wishing Ford had instead cast Maureen O'Hara. In the end, *The Horse Soldiers* is not a classic on par with Wayne and Ford's finest joint efforts, but it's still an extremely entertaining film. A flawed Ford-Wayne collaboration is comparable to a field goal rather than a touchdown; it may not be as flashy, but it's nonetheless effective.

1. Maj. Kendall's assistant is named Otis Hopkins. What is Hopkins's nickname?

2. What singular event caused John Ford first to stop the production while shooting in Louisiana and then eventually to distance himself from the film?

3. The producer of this film later remade John Ford's classic *Stagecoach* (1939) in 1966 because he wanted to see it "done right." Who is this?

4. What does Kendall say becomes impractical at a certain point?

5. A dying soldier named Bud Hoskins asks Col. Marlowe for a favor. What is this?

6. Where, according to the film's tagline, do *The Horse Soldiers* ride?

7. Where does Marlowe say there are thirty thousand potential votes to be found?

8. What does Sgt. Kirby say the second stripe on his sleeve indicates?

9. John Wayne made his directorial debut with a war film that was released the year after *The Horse Soldiers*. What is this film?

10. Hannah says Kendall is fighting for men's lives. What does Marlowe believe Kendall is fighting for?

11. What was Marlowe's occupation prior to the war?

12. Hannah's maid, Lukey, is played by a popular track star. Who is this?

13. *The Horse Soldiers* is one of two films starring John Wayne that were released in 1959. The other film was directed by Howard Hawks and costarred Dean Martin and Ricky Nelson. What is this film?

14. Why does Marlowe order Sgt. Kirby to be thrown into the river?

15. What event caused Marlowe's dislike for physicians?

16. What does Kendall suggest might make the coffee taste better?

17. With what does Kendall say his personal experience is limited?

18. Kendall delivers a baby. What is the baby's sex?

19. What does Marlowe proclaim to be his only orders after Newton Station?

20. What "Cheyenne Indian cure" does Kendall place on an axe wound?

21. Marlowe is modeled after a real-life person. Who is this?

22. After capturing a young cadet, Cpl. Wilkie asks what he should do with his prisoner. What is Marlowe's memorable response?

23. For what does Marlowe place Kendall under officer's arrest?

24. John Ford's only other film about the Civil War was released in 1962. This film, which Ford codirected with Henry Hathaway and George Marshall, also features John Wayne. What is this film?

25. What, according to Marlowe, is as valuable as ammunition?

Quiz No. 44:
IN HARM'S WAY
(1965)

Screenplay by Wendell Mayes (based on a novel by James Bassett)
Directed by Otto Preminger
Starring John Wayne, Kirk Douglas, and Patricia Neal
Paramount Pictures
Available on VHS, DVD

> *Now we all know the Navy is never wrong, but this time they're a little weak on being right.* —ADM. CHESTER W. NIMITZ

Most of Otto Preminger's epic naval war film *In Harm's Way* takes place in the wake of the Pearl Harbor attack. The sets and ship models are extremely realistic, the acting is good (considering we're dealing with John Wayne and Kirk Douglas here, both of whom generally gave the exact same performances over and over again), and the battle sequences are impressive. If only its storyline could have stuck to the basic war story, this could have been an exceptionally great film instead of being a merely good film. As it stands, the film is bogged down by silly melodramatics that don't always make sense. (Because he's grieving over his wife's death, Douglas's character rapes someone?) Still, at the end of the day the film's strengths outweigh its flaws—albeit not by much—and *In Harm's Way* remains an entertaining picture if nothing else.

In Harm's Way received one Academy Award nomination for Best Black-and-White Cinematography (Loyal Griggs), but did not win the Oscar. In addition, Patricia Neal received Best Foreign Actress honors from the British Academy of Film and Television Awards.

1. Who is Annalee Dorne's boyfriend?
2. Who saves RAdm. Rockwell Torrey's life?
3. *In Harm's Way* was the second film in which John Wayne and

Patricia Neal appeared together. The first film was also a naval war film. What is this film?

4. What, according to Cmdr. Egan Powell, was "like eating peanuts"?

5. From where did Capt. Paul Eddington receive his first transfer?

6. What was Ens. Jeremiah Torrey's major in college?

7. Who does McConnell say makes the crew look like a "bunch of pirates"?

8. How many days is "survivor's leave"?

9. In *Harm's Way* was the first of three collaborations between John Wayne and Kirk Douglas, all of which were released in consecutive years. What are the two films that followed?

10. What is the name of the top secret mission Powell says only twenty people should know about?

11. In what 1976 film would Henry Fonda reprise his role as Adm. Chester W. Nimitz?

12. What is the name of Eddington's wife?

13. Who does Culpepper say the men voted the "best officer to be shipwrecked on an island with"?

14. Torrey is injured at the beginning of the film when his first ship is torpedoed. What injury does he sustain?

15. Who does Eddington refer to as the "Rock of Ages"?

16. How many battleships are stationed at Pearl Harbor when it is attacked?

17. John Wayne was plagued with a terrible cough throughout the production. What is the significance of this?

18. How many hours does Torrey conclude they could add to their steaming time by navigating on a straight course as opposed to zigzagging?

19. What does Torrey say Eddington's record looks like?

20. What was Powell's occupation before the war?

21. How old was Torrey when his father left his mother?

22. Actress Paula Prentiss injured herself while filming her final scene in the film. How?

23. How is Eddington's wife killed?

24. The film's title refers to the following quotation, "I wish to have no connection with any ship that does not sail fast, for I intend to go in harm's way." Who said this?

25. Who does Nimitz jokingly say had the "audacity" to suggest the navy was wrong about Torrey?

Quiz No. 45:

IS PARIS BURNING?

(1966)

Screenplay by Gore Vidal and Francis Ford Coppola
Directed by René Clément
Starring Jean-Paul Belmondo, Charles Boyer, and Leslie Caron
Transcontinental Films
Available on VHS

> *The enemy must not occupy Paris! Be ruthless with the population! If they disobey, kill them! If you can't hold Paris, burn it!*
> —ADOLF HITLER

Is Paris Burning? is too long, refuses to be pinned down to a single point of focus, and features an inordinate number of big stars in cameo roles. In short, it's France's answer to *The Longest Day* (1962). Like its American predecessor, *Is Paris Burning?* doesn't give its big-name cast members much to do. The performances are, by and large, a mixed bag. This is not to say *Is Paris Burning?* is a bad film. While there are moments of greatness scattered throughout, the film is mediocre. Nevertheless, the wattage of the film's starpower coupled with its unlikely (and rather bizarre) teaming of screenwriters Gore Vidal and Francis Ford Coppola make this an interesting film worth checking out. The filmmakers should also be commended for the film's realistic recreation of wartime Paris; the use and integration of real war footage also lend the project a feeling of authenticity.

Is Paris Burning? received two Academy Award nominations for Best Black-and-White Cinematography (Marcel Grignon) and Best Black-and-White Art Direction–Set Decoration (Willy Holt, Marc Frederix, and Pierre Guffroy), winning for neither. In addition, composer Maurice Jarre received a Golden Globe nomination for Best Original Score.

1. By how many votes is the cease-fire rejected?

2. When asked why the church bells are ringing, what is Gen. Von Choltitz's memorable response?

3. Why do the German soldiers in the machine gun nest allow Maj. Gallois to cross the field and meet with the Americans rather than gun him down?

4. What, according to the proclamation, is to be done if any civilian shoots at a single German soldier?

5. *Is Paris Burning?* is one of two films released in 1966 in which Orson Welles appeared as an actor. In the second film, Welles plays a character named Cardinal Wolsey. What is this film?

6. To whom does Nordling say history will be grateful?

7. What is Nordling's drink of preference?

8. Gen. Bradley says three men are responsible for the decision to liberate Paris. Who are they?

9. What, according to Gen. Patton, is the business of the U.S. Army?

10. What happened to Bernard Labe on the day his wife discovered he was working for the resistance?

11. Von Choltitz carries a photograph of a new weapon in his wallet. What is this weapon?

12. Prior to *Is Paris Burning?* Charles Boyer and Leslie Caron had already appeared in two films together. Can you name them?

13. Nordling recalls eating mousse as a guest of the Labes. What type of mousse was this?

14. What is Nordling's occupational title?

15. What does Patton say the plans of the U.S. Army do *not* include?

16. Screenwriter Francis Ford Coppola later writes an entire film about one of the characters that appear in *Is Paris Burning?* What is this film?

17. Nordling reminds Von Choltitz that the Allied army is the enemy. Who does he say is *not* the enemy?

18. Who does Patton refer to as an "impatient lion"?

19. What is Von Choltitz's response when Nordling asks him why Adolf Hitler would want to destroy Paris?

20. What, according to the film's opening title card, was "terribly short"?

21. What does SS Commandant Patin say he believes all generals to be?

22. What, according to Von Choltitz, is the only way Paris can be saved from destruction?

23. What does Patin say will happen if any of the prisoners attempt to escape?

24. Von Choltitz says, "We are soldiers." What does he say they are *not?*

25. What happens when a group of college students attempt to purchase weapons from Capt. Serge?

Quiz No. 46:

KELLY'S HEROES
(1970)

Screenplay by Troy Kennedy Martin
Directed by Brian G. Hutton
Starring Clint Eastwood, Telly Savalas, and Don Rickles
Metro-Goldwyn-Mayer
Available on VHS, DVD

> *We see our roles as essentially defensive in nature. While our armies are advancing so fast and everyone's knockin' themselves out to be heroes, we are holding ourselves in reserve in case the krauts mount an offensive which threatens Paris, or maybe even New York. Then we can move in and stop them. But for $1.6 million, we could become heroes for three days.*
> —SGT. ODDBALL

Kelly's Heroes may have less pretentions than any other war film in the history of cinema. Viewers in search of a thought-provoking antiwar film should be advised that this is not that film. A light escapist adventure with elements of comedy, *Kelly's Heroes* is essentially a treasure hunt story set smack dab in the middle of World War II Europe.

When Kelly (Clint Eastwood) learns from a German prisoner that a nearby bank holds millions in gold bars, he begins planning the perfect heist. He then enlists a group of strange, offbeat characters (played by the likes of Don Rickles, Telly Savalas, and Donald Sutherland) to assist him. The only problem with the daring plan is that the gold is being kept thirty miles behind enemy lines. Humorously, U.S. Army brass mistakes the actions of Kelly and company as being acts of heroism.

Fresh from Sergio Leone's *Man with No Name* trilogy, Eastwood delivers a similar performance here (you know, a lot of squinting and sneering). The entire ensemble handles its lines well, and Brian G. Hutton's straightforward direction serves the material well. A fun comedic actioner, *Kelly's Heroes* is just as entertaining after the one-hundredth viewing as it is the first. Fans of the film will also enjoy David O. Russell's loose remake *Three Kings* (Quiz No. 88).

1. To what city does Capt. Maitland leave to deliver the confiscated yacht?

2. In what country was the majority of *Kelly's Heroes* shot?

3. Why does Maitland say he doesn't want the soldiers to sleep with the local women?

4. Which of the film's stars became extremely sick during filming?

5. What does Maj. Gen. Colt say he wants to give each of Kelly's men?

6. Clint Eastwood and Donald Sutherland reunited thity years later for a film that costarred Tommy Lee Jones and James Garner. What is this film?

7. The man who wrote the film's theme, "Burning Bridges," later served as the lieutenant governor of California. Who is this?

8. Big Joe says if he hears any one of three things, he'll strangle the soldier responsible. What are these?

9. According to the film's tagline, Kelly and his men "set out to rob a bank." What does the tagline say they did instead?

10. Oddball says he has only one way to keep the Tiger tanks busy. What is this?

11. What does Big Joe say is the first rule of war?

12. What is the name of the town where the gold is being kept?

13. What does Colt say he expects his communications officer to be able to do?

14. What actor plays Sgt. Mulligan?

15. How many Tiger tanks are protecting the town where the gold is being kept?

16. What was the film's working title?

17. What is the name of the hustling supply sergeant played by Don Rickles?

18. The man who later directed *Animal House* (1978) and *The Blues Brothers* (1980) served as a production assistant on *Kelly's Heroes*. Who is this?

19. The song "Sunshine" plays as Oddball destroys the German military installation. Who sings this tune?

20. *Kelly's Heroes* was the second war film directed by Brian G. Hutton and starring Clint Eastwood. What was the first?

21. What is the name of Oddball's "mechanical genius" played by Gavin MacLeod?

22. Why was Kelly demoted from the rank of lieutenant?

23. What is the significance of the plane that destroys Kelly's jeeps?

24. Whose "negative waves" does Oddball blame for the destruction of the bridge?

25. What does Oddball say can give you "an edge"?

Quiz No. 47:
KING RAT
(1965)

Screenplay by Bryan Forbes (based on a novel by James Clavell)
Directed by Bryan Forbes
Starring George Segal, Tom Courtenay, and James Fox
Columbia Pictures
Available on VHS

> *If the war ends, the Japs are gonna massacre every man in this camp.*
> *The only chance'll be if you have the big money to buy your way out.*
> *This is gonna be our ticket, Pete. Yours and mine. That's why we gotta*
> *go through with the deal tonight.* —CPL. KING

Films that take place in prisons and during wartime are generally quite effective because both situations provide filmmakers a wide canvas of desperation, despair, and fear with which to work. Because of this, prisoner of war stories that combine both elements are almost always effective. While films such as *The Bridge on the River Kwai* (1957) and *The Great Escape* (1963) tend to overshadow it, Bryan Forbes' *King Rat* is an equally impressive effort worthy of recognition. Like *The Great Escape,* which was also conceived by novelist James Clavell, *King Rat* focuses primarily on one American who is greatly outnumbered by British prisoners. While *King Rat* doesn't boast as many stars as *The Great Escape,* it is in many ways a superior film. There are no awkward motorcycle stunts to be found here, and George Segal gives a multilayered performance as the smug Cpl. King that is far more convincing than that of his *Great Escape* counterpart Steve McQueen. Equally impressive is Tom Courtenay as the comtemptuous Lt. Grey.

King Rat received two Academy Award nominations for Best Black-and-White Cinematography (Burnett Guffey) and Best Black-and-

White Art Direction–Set Decoration (Robert Emmet Smith and Frank Tuttle), but did not receive an Oscar for either. In addition, director Bryan Forbes was presented the British Academy of Film and Television Awards United Nations Award.

1. What type of animal is "Tojo"?
2. What is the name of the one-eyed teacher?
3. On whose real-life experiences was this film loosely based?
4. Who does King refer to as his "doggie"?
5. The film is introduced with a message informing the viewer that "this is not a story of escape." What are we then told this is a story of?
6. Tom Courtenay appeared in another film released the same year as *King Rat*, which was later listed to the American Film Institute's "100 Years, 100 Movies" list of the one hundred greatest American films. What is the title of this film?
7. How does Grey say King is like "all criminals"?
8. When Marlowe asks Chaplain Drinkwater what God can do, what is Drinkwater's response?
9. How does Marlowe injure his arm?
10. When Marlowe says there's nothing he can say, what is King's response?
11. What does Grey order Capt. Hawkins to destroy?
12. What does King say he will save if Marlowe can preserve the money?
13. At King's suggestion, Marlowe speaks Malay. What, according to Marlowe, is the "rough" translation of this sentence?
14. What is Tex ordered to do with Marlowe's infected bandages?
15. For what crime is Pvt. Gurble punished?
16. What contraband is discovered inside the headboard of Capt. Daven's bed?
17. Who does King plan to be his only rat meat customers?
18. Who is the camp's provost marshal?
19. Of what does Dr. Prodhomme say Capt. Masters died?
20. Who does King refer to as being a "poor man's Bela Lugosi"?
21. The film tells us the prisoners did not "live" at Changi. What does the film say they did do there?
22. What type of meat does King argue is no different from pig?

23. What does Col. Foster say the Japanese are generally overly polite in regard to?

24. Who makes a cameo as paratrooper Capt. Weaver?

5. King says he wants to put Marlowe on the payroll. How much does he offer to pay him per week?

Quiz No. 48:

THE LAST OF THE MOHICANS
(1992)

Screenplay by Michael Mann, Christopher Crowe, John L. Balderston, Paul
  Perez, Daniel Moore, and Philip Dunne (based on a novel by James
  Fennimore Cooper)
Directed by Michael Mann
Starring Daniel Day-Lewis, Madeleine Stowe, and Russell Means
Twentieth Century-Fox
Available on VHS, DVD

> *Death and honor are thought to be the same, but today I have learned*
> *that sometimes they are not.* —COL. EDMUND MUNRO

There can be no doubt that Twentieth Century-Fox executives greenlit
this adaptation of James Fennimore Cooper's classic novel because
they saw similarities between it and the wildly successful film *Dances
with Wolves* (1990), but screenwriter/director Michael Mann had
other ideas. In this sleek retelling of Cooper's story about a trapper
caught in the middle of the French and Indian War, the protagonist
Hawkeye (Daniel Day-Lewis) possesses all the attributes of the modern action film hero. While purists may scoff at Mann's decision to dis-
regard historical accuracy and stray from Cooper's original source
material, *The Last of the Mohicans* is a satisfying adventure film that
keeps the viewer glued to the screen. The film may not have the artistic
scope and overall depth of *Dances with Wolves,* but fidgety viewers will
be pleased by the fact that it's significantly shorter, clocking in right at
two hours.

 The Last of the Mohicans received one Academy Award nomination
for Best Sound (Chris Jenkins, Doug Hemphill, Mark Smith, and
Simon Kaye), and ultimately won the Oscar. Other honors include an
impressive seven British Academy of Film and Television Awards
nominations, nominations from both the American and British Societies

of Cinematographers, a Golden Globe nomination for Best Original Score (Trevor Jones and Randy Edelman), and Best Actor prizes for Daniel Day-Lewis from both the Evening Standard British Film Awards and the London Critics Circle Film Awards.

1. Who is the "last of the Mohicans"?

2. What two things does Duncan conclude to be a "reasonable basis" for a man and a woman to be together?

3. When Hawkeye says "someday I think you and I are going to have a serious disagreement," to whom is he speaking?

4. When does Magua say the hatchet will be buried?

5. Of what crime does Col. Munro say Hawkeye is guilty?

6. Numerous versions of *The Last of the Mohicans* had been made prior to this one. The most famous is the 1936 version, which served as the basis for this incarnation. What actor appeared as Hawkeye in the 1936 version?

7. The man who served as technical advisor on this film also served in this capacity on *Platoon* (1986) and *Saving Private Ryan* (1998). Who is this?

8. Who does Magua refer to as "Grayhair"?

9. Who is Hawkeye's adoptive father?

10. Gen. Webb concludes that the French "haven't the nature" for something. What is this?

11. Who does Magua say has become a "great war leader"?

12. What is Hawkeye's real name?

13. Whose death does Hawkeye say would be a "great honor" for the Huron?

14. What is the name of Cora's younger sister?

15. What does Cora say is "on fires"?

16. The actor who plays Col. Beams also appears in *The Usual Suspects* (1995), *Amistad* (1997), and *The Shipping News* (2001). Who is this?

17. Screenwriter Philip Dunne, who died the year the film was released, is credited as a writer on the film despite his having nothing to do with the production. Why?

18. Where are Duncan's men taking Cora and her sister when they are ambushed and ultimately saved by Hawkeye?

19. What does Magua say Hawkeye speaks with two tongues?

20. How does Cora's younger sister die?

21. Munro says he's lived to see something he never expected. What is this?
22. Who does Magua say the white man is a doe to?
23. Why does Duncan say Cora is defending Hawkeye?
24. In what state was *The Last of the Mohicans* filmed?
25. Why does Hawkeye shoot Duncan?

Quiz No. 49:
LAWRENCE OF ARABIA
(1962)

Screenplay by Robert Bolt and Michael Wilson (based on the memoirs of
   T. E. Lawrence)
Directed by David Lean
Starring Peter O'Toole, Omar Sharif, Alec Guiness, and Anthony Quinn
Columbia Pictures
Available on VHS, DVD

> *Young men make wars and the virtues of war are the virtues of young*
> *men—courage and hope for the future. Then old men make the peace*
> *and the vices of peace are the vices of old men—mistrust and caution.*
> *It must be so.*   —PRINCE FEISAL

David Lean's *Lawrence of Arabia* is the king of all epics. This magnificent, sprawling masterpiece chronicles the life of T. E. Lawrence, an eccentric Englishman who assisted the Arabs in their struggle for
independence. The performances of Peter O'Toole, Omar Sharif, Alec
Guiness, Anthony Quinn, and the rest of the cast are precise and carefully measured. The real-life Lawrence was an extremely complex man
whose actions sometimes defied logic, and it is to the credit of screenwriter Robert Bolt that he left these actions unexplained and enig-
matic rather than attempting to assign clearly defined motivations for
them. Shot in 70mm, Freddie Young's cinematography is breathtaking.
Lean's direction is superb, and first-time screenwriter Bolt's script is
lean and mean, even at the film's staggering length (221 minutes).
Today, *Lawrence of Arabia* is widely recognized as one of the greatest
films ever made, and deservedly so. In an era in which the words
"great" and "classic" are bandied about in a cavalier fashion, there are
no sufficient words to adequately describe the level of greatness this
film achieves.

   Lawrence of Arabia received ten Academy Award nominations for

Best Picture (Sam Spiegel), Best Director (Lean), Best Adapted Screenplay (Bolt), Best Actor (O'Toole), Best Supporting Actor (Sharif), Best Color Cinematography (Young), Best Film Editing (Anne V. Coates), Best Sound (John Cox), Best Substantially Original Score (Maurice Jarre), and Best Art Direction–Set Decoration (John Box, John Stoll, and Dario Simoni). These nominations resulted in seven Oscars for Best Picture, Best Director, Best Cinematography, Best Film Editing, Best Sound, Best Art Direction–Set Decoration, and Best Substantially Original Score. Other honors include four British Academy of Film and Television Awards, four Golden Globe Awards, a Writers Guild of Great Britain Award, and a National Board of Review Award for Best Director. The film was listed to the National Film Registry as a classic in 1991. In 1998, *Lawrence of Arabia* was listed to the American Film Institute's "100 Years, 100 Movies" list of the one hundred greatest American films at number five.

1. Because he found the name Omar Sharif to be too fancy a moniker, Peter O'Toole referred to Sharif by a nickname during production. What was this?

2. What does Prince Feisal conclude that England has a great hunger for?

3. Who was the first screenwriter hired to write *Lawrence of Arabia*?

4. What actor was nearly cast in the lead, causing T. E. Lawrence's brother A. W. Lawrence to conclude would "almost inevitably mean the film will be a flop"?

5. What legendary actor was initially signed to appear in the role of Gen. Allenby in 1961?

6. What does Feisal believe young men are?

7. The director of *All Quiet on the Western Front* (1930) had attempted to direct Lawrence's life story in 1926. Who was this?

8. According to legend, Peter O'Toole had something cosmetically altered to make him look more like Lawrence. What was this?

9. David Lean used four assistant directors on *Lawrence of Arabia*. Two of them later became accomplished filmmakers. Can you name them?

10. What are the two things Feisal says his people are not used to?

11. Who provides the voice of the motorcyclist who hails Lawrence by the Suez Canal?

12. What does Feisal say no man can provide?

13. What actress suggested Peter O'Toole for the role of Lawrence after seeing him in a London stage production?

14. A sequel entitled *A Dangerous Man: Lawrence After Arabia* (1990) was later produced. Who assumes the role of Lawrence in this film?

15. At Lawrence's funeral, a man becomes angered by a remark made by Jackson Bentley. The man tells Bentley he once shook Lawrence's hand. Where was this?

16. How many female speaking roles are there in this film?

17. Where does Sherif Ali ibn el Kharish say he was educated?

18. Lawrence says there is a trick to putting out burning matches with his fingers. What is this?

19. What does Brighton conclude regarding British and Arab interests?

20. After being called a clown, Lawrence says "we can't all be" something. What is this?

21. Peter O'Toole lost in his bid for Best Actor. To whom did he lose?

22. Who, according to Gasim, does Allah favor?

23. What does Mr. Dryden say have small beginnings?

24. How many men does Auda say he has killed with his hands?

25. What is the first line of dialogue in the film?

Quiz No. 50:
THE LONGEST DAY
(1962)

Screenplay by Romain Gary, James Jones, David Pursall, Cornelius Ryan, and
   Jack Seddon (based on a novel by Cornelius Ryan)
Directed by Ken Annakin, Andrew Marton, Gerd Oswald, and Bernhard
   Wicki
Starring Richard Burton, Sean Connery, and John Wayne
Twentieth Century-Fox
Available on VHS, DVD

> *This is history! We are living an historical moment. We are going to*
> *lose the war because our glorious Fuhrer has taken a sleeping pill and*
> *is not to be awakened. Think of it, Kurt. We are witnessing something*
> *which historians will always say is completely improbable, and yet it*
> *is true.*   —MAJ. GEN. BLUMENTRITT

Like *How the West Was Won* (1962), which was released the same year,
The Longest Day is a huge sweeping epic crafted by multiple screenwriters and directors, and features a virtual who's who of Hollywood's
hottest stars. The Daryl F. Zanuck–produced film depicts D day
through the eyes of many different soldiers of various ranks on both
sides of the conflict. This rather profitable formula—a long, bloated
film featuring a cavalcade of stars—would be revisited numerous
times in the years to come (*Is Paris Burning?* [1966], *Tora! Tora! Tora!*
[1970], *Midway* [1976], *A Bridge Too Far* [1977], and so on). Such
films are comparable to the Major League Baseball All-Star Game in
that these exhibitions are rarely as thrilling as the normal games and
the performers aren't giving 100 percent, but the sheer volume of talent involved makes it interesting nonetheless. While this is certainly
the case here, *The Longest Day* still stands head and shoulders above
the aforementioned battle epics.

   The Longest Day received five Academy Award nominations in the categories of Best Picture (Zanuck), Best Black-and-White Cinematography (Jean Bourgoin and Walter Wotitz), Best Film Editing (Samuel E. Beetley), Best Special Effects (Robert MacDonald and Jacques Maumont), and Best Black-and-White Art Direction–Set Decoration (Ted Haworth, Leon Barsacq, Vincent Korda, and Gabriel Bechir). These five nominations resulted in two Oscars for the film's special effects and cinematography. Other honors include a Laurel Award for Top Action Drama, a Laurel Award nomination for Top Action Performance (Robert Mitchum), a Golden Globe Award for Best Black-and-White Cinematography, an American Cinema Editors Award for Best Edited Feature Film, and a David di Donatello Award for Best Foreign Film.

1. During his briefing prior to the invasion, Lt. Col. Vandervoort tells the men to send the German soldiers somewhere. Where is this?

2. Brig. Gen. Cota says only two kinds of men will stay on the beach. What are they?

3. *The Longest Day* was one of two films released in 1962 that starred both John Wayne and Henry Fonda. What is the other film?

4. What do the Allies drop attached to parachutes as a diversion?

5. Where have the Germans long presumed the Allies would attack?

6. *The Longest Day* is one of only two films featuring both John Wayne and Robert Mitchum. The second film, which was directed by Howard Hawks, was released five years later. What is this film?

7. A Frenchman arrives on the beach riding a bicycle. He welcomes Lord Lovat's commandos and offers them a gift. What is this?

8. Sean Connery, Curt Jurgens, and Gert Fröbe all appear in *The Longest Day*. What is the significance of this?

9. Brig. Gen. Theodore Roosevelt Jr. is told that he shouldn't attack in the first wave because he's too important to the operation. What does he conclude to be the real reason his superiors don't want him killed?

10. Flight Officer Campbell says he's noticed something peculiar regarding the German he killed. What is this?

11. What are the words of wisdom involving technology that Capt. Maud says his grandmother always offered?

12. What does Campbell say has always worried him about being "one of the few"?

13. How many Allied soldiers does Field Marshal Rommel say will reach the shore?

14. Bill Millin appears as the man who plays the bagpipes as Lord Lovat's men storm the beach. What is the significance of this?

15. What does Lord Lovat say England has earned?

16. The British padre dives beneath the water to search for something he's lost. What is this?

17. The Nazis say the Americans have always done two things when attacking in the past. What are these?

18. The German director responsible for *A Kiss Before Dying* (1956) and *Brainwashed* (1960) directed portions of the film but did not receive credit. Who is this?

19. Dwight D. Eisenhower was interested in portraying himself in this film, but the filmmakers decided against it. Why?

20. What is the "five-cent toy" that is issued to the American GIs?

21. What is the name of Maud's dog that accompanies him on the invasion?

22. What does Maj. Gen. Blumentritt have in his quarters that he has been keeping for a "fitting occasion"?

23. Which member of the legendary "Rat Pack" appears in the film?

24. What does RAdm. Janjard tell his men they must do to drive out the enemy?

25. Who wrote and performed the film's theme song?

Quiz No. 51:

M*A*S*H

(1970)

Screenplay by Ring Lardner Jr. (based on a novel by Richard Hooker)
Directed by Robert Altman
Starring Donald Sutherland, Elliott Gould, and Tom Skerritt
Twentieth Century-Fox
Available on VHS, DVD

> *This isn't a hospital! It's an insane asylum!*
> —MAJ. MARGARET O'HOULIHAN

Director Robert Altman has made a number of classic films, and *M*A*S*H* may well be the finest of them all. Although *M*A*S*H* actually takes place during the Korean War, Altman's film was meant as an allusion to the Vietnam conflict, which was still raging at the time. In an era of blatant rebellion, Altman crafted a film as rebellious as the characters it depicts. Through racially stereotyped characters (a black footballer is named "Spearchucker"), sexist attitudes, homophobic themes, and an antimilitary sentiment, *M*A*S*H* thumbs its nose (and maybe even raises a middle finger) at the establishment in general. Although the film takes place during the war, which is directly responsible for most of what transpires in the story, the film doesn't concern itself much with the war. Instead, the film searches for humor—generally at the expense of others—in what is perhaps the darkest of situations. Though many of the situations presented in the film are a tad bit outrageous, its most humorous moments are among the funniest of the past thirty-five years. Those who haven't seen the film and imagine it being similar to the long-running television series it inspired are likely to be shocked by its ballsiness.

*M*A*S*H* received five Academy Award nominations for Best Picture (Ingo Preminger), Best Director (Altman), Best Adapted Screenplay (Ring Lardner Jr.), Best Supporting Actress (Sally Kellerman), and

Best Film Editing (Danford B. Greene). These nominations resulted in a single Oscar awarded to Kellerman for Best Supporting Actress. Other honors include the prestigious Palme de Or at the Cannes Film Festival, five British Academy of Film and Television Awards nominations, a Golden Globe Award for Best Comedy Motion Picture, Laurel Awards for Best Picture (second place), Best Male Comedy Performance (Elliott Gould), Best Female Comedy Performance (Kellerman), and a second-place award for Best Male Comedy Performance (Donald Sutherland).

1. In one scene, it is announced that "tonight's movie is *The Glory Brigade*." Why would it have been impossible for this film to be shown?

2. How many African American surgeons actually served in the Korean War?

3. What are Walt's nicknames?

4. What is Radar's real name?

5. What 1975 cartoon parodied *M*A*S*H* and featured characters named Coldlips, Col. Flake, and Maj. Sideburns?

6. When O'Houlihan asks how someone like Hawkeye Pierce could have "reached a position of responsibility in the Army Medical Corps," what is is Col. Blake's memorable response?

7. What, according to the film's tagline, does *M*A*S*H* give?

8. To how many women is Walt engaged?

9. Only one regular character on the television series was played by the same actor who played the character in the film. Which character is this?

10. G. Wood plays the same character in the film and the first three episodes of the television series. Who is this?

11. Where does O'Houlihan say she calls home?

12. What does O'Houlihan say she cannot forgive?

13. Most of the football scenes were actually directed by the filmmaker responsible for films like *Stacey* (1973) and *Seven* (1979). Who is this?

14. What is Hawkeye's real name?

15. What does O'Houlihan say her letter to the army brass is written in the interest of?

16. The actor playing Capt. "Ugly" John Black is an accomplished screenwriter. Who is this?

17. This film served as the basis for four television series. Can you name them?

18. Who does Henry say have "all the fun"?

19. What bizarre *M*A*S*H*-related events occurred on February 15 and February 16, 1996?

20. What is Father Mulcahy's nickname?

21. When Hawkeye laments that one makes "certain concessions to the war," to what is he referring?

22. What is Duke's real name?

23. Fred Williamson and Buck Buchanan, both of whom appear in *M*A*S*H*, played for the same professional football team. Can you name this team?

24. What kind of women does Duke say he prefers?

25. What does Hawkeye believe Walt needs for "therapeutic value"?

Quiz No. 52:

MERRILL'S MARAUDERS

(1962)

Screenplay by Samuel Fuller, Charlton Ogburn Jr., and Milton Sperling
Directed by Samuel Fuller
Starring Jeff Chandler, Ty Hardin, and Peter Brown
United States Pictures
Available on VHS

When you lead, you have to hurt people; the enemy and sometimes your own.
                                        —BRIG. GEN. MERRILL

Few filmmakers in history have been so successful that their names became synonymous with the genre in which they worked. Just as one cannot discuss the Western genre without mentioning John Ford or Howard Hawks, a discussion of the war film among knowledegable cineastes cannot be conducted without speaking of Samuel Fuller. Like other Fuller-helmed projects, such as *Fixed Bayonets* (1951) and *The Steel Helmet* (1951), *Merrill's Marauders* is a grimly realistic no-nonsense war film. There are no love stories to be found in Fuller's films, which instead focus on the war itself. *Merrill's Marauders,* which tells the true story of three thousand American soldiers who traveled two hundred miles on foot through the jungles of Burma in 1944 to strike strategic posts at Walawbaum and Myitkyina, provides a down-and-dirty look at the operation through the eyes of the soldiers involved. As is the case with most of Fuller's films, less becomes more. Despite having an incredibly small budget with which to work, Fuller crafts a lean, mean, action-packed picture that is far better than bigger budget war films that tell essentially the same story.

    1. *Merrill's Marauders* was Jeff Chandler's final film before his untimely death. From what did Chandler die?
    2. Merrill's radio handle is a football term. What is this?

3. Where do Franklin D. Roosevelt and Winston Churchill meet at the beginning of the film?

4. Who suggests eating Muley's pet mule?

5. What does Merrill say the men can do if they have a single ounce of strength left in them?

6. What does Kolowicz say is "holding up" their British replacements?

7. What, according to Gen. Stilwell, is his "big nightmare"?

8. Who does Kolowicz say looks sloppy?

9. Samuel Vaughan Wilson plays Bannister. What is the significance of Wilson's appearance in the film?

10. What, according to Merrill, is "gonna drive [him] nuts"?

11. What is the name of Muley's pet mule?

12. What is Chowhound's real name?

13. On what date was the invasion launched?

14. What does Merrill say is "all you have to do" when at the end of your rope?

15. To whom does Stockton write, informing them that O'Brien is wounded?

16. What does Merrill say he'd rather be than dead?

17. Where were the film's jungle scenes shot?

18. What does Bullseye warn Chowhound to stay away from?

19. What does Kolowicz say Stockton is "too close" to?

20. Where does Merrill say he was when he suffered his first heart attack?

21. What is Stockton's response when Bullseye tells him to have Merrill pick up his own ammo?

22. Who does Doc say looks good to him?

23. Who does Merrill say a captain always believes?

24. What is Merrill's first name?

25. Who advises Lt. Stockton not to take the point?

Quiz No. 53:

A MIDNIGHT CLEAR

(1992)

Screenplay by Keith Gordon (based on a novel by William Wharton)
Directed by Keith Gordon
Starring Peter Berg, Kevin Dillon, and Arye Gross
A&M Films
Available on VHS, DVD

> *I'm having my usual trouble—noticing how beautiful the world is just*
> *when I might be leaving it.*   —WILL KNOTT

Although *A Midnight Clear* begins like virtually every other World
War II film, it quickly shifts gears, strays from the formula, and establishes itself as a uniquely unconventional war film. Ordered to secure
an abandoned chateau in the middle of the woods for use as an observation post, a weary, tattered American squad finds itself surrounded
by a group of unusual German soldiers. After a number of signs—
among them an unlikely snowball fight—they come to the realization
that the Germans don't want to fight them. Deftly adapted by screen-
writer/director Keith Gordon, the film has a cold, dark, eery tone that
is not generally associated with war films. The ensemble, which includes Peter Berg, Kevin Dillon, Arye Gross, Ethan Hawke, Gary
Sinise, and Frank Whaley, work well together and deliver Gordon's
often-poetic dialogue with ease. Despite being overlooked—perhaps
due in part to its lack of carnage—*A Midnight Clear* is one of the
finest, most effective antiwar films ever produced.

The film received an Independent Spirit Award nomination for Best
Screenplay, but did not win.

1. Only one member of the I&R platoon was not a virgin at the
beginning of the war. Who was this?
2. What does Miller say it's hard to do with a "frozen butt"?

3. What is the name of the camp where Knott talks with Maj. Griffin?

4. How many men are there supposed to be in an intelligence recon squad?

5. What is the name of the girl the soldiers bring back to the hotel?

6. Which of the men first comes to the realization that the Germans want to surrender?

7. The soldier who possessed the platoon's only deck of cards is now dead. What is his name?

8. Which cast member later appears as a regular on the television series *Scrubs*?

9. Shutzer writes a message in front of the snowman. What is this?

10. What news does Knott say "did [Mother] in for sure"?

11. What does Knott believe to be "about the same thing" as an officer?

12. Why does Shutzer believe the Germans don't want to surrender to him?

13. What was Griffin's civilian occupation?

14. Mundy gives one of the German soldiers a grenade. What does the German do with it?

15. Another William Wharton novel dealing with war had been previously adapted in 1984. The film, which was directed by Alan Parker, starred Nicholas Cage and Matthew Modine. What is this film?

16. Of what does Mother say he didn't believe there "was any" left?

17. What is Mother's real name?

18. What "squad rule" was established by Father?

19. *A Midnight Clear* was the second William Wharton adaptation in which Ethan Hawke appeared. Can you name the first?

20. What, according to Knott, doesn't mean surrender?

21. What affliction does Knott say kept Mel from being squad leader?

22. The squad finds the frozen bodies of an American soldier and a German soldier posed. What do they appear to be doing?

23. Knott drops two things when he is startled by the three disappearing Germans. What are these?

24. *A Midnight Clear* was the second war film in which John C. McGinley and Kevin Dillon appeared together. What was the first?

25. Who does Miller lament about having "finally found a date"?

Quiz No. 54:

MIDWAY

(1976)

Screenplay by Donald S. Sanford
Directed by Jack Smight
Starring Charlton Heston, Edward Albert, and Henry Fonda
Universal Pictures
Available on VHS, DVD

> *You know, you're being paid to fly fighter planes. Not sit down in your*
> *cabin and cry over your girl's picture. You'd better shape up, Tiger, or*
> *some hotshot Jap pilot's gonna flame your ass!*
> —CAPT. MATTHEW GARTH

Based on the 1942 Pacific theater "battle to end all battles," Jack
Smight's epic film *Midway* features a cavalcade of stars, including
Charlton Heston, Edward Albert, Henry Fonda, James Coburn, Glenn
Ford, Hal Holbrook, Toshiro Mifune, Robert Mitchum, Cliff Robertson,
and Robert Wagner, all apparently cast simply for the sake of having a
big-name cast. Many of these legendary actors are given little to do
here, and the inept overdubbing of Japanese icon Mifune leaves him
sounding like an angry robot. As we tend to remember Charlton
Heston only for his greatest roles, his at-times cartoonish overacting in
Midway serves as a reminder that Heston was more than capable of
being a ham when presented with the opportunity to do so. Equally
easy to dislike is the screenplay's unneeded subplot focusing on the
budding relationship between the son of Heston's character and a
Japanese woman.

Yet, despite its many flaws, *Midway* is a thoroughly entertaining
film. Although it had been done before (and done better, I might add),
the filmmakers' decision to show the conflict from both the American
and Japanese points of view was a wise choice that only makes the film
more entertaining. However, *Midway* fails (in terms of realism) where

so many other World War II films have before and since: In what is likely a monetary consideration regarding the Japanese box office, the Japanese are cast in an unrealistic overly sympathetic light rather than given equal treatment to their American counterparts.

1. What is the question Adm. Chester W. Nimitz says he believes Capt. Matthew Garth would have asked himself after the battle?

2. Henry Fonda had previously portrayed Nimitz in a 1965 Otto Preminger film. What is this film?

3. Shots from a 1956 Joseph Pevney war film were integrated into *Midway*. What is this film?

4. The son of a legendary filmmaker known primarily for directing war films appears in this film. Who is this?

5. What does Cmdr. Jessop believe to be Lt. Thomas Garth's only weakness?

6. Who does Adm. Halsey name as his replacement?

7. Robert Mitchum and Henry Fonda had appeared together previously in a 1962 war film directed by Ken Annakin, Andrew Marton, Gerd Oswald, and Bernhard Wicki. What is this film?

8. The film ends with a quotation. Who is it from?

9. Who does Lt. Cmdr. Blake refer to as a "goddamn scalp hunter"?

10. What does Nimitz say might be the "smart play"?

11. In how many Westerns do *Midway* costars Glenn Ford and James Coburn appear together?

12. What is the film's alternate video title?

13. Why does Vice Adm. Nagumo say his ninety-three zeroes are ill-prepared to destroy an airstrip?

14. The man who overdubbed Toshiro Mifune's voice is best known as the narrator on *Bullwinkle*. Who is this?

15. What is Adm. William Halsey Jr.'s nickname?

16. What does Cmdr. Rochefort say he believed would have Capt. Garth "dancing in the streets"?

17. On what ship is Adm. Yamamoto during the battle?

18. Capt. Garth says Nagumo is doing the same thing he's doing. What is this?

19. Footage from a 1970 war film directed by Richard Fleischer, Kinji Fukasaku, and Toshio Masuda was integrated into *Midway*'s battle scenes. What is this film?

20. Where was the USS *Yorktown* damaged one week prior to the Battle of Midway?

21. A year before appearing together in *Midway,* Tom Selleck and Dabney Coleman starred together in a made-for-television remake of *The Best Years of Our Lives* (1946). What is this title of this telefilm?

22. Erik Estrada appears in the film as Lt. Ramos. What is Ramos's nickname?

23. What does Capt. Garth conclude to be a "problem we all have once a year"?

24. What fruit are the PBY scout planes named after?

25. What is the name of Lt. Garth's Japanese girlfriend?

Quiz No. 55:

MISTER ROBERTS

(1955)

Screenplay by Frank S. Nugent, Joshua Logan, and Thomas Heggen (based
  on a novel by Thomas Heggen)
Directed by John Ford and Mervyn LeRoy
Starring Henry Fonda, James Cagney, and William Powell
Warner Bros.
Available on VHS, DVD

> *This is a tough crew on here and they have a wonderful battle record.
> But I've discovered, Doc, that the unseen enemy of this war is the
> boredom that eventually becomes a faith, and therefore a terrible
> form of suicide. I know now that the ones who refuse to surrender to it
> are the strongest of all.* —LT. DOUG A. ROBERTS

That *Mister Roberts* wound up being a highly qualitative picture is a
miracle considering the problems that plagued its production. Despite
its being adapted from a hugely successful play (both of which were
adapted from Thomas Heggen's novel), Warner Bros. initially wanted
its lead, Henry Fonda, replaced with someone younger and more
bankable. However, director John Ford fought for Fonda, and won—
something he later regretted. Then, the U.S. Navy decided against assisting the film, but later, after Ford called on Adm. Robert Carney, the
chief of naval operations, for a personal favor, the navy changed its
mind. When shooting began, Ford and Fonda found themselves at
odds over the film's direction, and the long-time friendship between
the two men ultimately suffered as a result. After punching Fonda during a discussion regarding the comedic timing of the film, Ford became ill-tempered and began drinking heavily. Midway through the
production, Ford suffered medical problems and had to be removed
from the project. Mervyn LeRoy then came onboard the production
and completed filming. While LeRoy made no attempts to reshape the

film as his own, Warner Bros. decided to add scenes that Ford had ordered cut from the final print. When events such as these transpire during a film's production, the finished result is generally poor. However, this is not the case with *Mister Roberts*. The film quickly became a box-office hit and launched Jack Lemmon's career into the stratosphere.

Mister Roberts received three Academy Award nominations for Best Picture (Leland Hayward), Best Supporting Actor (Lemmon), and Best Sound (William A. Mueller), resulting in one Oscar awarded to Lemmon. Other honors include a British Academy of Film and Television Awards nomination for Best Foreign Actor (Lemmon) and a Writers Guild Award for Best Written American Comedy.

1. What does Lt. Roberts say will happen the day Ens. Pulver follows through with something?

2. What happened to John Ford that caused him to leave the production?

3. Who does Capt. Morton refer to as a "man who keeps his word"?

4. A line from the play this film was adapted from had to be cut because it was deemed inappropriate. What was this?

5. What, according to Doc, is "mostly what makes heroism"?

6. What is the significance of William Powell's performance in *Mister Roberts*?

7. What, according to Roberts, does Pulver do for sixteen hours each day?

8. Roberts raises his glass to toast a "great American." Who is this?

9. The film was adapted from an ultrasuccessful stage play. For how many years did the play run on Broadway?

10. What does Morton call the "rankest piece of insubordination" he's ever seen?

11. What does Roberts say scotch tastes like?

12. Fornell sends Pulver a letter informing him of something. What is this?

13. Warner Bros. head Jack Warner had wanted to cast one of two actors in the role of Lt. Doug A. Roberts. Who were these two actors?

14. What is the name of the ship on which the film takes place?

15. What does Morton say he doesn't like in his pajamas?

16. A cast member was married in Honolulu one week before film-

ing. Henry Fonda gave the bride away and John Ford served as the best man. Who was this?

17. Who does Roberts allow to read his request for a transfer at the beginning of the film?

18. What is the occupation of the showering women the men observe through binoculars?

19. John Ford and James Cagney had collaborated previously on a 1952 World War I film. What is this film?

20. Morton times Roberts after his announcement that there will be no liberty. How many seconds does it take for Roberts to arrive at his cabin?

21. Henry Fonda and John Ford worked together on one final film seven years after *Mister Roberts*. What is this film?

22. Who does Doc say is the "most absolute Monarch left in the world"?

23. Why does Morton sound the general alarm?

24. What has Roberts been hiding in a shoebox?

25. How many soldiers are hospitalized after the army-navy brawl?

Quiz No. 56:

MOTHER NIGHT

(1996)

Screenplay by Robert B. Weide (based on a novel by Kurt Vonnegut Jr.)
Directed by Keith Gordon
Starring Nick Nolte, Sheryl Lee, and Alan Arkin
Fine Line Features
Available on VHS, DVD

> *I suppose the moral here is you must be careful what you pretend to be*
> *because in the end you are what you pretend to be.*
> —HOWARD W. CAMPBELL JR

Director Keith Gordon's *Mother Night* is the first film adapted from a novel by Kurt Vonnegut Jr. to fully capture the essence and spirit of his work. Actor Nick Nolte does the finest work of his career here as a successful American playwright named Howard W. Campbell Jr., who resides in Germany at the outbreak of World War II. If we are to believe Campbell, who narrates the film, he is then approached by an American intelligence agent (John Goodman) and persuaded to work as a spy. By befriending the Nazis and positioning himself as a propagandistic anti-Semitic radio personality, Campbell delivers veiled messages to Allied operatives through his weekly broadcasts. In his mind, Campbell is a hero fighting fascism. To the rest of the world, he is the singular voice of Nazism and racial hatred. When the war grinds to a halt and Adolf Hitler's regime is toppled, Campbell becomes a hunted war criminal. As with other works of Vonnegut, as well as Gordon's 1999 follow-up, *Waking the Dead,* it becomes difficult to differentiate between reality and the perceived reality of the film's protagonist. Whether or not Campbell is truly working as a spy or this is simply a fantasy he has concocted to rationalize his actions is never made clear. Gordon's subtle, straightforward style of direction serves the material well, and the voice of screenwriter Robert B. Weide—a close friend of Vonnegut's—

meshes so flawlessly with that of the author that it almost seems as though Vonnegut himself penned the screenplay. *Mother Night* is a complex, richly textured film and is an example of a project where seemingly everything comes together to create an extraordinary film.

1. For what country does George Kraft work as a spy?

2. What does Adolf Eichmann say in regard to the six million Jews he was responsible for killing?

3. What city does Campbell refer to as the "heart of the free world"?

4. Why doesn't Campbell inform his wife he's a spy?

5. What does Campbell call "every playwright's secret dream"?

6. George Kraft declares that both he and Campbell are members of the "largest organization in the world." What is this?

7. Who does Campbell refer to as his "blue fairy godmother"?

8. By what name does Campbell refer to the president of the United States?

9. What is the name of the German actress Campbell is married to?

10. How many weeks do Campbell's captors give him to complete his memoirs?

11. What is Robert Sterling Wilson's title?

12. What is the title of Dr. Lionel Jones's self-published book that Kraft jokes about never being able to find?

13. Nick Nolte later appears in a 1999 Vonnegut adaptation directed by Alan Rudolph. What is this film?

14. What song plays over the film's opening credits?

15. What is the occupation of Campbell's father-in-law?

16. How many people does Wirtanen say knew that Campbell was an American spy?

17. Who provides the voice of Eichmann?

18. The character Howard W. Campbell Jr. also appears in a 1972 film adapted from another novel by Kurt Vonnegut Jr. In this film, directed by George Roy Hill, the role is played by Richard Schaal. What is this film?

19. Whose death does Campbell later learn was "one of the pieces of information" he broadcast without his knowing?

20. Why does Eichmann say Campbell is lucky?

21. What notion does Wirtanen say he believes Campbell is obsessed with?

22. Director Keith Gordon took a small role in a 1994 film in order to get the script for *Mother Night* to Nick Nolte. What is this film?

23. With what phrase of praise does Campbell conclude each broadcast?

24. Who makes a cameo in the film as "Sad Man on Street"?

25. What is the name of the racist newsletter that reports Campbell's home address?

Quiz No. 57:

NAPOLEON

(1927)

Screenplay by Abel Gance
Directed by Abel Gance
Starring Albert Dieudonne, Vladimir Roudenko, and Edmond Van Daele
Metro-Goldwyn-Mayer
Available on VHS

> *I have pushed back the frontiers of glory. That's quite something.*
> —NAPOLEON BONAPARTE

Abel Gance's 1927 landmark epic is perhaps the finest silent film ever produced. While silent films are often choppy and known for a certain style of melodramatic overacting, this is not the case with *Napoleon*. Gance's film holds up remarkably well seven decades after its creation. While the film excels in nearly every aspect, it is Gance's innovative experimentation in the editing room that remains the most impressive; looking back at his work here, it's now obvious that Gance's editing techniques were decades ahead of their time. However, Gance's experimentation didn't end there. Other successful innovations include the use of overlapping superimposed images, experimental camerawork, and the now-obsolete but nonetheless fascinating Polyvision, which allowed Gance to show three scenes simultaneously. A less-successful innovation is his early use of color. It's ironic that, while this was no doubt one of the film's most modernistic high-tech features in 1927, it is precisely this element of the film that dates it more than anything else. The film, which chronicles Napoleon Bonaparte's life from a snowball fight as a young schoolboy to his adult life as a conquering military commander, was restored by film historian Kevin Brownlow for a 1981 rerelease.

Napoleon received special awards from the New York Film Critics

Circle, the National Board of Review, and the Los Angeles Film Critics Circle for the 1981 restored version.

1. Director Abel Gance made another film based on the life of Napoleon Bonaparte in 1971. What is the name of this film?

2. What is the name of the school where Napoleon is shown engaging in a snowball fight?

3. Who appears in the film as Saint-Just?

4. Who gives Napoleon a pet eagle as a gift?

5. What does the film say the fallen drummers were replaced with?

6. A reward is offered for the capture of Napoleon when he is declared a traitor. How much is the reward?

7. When the commissioners of the Army ask Napoleon for his opinion, he instead gives them an ultimatum. What is this?

8. Abel Gance initially planned to make *Napoleon* a series of films. How many films did he envision?

9. What are the names of Napoleon's brothers?

10. Who does Robespierre refer to as "chatterers"?

11. What is the name of Napoleon's childhood adversary who puts stones inside his snowballs?

12. What conductor provided a new score for *Napoleon* when it was rereleased by Francis Ford Coppola's Zoetrope Studios in 1981?

13. When the commissioners of the army arrive on the battlefield to promote Napoleon to the rank of brigadier general, they find him asleep. What is he resting his head on?

14. What is said to be the "final refuge for fugitives"?

15. What body of land does Napoleon's geography instructor refer to as a "half-civilized island"?

16. What is Josephine's full name?

17. Who portrays Charlotte Corday in the film?

18. Who are referred to as "the three gods"?

19. In the snowball fight at the beginning of the film, Napoleon's army is outnumbered. His army consists of twenty boys. How many boys are on the opposing side?

20. What weapons does Gen. Carteaux say his army will use to take Toulon?

21. What, according to Napoleon, will be the worth of "all that results from carnage"?

22. Who is the "friend" Napoleon discusses the future with at the Sanguinaires?

23. Carteaux says that artillery is not only useless, but also something else. What is this?

24. Who is said to be the Bonaparte family's best friend?

25. Film historian Kevin Brownlow's restored version of *Napoleon* was released in 1981. Something else significant regarding the film occurred later that same year. What was this?

Quiz No. 58:

1941

(1979)

Screenplay by Robert Zemeckis, Bob Gale, and John Milius
Directed by Steven Spielberg
Starring Dan Aykroyd, Ned Beatty, and John Belushi
Columbia Pictures
Available on VHS, DVD

> *This time we win or we die trying. We sure as hell didn't start this war,*
> *but by God we're gonna finish it.* —SGT. FRANK TREE

Loosely based on a real-life incident in which a Japanese submarine sighting off the coast of California sent locals into a frenzy, Steven Spielberg's *1941* is a madcap examination of the paranoia that ran rampant on the West Coast at the onset of World War II. Although the script has some pacing problems, very little plot, and more than a few scenes that simply don't work, *1941* is still an above-average comedy filled with memorable moments. While it's unlikely the film will be re-membered as Spielberg's finest war film, *1941* is an all-star collabora-tion by many of Hollywood's brightest stars. It's significant anytime filmmakers such as Spielberg, Robert Zemeckis, and John Milius (pulling double duty here as screenwriter and executive producer) join forces for a project. The film also features a stellar cast that includes Dan Aykroyd, Ned Beatty, John Belushi, Christopher Lee, Tim Matheson, Toshiro Mifune, Warren Oates, Robert Stack, Treat Williams, Nancy Allen, John Candy, Elisha Cook Jr., Slim Pickens, Lionel Stander, Samuel Fuller, Mickey Rourke, and Michael McKean. This film may be far from Spielberg's best, but it's still a wildly enjoyable romp that only improves with time.

1941 received three Oscar nominations in the categories of Best Cinematography (William Fraker), Best Visual Effects (Fraker, A. D.

Flowers, and Gregory Jein), and Best Sound (Robert Knudson, Robert J. Glass, Don MacDougall, and Gene S. Cantamessa).

1. What is the name of the amusement park the Japanese submarine destroys?

2. David Lander and Michael McKean are cast as antiaircraft gunners. What is the significance of this?

3. Who was jailed for stealing Ward Douglas's car?

4. What is the name of the gas station where Captain "Wild" Bill Kelso refuels his plane?

5. What is the name of Sal Stewart's band that performs at the USO dance?

6. As the film opens, a woman removes her robe and goes skinny-dipping in the ocean. What is printed on the back of her robe?

7. What type of food does Cpl. Chuck Sitarski hate?

8. What is Stewart's real name?

9. *1941* was the first of three films Dan Aykroyd and John Belushi made together. Can you name the other two films?

10. Under what working title was *1941* filmed?

11. Who does Cmdr. Akiro Mitamura say his men are the descendants of?

12. The opening scene is an homage to another Spielberg film. What is this film?

13. Whose house does Hollis Wood believe the Japanese want to attack?

14. What is the toy prize inside Wood's Popper Jacks box?

15. What is the significance of Mr. and Mrs. Douglas's first names?

16. What are Kelso's final words in the film?

17. How many components, according to Sgt. Frank Tree, make up a General Electric refrigerator?

18. Who does Maj. Gen. Joseph W. Stilwell call the "craziest son-of-a-bitch" he's ever seen?

19. What, according to Stilwell, can you not have an air raid without?

20. A talent scout named Meyer Mishkin attends the USO dance. Which studio does Mishkin represent?

21. What is the one thing Donna Stratton is obsessed with?

22. What does Hollis throw into the toilet to trick his captors?

23. From what state does Pvt. Ogden Johnson Jones hail?

24. Which cast member also appears in the war films *Hell in the Pacific* (1968) and *Midway* (1976)?

25. What Hollywood icon was first offered the role of Maj. Gen. Joseph W. Stilwell, but rejected it because he felt the film was anti-American?

Quiz No. 59:
NO MAN'S LAND
(2001)

Screenplay by Danis Tanovic
Directed by Danis Tanovic
Starring Branko Djuric, Rene Bitorajac, and Filip Sovagovic
United Artists
Available on VHS, DVD

> *What's your problem? You want what? An introduction? To exchange*
> *phone numbers and visiting cards? We don't need an introduction.*
> *The next time we see each other, it'll be through a gun's sight.*
>
> —CIKI

When this Bosnian antiwar film was released in 2001, it was rightfully hailed as a masterpiece. Written and directed by Danis Tanovic, this loose remake of a 1931 film with the same title (directed by Victor Trivas and George Shdanoff) is the story of three soldiers, two Bosnian and one Serbian, who find themselves trapped together in a trench located between gunposts from each army. Making things more complicated, one of the Bosnian soldiers is lying on top of a mine that will explode if he moves. While *No Man's Land* begins down the beaten path of films such as *Grand Illusion* (1937) and *Hell in the Pacific* (1968)—storylines where enemy soldiers become unlikely companions under extreme conditions—the film then veers off; stuck together or not, these stubborn warriors vow to remain bitter enemies till the end. A fine mixture of comedy and drama, *No Man's Land* is easily one of the finest war films produced in the past twenty years.

In 2002, *No Man's Land* was awarded the Oscar for Best Foreign Language Film. Other honors include a Palme de Or nomination and a win for Best Screenplay at the 2001 Cannes Film Festival.

1. What is Ciki's response when Nino asks if he's going to set him free?

2. According to the old Serbian soldier, how many lead bearings does a bouncing mine spray when detonated?

3. Ciki's shirt bears the logo of a rock band. What is this band?

4. Capt. Dubois tells reporters that they must have three items before they will be permitted to visit the site. What are these?

5. From what does Ciki say he hopes Cera will die?

6. What is the name of Jane Livingston's cameraman?

7. Before the Bosnian relief squad is gunned down, one of the soldiers explains the difference between a pessimist and an optimist. What is this?

8. Nino asks Ciki why he wants him to empty his pockets. What is Ciki's response?

9. Ciki asks Nino why he cannot have a cigarette. What is Nino's response?

10. What is Sgt. Marchand's first name?

11. What does Livingston offer Nino just before requesting an interview?

12. Ciki says he had a girlfriend who lived in Banja Luka. What is her name?

13. Dubois says his superiors are attending a seminar in Geneva. What is the subject of the seminar?

14. According to the news report shown in the film, how many United Nations troops have been dispatched to Bosnia?

15. From what country is the bomb disposal officer who attempts to aid Cera?

16. What is Nino's response when Livingston asks if he placed the mine beneath Cera?

17. Why does the old Serbian soldier advise Nino not to touch anything in the trench?

18. What network employs Livingston?

19. Marchand speaks fluently in two languages. What are these?

20. When Michel says that a bomb expert makes only one mistake, Marchand disagrees, saying he makes two. What, according to Marchand, is his first mistake?

21. Ciki finds something in the old Serbian soldier's wallet that disgusts him. What is this?

22. Ciki shoots Nino to stop him from leaving with the United Nations officers. Where does he shoot him?

23. What, according to Marchand, can one not be neutral when facing?

24. What does the old Serbian soldier complain to his commanding officer that Nino does not know how to do?

25. Just after being shot, Ciki climbs out of the trench to retrieve something from his bag. What?

Quiz No. 60:

OBJECTIVE, BURMA!

(1945)

Screenplay by Alvah Bessie, Ranald MacDougall, and Lester Cole
Directed by Raoul Walsh
Starring Errol Flynn, James Brown, and William Prince
Warner Bros.
Available on VHS

> *Don't make sense to me. Swamps, jungle, rivers, flies, fleas, beetles,*
> *bugs, snakes, beetles, bugs, snakes. . . . It's monotonous!*
> —CPL. GABBY GORDON

Detractors of *Objective, Burma!* will quickly point out that the film
isn't historically accurate (such as its suggestion that only U.S. forces
were involved in the war with Japan in the Burmese jungles) and is
filled with flag-waving jingoistic propaganda. So what? Skillfully directed by legendary helmer Raoul Walsh, this is an entertaining adventure. Dropped behind enemy lines, Errol Flynn leads a group of
paratroopers on a mission to destroy a Japanese radar installation.
After achieving this, the soldiers must then travel many miles on
foot—behind enemy lines—without support. Despite being filmed in
the United States, Walsh gets the most out of the scenery, which actually passes for Burmese jungle. Flynn and the rest of the cast turn in
fine performances, the film's cinematography is first rate, and editor
George Amy does an excellent job maintaining the film's pace.

Objective, Burma! received three Academy Award nominations in
the categories of Best Original Story (Alvah Bessie), Best Film Editing
(Amy), and Best Original Score (Franz Waxman). However, these
nominations failed to yield a single Oscar.

1. What does Capt. Nelson say one should expect when "dealing
with monkeys"?

2. Director Raoul Walsh once played a horrendous practical joke on his friend Errol Flynn, who stars in *Operation, Burma!* Walsh stole the body of a recently deceased mutual friend and propped it up inside Flynn's home. Whose body was this?

3. The actor who appears in the film as Capt. Hennessey later becomes a television star. Who is this?

4. Lt. Jacobs was a teacher before the war. What subject did he teach?

5. Nelson tells a story about a time when he was afraid to jump. Someone then threatened to shoot him if he didn't. Who was this?

6. How old is Col. Carter?

7. *Operation, Burma!* was one of two films released in 1945 starring Errol Flynn and directed by Raoul Walsh. On the other film, Walsh did not receive credit. What is this film?

8. When asked where he would like to be if he could be any place in the world, where does Nelson say he would be?

9. What does Nelson order the men not to do until they reach the radar station?

10. How long does Nelson say it will take "at most" for the men to march from the airstrip to the radar station?

11. The film begins with a quotation. Who is it from?

12. Why does Nelson say the air force can't bomb the radar station?

13. The squad splits up into two groups. One group is led by Nelson. Who leads the second group?

14. When Williams receives his gear, he remarks that something is missing. What is this?

15. What would later happen to screenwriters Alvah Bessie and Lester Cole?

16. When Williams asks what will happen if his chute doesn't open, what is Nelson's memorable response?

17. How many men does Sgt. Treacy take with him to cover the radio shack?

18. What does Williams say he's liable to find in his typewriter?

19. Raoul Walsh later reworked the film's plot for a 1951 western. What is this film?

20. Where were the jungle scenes shot?

21. What does Williams say the cat told the canary before eating him?

22. The jump sergeant says he keeps a bucket on the plane. What is this for?

23. Errol Flynn and George Tobias had appeared together in a film two years prior to *Objective, Burma!* The film, which was a musical, was directed by David Butler. What is this film?

24. What does Williams joke about being a "military secret"?

25. Where does Nelson say he was when he was attacked by the Japanese while skinnydipping?

Quiz No. 61:

OPERATION PETTICOAT

(1959)

Screenplay by Stanley Shapiro, Maurice Richlin, Paul King, and Joseph Stone
Directed by Blake Edwards
Starring Cary Grant, Tony Curtis, and Joan O'Brien
Universal International Pictures
Available on VHS, DVD

> *Lt. Holden has reached new heights in the art of scavenging. Like a spider in a web, he sits there and his victims come to him like flies bearing gifts. He's the only man I know who will probably be presented the Navy Cross at his court-martial.*
>
> —CMDR. MATT SHERMAN

Throughout his career, Cary Grant was able to mine expressions of confusion, befuddlement, and surprise for laughs. Here, in this light World War II naval comedy, Grant works his magic playing straight man to Tony Curtis. While not nearly as talented as Grant's frequent screwball comedy partner Katharine Hepburn, Curtis is brilliant here as the resourceful con man/supply officer Lt. Nicholas Holden. As is the case with director Blake Edwards's most humorous works, the situations the crew face in *Operation Petticoat* are so unrealistically silly that they're funny. The cast is terrific, and screenwriters Stanley Shapiro, Maurice Richlin, Paul King, and Joseph Stone provide colorful characters, truly bizarre situations, and sharp, biting dialogue. While few comedy films dealing with the subject of war succeed in hilarity, *Operation Petticoat* is a delightfully entertaining picture that has lost little of its luster since its initial release.

Operation Petticoat received a single Oscar nomination for Best Original Screenplay (Shapiro, Richlin, King, and Stone), but did not win. Other honors include a Laurel Awards nomination for Top

Comedy, a Laurel Award for Top Male Comedy Performance (Grant), and a Writers Guild Award.

1. Why does Cmdr. Sherman say Lt. Holden wouldn't want to be his supply officer?
2. How many seconds does Sherman give each nurse to shower in the morning?
3. Tony Curtis performed an impression of his costar Cary Grant in the film in which he had just appeared prior to *Operation Petticoat*. What is this film?
4. What is the name of Sherman's damaged submarine at the beginning of the film?
5. Who does Sherman suggest may be a "Japanese agent"?
6. Why does Sherman say Seaman Hornsby acts like a "perfect swine"?
7. Where does Holden say he coordinated the naval parade?
8. What color do the sailors accidentally paint the submarine?
9. Where does Holden say he had his clothes made?
10. What does Holden say poor men and poor women end up with?
11. *Operation Petticoat* is one of two films directed by Blake Edwards and starring Tony Curtis that was released in 1959. The other film costars Janet Leigh. What is this film?
12. Sherman says he's "running" a submarine. What does he say he is *not* running?
13. What does Sherman tell Fox to neutralize his cologne with?
14. In his daily log, Sherman says the crew's morale is high, but there is one concern. What is this?
15. When Holden says "there isn't a burglar, swindler, pickpocket, or fence on the islands that doesn't know and respect him," of whom is he speaking?
16. Sherman says that women under the age of twenty-one are protected by law. Who does he say protects women over the age of sixty-five?
17. What, according to Sherman, is the last thing his men need?
18. What does Sherman order Stovall to refer to the casino as?
19. When asked why he joined the navy, what is Holden's response?
20. Why does Sherman say he likes having gray hair?

21. What is Lt. Reed borrowing when she strikes Hunkle?

22. A television series based on this film aired in 1977. Tony Curtis's daughter appears on this series. Who is this?

23. What is the name of the woman tattooed on Hunkle's chest?

24. What does Sherman say he has a "rather unreasonable" desire to do?

25. When asked if his fiancée is from the "right side of the tracks," what is Holden's response?

Quiz No. 62:

PATHS OF GLORY

(1957)

Screenplay by Stanley Kubrick, Calder Willingham, and Jim Thompson
Directed by Stanley Kubrick
Starring Kirk Douglas, Ralph Meeker, and Adolphe Menjou
United Artists
Available on VHS, DVD

> *Col. Dax, you're a disappointment to me. You've spoiled the keenness*
> *of your mind by wallowing in sentimentality. You really did want to*
> *save those men, and you were not angling for Mireau's command. You*
> *are an idealist—and I pity you as I would the village idiot.*
> —GEN. BROULARD

A thoroughly engaging antiwar classic, Stanley Kubrick's *Paths of Glory* is an indictment of both the military and war itself. The army is represented by the selfish, cold-hearted Gen. Mireau (George Macready), who proves himself more than willing to sacrifice the lives of his men for his own benefit. Throughout the film, Mireau shows very little regard for human life and reasons that this is because he's a military man. Other officers are depicted as being equally incompetent. *Paths of Glory* is a grim film that shows war for what it is: bleak, tragic, and pointless. *Paths of Glory* was one of Kubrick's first successes, and it remains one of his most enjoyable films because of its humanistic qualities that are absent in his later works.

Although *Paths of Glory* was ignored by the Academy of Motion Picture Arts and Sciences, it did manage to snag a number of other honors. The Italian National Syndicate of Film Journalists presented Kubrick the silver ribbon for Best Director of a Foreign Film. In addition, *Paths of Glory* received a British Academy of Film and Television Awards nomination for Best Film, a Laurel Award nomination for Top Male Supporting Performance (Adolphe Menjou), and a Writers

Guild Award nomination. The film was listed to the National Film Registry as a classic in 1992.

1. Kirk Douglas served as a producer on *Paths of Glory*. How many films had he produced prior to this one?

2. Col. Dax apologizes to Gen. Broulard. What does he apologize for?

3. Where does the film's tagline say Dax led his regiment?

4. When he sees a moving figure, Lt. Roget hurls a hand grenade at it. Who does he kill?

5. What does Broulard consider a soldier's best friend?

6. Stanley Kubrick directed Kirk Douglas in a second film three years after *Paths of Glory*. What is this film?

7. What is the name of the "key position" that Broulard wants to take?

8. What are Paris, Arnaud, and Ferol charged with?

9. What decision does Mireau say cannot be left up to the men?

10. What does Dax say he is occasionally ashamed to be a member of?

11. The title of the film is derived from a line in "Elegy Written in a Country Churchyard." Who wrote this?

12. Whose body does Cpl. Paris say fell on him, knocking him unconscious?

13. What must the officer supervising an execution do after the men are shot?

14. Broulard calls one soldier a "baby" and orders him to be transferred from his regiment so he cannot "contaminate" the others. From what is this soldier suffering?

15. What does Paris say Roget has instead of a spine?

16. What habit does Mireau say he never "got"?

17. What is the name of the cult actor who appears in the film as Maurice Ferol?

18. Paris observes a cockroach and angrily points out that the cockroach is likely to outlive him. At this, Ferol then crushes the cockroach. What does Ferol say after crushing the cockroach?

19. In what countries was *Paths of Glory* banned?

20. Mireau says, "Patriotism is the last refuge of a scoundrel." Who is he quoting here?

21. What does Mireau say will happen if his soldiers "won't face German bullets"?

22. Several actors were initially considered for the role of Col. Dax. Which of the following actors was not: Richard Burton, James Mason, Gregory Peck, or Burt Lancaster?

23. What is the name of the castle where the film begins?

24. What does Dax say is an ugly word?

25. Susanne Christian appears as the German girl singing at the end of the film. What is the significance of this?

Quiz No. 63:

THE PATRIOT

(2000)

Screenplay by Robert Rodat
Directed by Roland Emmerich
Starring Mel Gibson, Heath Ledger, and Joely Richardson
Columbia Pictures
Available on VHS, DVD

> *I consider myself fortunate to be serving the cause of liberty. And though I fear death, each day in prayer I reaffirm my willingness, if necessary, to give my life in its service. Pray for me, but above all, pray for the cause.*
> —CPL. GABRIEL MARTIN

Actor Mel Gibson's interest in this project should be of little surprise considering *The Patriot* is very similarly structured to his own epic war film *Braveheart* (1995). While director Roland Emmerich's previous efforts are nearly unwatchable, *The Patriot* is a highly entertaining film that stands up to repeated viewings. This story of the American Revolution is not historically accurate and occasionally enters into the territory of melodrama. However, when looked on as sheer popcorn entertainment, the film does not disappoint. While *The Patriot* is, in many ways, simply a Rambo-type action flick set during the Revolution, it occasionally rises above the typical action movie fare. And, while it never quite succeeds in being the epic film it aspires to be, *The Patriot* is far and away one of the finest films about the American Revolution that have been produced to date.

The Patriot received three Oscar nominations in the categories of Best Cinematography (Caleb Deschanel), Best Original Score (John Williams), and Best Sound (Kevin O'Connell, Greg P. Russell, and Lee Orloff).

1. How many members of the militia are held captive at Ft. Carolina?

2. What is Gabriel Martin's middle name?

3. Screenwriter Robert Rodat wrote a World War II film that was released two years prior to *The Patriot*. What is this film?

4. What nickname is Benjamin Martin given after singlehandedly wiping out twenty soldiers?

5. What color does Maj. Jean Villeneuve say his daughters' eyes were?

6. What are the names of Gen. Cornwallis's two great danes?

7. How many children does Benjamin have?

8. What actor was first offered the lead role, but turned it down?

9. What did Gabriel pour into Ann's tea when she was eleven?

10. How many infantrymen are there under Cornwallis's command?

11. What is Thomas's age when he is killed?

12. Col. Tavington says his father squandered two things. One of these is his inheritance. What is the other?

13. What does Benjamin promise to order as long as Cornwallis's men continue to kill civilians?

14. *The Patriot* is one of four films starring Mel Gibson that were released in 2000. Can you name at least one of the others?

15. What is the name of Benjamin's tight-lipped daughter?

16. What, according to Benjamin, "can trample a man's rights" the same as a king?

17. What does Benjamin observe to be Cornwallis's weakness?

18. What type of tactics does Tavington say will be necessary to capture Benjamin?

19. Two years after his turn in *The Patriot*, Heath Ledger appeared in another period/war film. In this film, he plays a character named Harry Faversham. What is this film?

20. Why does John Billings commit suicide?

21. What color does Benjamin say Villeneuve looks good in?

22. What, according to Benjamin, does a parent not have the luxury of?

23. What creature does Benjamin jokingly refer to as being "a fine meal"?

24. How many drafts of the screenplay did Robert Rodat write?

25. What is the name of Gabriel's friend who was killed at Elizabethtown?

Quiz No. 64:

PATTON

(1970)

Screenplay by Francis Ford Coppola and Edmund H. North (based on books by Omar Bradley and Ladislas Farago)
Directed by Franklin J. Schaffner
Starring George C. Scott, Karl Malden, and Stephen Young
Twentieth Century-Fox
Available on VHS, DVD

> *Now I want you to remember that no bastard ever won a war by dying for his country. He won it by making the other poor dumb bastard die for his country.*   —GEN. GEORGE S. PATTON JR.

Few film characters this side of James Bond or Superman have made as lasting an impression on audiences as George C. Scott's Patton. His performance so realistically captured the imagination and enthusiasm of viewers that he and the famous general he portrayed became nearly inseparable in the public's perception. Such strong character identification is a testament to both the film's magnificent screenplay and Scott's convincing performance. In the film, Scott seems to be channeling the spirit of Gen. George S. Patton Jr., embracing the legendary warrior's mannerisms and eccentric idiosyncracies as his own. Franklin J. Schaffner's film received critical acclaim after its initial release in 1970, and its stature continues to grow. In short, *Patton* is one of the rare instances in which virtually every single aspect of a film's production comes together perfectly to create a masterpiece that improves with each viewing.

Patton received ten Academy Award nominations in the categories of Best Picture (Frank McCarthy), Best Director (Schaffner), Best Adapted Screenplay (Francis Ford Coppola and Edmund H. North), Best Actor (Scott), Best Cinematography (Fred J. Koenekamp), Best Film Editing (Hugh S. Fowler), Best Art Direction–Set Decoration

(Urie McCleary, Gil Parrondo, Antonio Mateos, and Pierre-Louis Thevenet), Best Visual Effects (Alex Whedon), Best Sound (Douglas O. Williams and Don J. Bassman), and Best Original Score (Jerry Goldsmith). These nominations resulted in seven Oscars awarded for Best Picture, Best Director, Best Adapted Screenplay, Best Actor, Best Film Editing, Best Sound, and Best Art Direction–Set Decoration. Other honors include two British Academy of Film and Television Awards nominations, an American Cinema Editors Award, a Directors Guild Award, and a Writers Guild Award. In 1998, the American Film Institute listed *Patton* to its "100 Years, 100 Movies" list of the greatest American films ever produced at number eighty-nine.

    1. What does Gen. Patton declare glory to be in his final words in the film?

    2. *Patton* was the second film cowritten by Francis Ford Coppola that featured Gen. George S. Patton Jr. as a character. The first was cowritten by Gore Vidal. What is the title of this 1966 film?

    3. What general served as a consultant on this film?

    4. Patton becomes angered when he sees a political cartoon of himself kicking a GI. In the cartoon, a symbol appears on his boot. What is this?

    5. George C. Scott later reprises the role of *Patton* in a 1986 telefilm. What is this film?

    6. Which U.S. president is known to have screened *Patton* a number of times, and even quoted from the film when speaking to reporters?

    7. Patton says he read a book that was written by a "magnificent bastard." Who is this?

    8. Patton says Morocco is a combination of two things. What are these?

    9. From what two books was *Patton* adapted?

    10. What, according to Patton, is the proper way for a professional soldier to die?

    11. What does Patton say only a "pimp from a cheap New Orleans whorehouse" would do?

    12. After Patton is nearly killed in a Luftwaffe attack, he says he would like to do something to each of the two German pilots. What?

    13. What does Patton say he does "every Goddamn day"?

    14. What is the name of Patton's dog?

15. What was the film's working title?

16. Actor George C. Scott received his third Oscar nomination for *Patton*. For what films did he receive his first two nominations?

17. What does Patton say he wouldn't give for any soldier who lost and then laughed?

18. *Patton* was released in England under two alternate titles. Can you name them?

19. Why does Gen. Bradley say he does his job?

20. From what do the two soldiers Patton orders be removed from the hospital suffer?

21. The North African battle scene depicts M47 tanks fighting M48 tanks. What is the significance of this?

22. Twenty minutes of the film was excised for the Italian version. What did these scenes depict?

23. The first actor offered the role of Patton shares the surname of a Nazi officer in the film. Who is this?

24. Why was the opening scene filmed last?

25. Who does Patton refer to as a "nasty-faced son-of-a-bitch"?

Quiz No. 65:

PEARL HARBOR

(2001)

Screenplay by Randall Wallace
Directed by Michael Bay
Starring Ben Affleck, Josh Hartnett, and Kate Beckinsale
Touchstone Pictures
Available on VHS, DVD

> *Victory belongs to those who believe in it the most and believe in it the*
> *longest. We're gonna believe. We're gonna make America believe, too.*
> —LT. COL. JIMMY DOOLITTLE

In this age of ultrarealistic, gritty war films à la *Saving Private Ryan*
(1998), Michael Bay's *Pearl Harbor* seems as much a relic of the past as
the Egyptian pyramids, which are now surrounded by a modern
Cairo, complete with a Pizza Hut and other American fast-food
chains. Like the epic all-star war films of the past, Bay's film is long,
overly sentimental, and boasts an impressive cast whose talents it
doesn't quite know how to fully utilize.

Often melodramatic to the point of hilarity, *Pearl Harbor* would be
a ripe target for parody if this film weren't already an unintentional
parody of sorts. While much of the film's dialogue is silly, it appears
that Alec Baldwin, cast as Lt. Col. Jimmy Doolittle, drew the short
straw and got stuck with the worst of it. Baldwin, who can deliver
long-winded bravura monologues with the greatest of ease (see
Glengarry Glen Ross [1992]), is given so much unrealistic jingoistic
banter to recite here that he's left sounding like a constipated military
recruiter during wartime. Another major problem with the screenplay
is that its romantic subplot is so contrived that it would be better
suited to a daytime soap opera than a war film. Although Bay is largely
successful in crafting an obvious homage to war films of the 1940s,
Pearl Harbor seems so quaint and out of touch that it alienates its pri-

mary audience. The film does, however, succeed magnificently in one key area: With its incredible special effects and sizable budget, it features some of the most exciting battle scenes ever captured on film. The camerawork is superb in these scenes, and here the film provides on-the-edge-of-your-seat entertainment. It is for this reason alone that *Pearl Harbor* must be listed among the greatest war films of all time.

Pearl Harbor received four Academy Award nominations in the categories of Best Visual Effects (Eric Brevig, John Frazier, Edward Hirsh, and Ben Snow), Best Sound Effects Editing (Christopher Boyes and George Watters II), Best Sound (Gregg P. Russell, Peter J. Devlin, and Kevin O'Connell), and Best Song (Diane Warren). These nominations resulted in a single Oscar awarded for Best Sound Effects Editing. Other honors include an MTV Movie Award for Best Action Sequence, a Grammy nomination for Best Song, three Golden Satellite Award nominations, and two Golden Globe nominations.

1. Who was the first actor approached to play Franklin D. Roosevelt?

2. Alec Baldwin plays the same character in *The Hunt for Red October* (1990) that his *Pearl Harbor* costar Ben Affleck plays in *The Sum of All Fears* (2002). What is the name of this character?

3. Alec Baldwin plays a character named Blake in *Glengarry Glen Ross* (1992) that later serves as the direct model for a character named Jim Young played by Ben Affleck in a 2000 film directed by Ben Younger. What is this film?

4. What was the first draft of the film's screenplay titled?

5. What does President Roosevelt say submarine commanders have no time for?

6. Cuba Gooding Jr. portrays Petty Officer Dorie Miller—the first African American awarded the distinguished Naval Cross. A year before his appearance in *Pearl Harbor,* Gooding portrayed another African American naval hero in *Men of Honor* (2000). Who was this?

7. What does Evelyn Johnson say she'll never look at without thinking of Rafe McCawley?

8. What does Lt. Col. Doolittle wire to the bombs his men drop over Japan?

9. Where does Adm. Kimmel conclude that a "smart enemy" will attack?

10. What does Adm. Yamamoto say he believes the Japanese have awakened?

11. On what day of the week is the attack on Pearl Harbor?

12. What does McCawley say wasn't all that he'd expected?

13. In what state were the Tennessee farm scenes filmed?

14. When McCawley is asked if he's anxious to die, what is his response?

15. *Pearl Harbor* is one of two Jerry Bruckheimer–produced war films released in 2001 featuring both Josh Hartnett and Tom Sizemore. What is the other film?

16. What term does McCawley define as being "the kind of mission where you get medals, but they send them to your relatives"?

17. Whose dog appears in the film as Doolittle's pet?

18. After Danny Walker is shot, McCawley says, "I wasn't supposed to tell you—you're gonna be a father." What is Walker's memorable response?

19. Walker tells McCawley that he's a "lousy drunk" and always has been. What is McCawley's memorable response?

20. How many times did director Michael Bay resign during filming?

21. Johnson asks Miller what he gets for winning a boxing match. What is Miller's response?

22. What does Yamamoto conclude that a brilliant man would do?

23. Who was the first actor cast in the role of Danny Walker?

24. Whose heart does Doolittle say there's nothing stronger than?

25. Who was the first actress offered the role of Evelyn Johnson?

Quiz No. 66:
PLATOON
(1986)

Screenplay by Oliver Stone
Directed by Oliver Stone
Starring Tom Berenger, Willem Dafoe, and Charlie Sheen
Orion Pictures
Available on VHS, DVD

> *Well, here I am, anonymous all right. With guys nobody really cares about. They come from the end of the line, most of 'em. Small towns you never heard of: Pulaski, Tennessee; Brandon, Mississippi; Pork Van, Utah; Wampum, Pennsylvania. Two years' high school's about it. Maybe if they're lucky a job waiting for them back at a factory, but most of 'em got nothing. They're poor, they're unwanted, yet they're fighting for our society and our freedom. It's weird, isn't it? They're the bottom of the barrel and they know it. Maybe that's why they call themselves grunts—cause a grunt can take it, can take anything.*
> —PVT. CHRIS TAYLOR

One often hears *Saving Private Ryan* (1998) bandied about by cineastes as the film responsible for transforming the war movie genre. While Steven Spielberg's bloody World War II epic deserves the considerable praise critics heap on it, *Saving Private Ryan* would not have been possible had *Platoon* not preceded it. Prior to *Platoon*, films about the Vietnam conflict were largely unrealistic in their depictions of what went on there. While films like *The Deer Hunter* (1978) and *Apocalypse Now* (1979) were much grittier than many of their predecessors, they still presented a fantasy Vietnam that was very much the creation of the filmmakers responsible for them. Oliver Stone's *Platoon* was the first film to fully capture the feeling of life in Vietnam. Stone—a Vietnam veteran himself—creates fully dimensional characters that have since become the model for virtually every film about the conflict. The dialogue is sharp, the entire ensemble does quality work here, and everything seen onscreen has an air of authenticity to it.

Platoon received eight Academy Award nominations in the categories of Best Picture (Arnold Kopelson), Best Director (Stone), Best Screenwriter (Stone), Best Supporting Actor (Tom Berenger), Best Supporting Actor (Willem Dafoe), Best Cinematography (Robert Richardson), Best Film Editing (Claire Simpson), and Best Sound (John Wilkinson, Richard D. Rogers, Charles Grenzbach, and Simon Kaye). These nominations resulted in four Oscars for Best Picture, Best Director, Best Film Editing, and Best Sound. Other honors include an American Cinema Editors Award, two British Academy of Film and Television Awards, the Best Director Prize at the Berlin International Film Festival, a Directors Guild Award, and three Golden Globe Awards. In 1998, the American Film Institute listed *Platoon* to its "100 Years, 100 Movies" list of the greatest American films ever produced at number eighty-three.

1. The actor who appears in the film as Capt. Harris also appears in the war films *Casualties of War* (1989), *84 Charlie Mopic* (1989), and *Saving Private Ryan* (1998). Who is this?

2. Willem Dafoe's character, Elias, is said to believe he's Jesus Christ. What is the significance of this?

3 How many times does Barnes shoot Elias?

4. Charlie Sheen's character stops his platoon from raping a villager. In *Casualties of War,* Michael J. Fox's character attempts to stop his platoon from raping a villager. In 2000, Sheen replaced Fox on a popular television series. What is this series?

5. To whom does Taylor write throughout the film?

6. Charlie Sheen appeared in a second film directed by Oliver Stone one year after *Platoon* was released. What was this film?

7. What does Junior say Christians don't do?

8. What does O'Neal observe to be "like assholes"?

9. Johnny Depp and Willem Dafoe reunited in a 1990 film directed by John Waters. What is this film?

10. Why did Johnny Depp write "Sherilyn" on the helmet his character wears in the film?

11. Who was the first actor to be offered the role of Chris Taylor?

12. The platoon is divided into two factions. Who are the leaders of these groups?

13. King says he is "short." What does this mean?

14. Oliver Stone's script was optioned in 1976. What director was attached to the project at that time?

15. Why does Taylor's helmet say "when I die, bury me upside down"?

16. When Barnes says "I am personally gonna take an interest in seeing them suffer," to whom is he referring?

17. Willem Dafoe, Tom Berenger, John C. McGinley, Dale Dye, David Neidorf, Corkey Ford, Chris Pedersen, and Mark Moses all reunited in a 1989 film that also dealt with the Vietnam War. What is this film?

18. Who does King label as being a "crusader"?

19. Who appears in a cameo as the officer at the bunker that is destroyed by a suicide runner?

20. What, according to Barnes, is reality?

21. What, according to Bunny, is the only thing that might be as good as "pussy"?

22. In what 1992 film did actors John C. McGinley, Forest Whitaker, and Keith David reunite?

23 Corey Glover, who appears in the film as Francis, later came to prominence as the lead singer for a popular rock band. What was this band?

24. What is O'Neal's nickname?

25. What, according to King, will happen if one keeps his "pecker hard and [his] powder dry"?

Quiz No. 67:

PORK CHOP HILL
(1959)

Screenplay by James R. Webb (based on a book by S.L.A. Marshall)
Directed by Lewis Milestone
Starring Gregory Peck, Harry Guardino, and Rip Torn
United Artists
Available on VHS, DVD

> *No time for reconnaissance. We'll have to go by the book. Don't ask me*
> *how we're gonna read it in the dark.*   —LT. JOE CLEMONS

While it never flies quite as high as Lewis Milestone's previous war film *All Quiet on the Western Front* (1930), *Pork Chop Hill* is a superb anti-war picture. The film takes place during the Korean War and focuses on an army lieutenant (Gregory Peck) and the insignificant mound of dirt he's ordered to take and hold—no matter how many of his men he must sacrifice to do so. The pointlessness of war is hardly a new subject, but few films manage to make their point as well as *Pork Chop Hill.* Featuring a slew of accomplished supporting actors, such as Rip Torn, Woody Strode, Martin Landau, Gavin MacLeod, James Edwards, and Robert Blake, the film's acting is exemplary. The battle scenes are well crafted and possess a feeling of authenticity. The film's tagline promises it to be bold, blunt, and blistering, and *Pork Chop Hill* more than succeeds in meeting this promise.

    1. Lt. Clemons orders a soldier who has no rifle to serve as a runner. What is this soldier's name?

    2. Who appears in an uncredited cameo as a BAR man?

    3. Who does Clemons believe may be remembered as the last man ever to lead a bayonet charge?

    4. What company is "supposed to handle the ridge"?

5. How many members of Easy Company does the Chinese propagandist say were killed?

6. *Pork Chop Hill* was loosely remade in a Vietnam setting in a 1987 film directed by John Irvin. What is this film?

7. Who served as the film's technical advisor?

8. What is the "simple truth" the Chinese propagandist points out?

9. Veteran director Lewis Milestone followed up *Pork Chop Hill* with a 1960 film starring Frank Sinatra, Dean Martin, and Sammy Davis Jr. What is this film?

10. How many points shy of thirty-six does Battalion say Forstman is?

11. The actor who appears as Pvt. Franklin was a former UCLA football star and also appears in *The Ten Commandments* (1956), *Spartacus* (1960), and *The Man Who Shot Liberty Valance* (1962). Who is this?

12. The actor who appears as Pvt. Velie is accused of murdering his wife forty years later. Who is this?

13. What does Pvt. Saxon say his bulletproof vest didn't stop him from doing?

14. By what does Clemons say his men are hanging on?

15. What does Clemons say no American would pay one dollar for?

16. What is the name of the company Clemons leads?

17. The actor who appears as Sgt. Coleman later comes to prominence as Stanley Roper on the television series *Three's Company.* Who is this?

18. What, according to its tagline, is *Pork Chop Hill* the "battle picture without"?

19. How many men are in Clemons' company prior to the attack?

20. James R. Webb's next produced screenplay after *Pork Chop Hill* was another film starring Gregory Peck. The film, based on a novel by John D. MacDonald, also stars Robert Mitchum. What is this film?

21. Of what does Clemons say the Americans must convince the Chinese?

22. The actor who appears as Pvt. Saxon also appears in the war-themed films *Operation Petticoat* (1959), *The Sand Pebbles* (1966), and *Kelly's Heroes* (1970). He later made a name for himself as a regular on the television series *The Mary Tyler Moore Show* and *The Love Boat.* Who is this?

23. The men become angry when they are shelled in the trenches. Why?

24. Why does Lt. Ohashi say it always scares him when Clemons addresses him by his first name?

25. What kind of automobile did Forstman win in a raffle?

Quiz No. 68:
RAN
(1985)

Screenplay by Masato Ide, Akira Kurosawa, and Hideo Oguni (based on a
   play by William Shakespeare)
Directed by Akira Kurosawa
Starring Tatsuya Nakadai, Akira Terao, and Jinpachi Nezu
Nippon Herald Films
Available on VHS, DVD

> *I, Hidetora, was attacked by my own sons. I was betrayed by my own
> vassal. That's not the worst. Because of me, my loyal men died a use-
> less death. As fate would have it, only I survived. I, who should have
> died.* —LORD HIDETORA ICHIMONJI

Akira Kurosawa was Japan's greatest filmmaker and *Ran,* is his finest
film. This adaptation of William Shakespeare's *King Lear* set in
sixteenth-century feudal Japan is an examination of loyalty and
betrayal—themes that recur throughout Kurosawa's body of work.
The film's storyline focuses on the jealous rivalry between three brothers after their powerful father names one of them as his successor.
These feelings of envy lead to acts of betrayal and massive bloodshed.
The epic battle scenes are beautifully choreographed, and Kurosawa's
use of color is so breathtakingly gorgeous that these striking images
linger in the viewer's mind long after the final credits have rolled. The
film's photography (handled by Asakazu Nakai, Takao Saito, and Masa-
haru Ueda) is so flawless it should be screened daily by all aspiring cinematographers. The film's elaborately detailed sets and costumes are
also impressive. Easily one of the ten greatest films ever produced, *Ran*
is a film so beautiful and well crafted that words cannot do it justice.

   Ran received four Academy Award nominations for Best Director
(Kurosawa), Best Cinematography (Nakai, Saito, and Ueda), Best Art
Direction–Set Decoration (Yoshio Muraki and Shinobu Muraki), and

Best Costume Design (Emi Wada). These nominations led to one Oscar, for Best Costume Design. Other honors include six British Academy of Film and Television Awards nominations, a Bodil Award for Best Non-American Film, National Board of Review Prizes for Best Foreign Language Film and Best Director, two nominations at France's César Awards, and nominations and/or awards from virtually every organized film awards group in existence.

1. Who does Hidetora say are the only ones who live in solitude?
2. What was Lord Ichimonji's age when he first flew his banner over the castle in which he was born?
3. What, according to Kurogane, does not win wars?
4. What is the name of Taro's general?
5. Director Akira Kurosawa often called one of his films a "dress rehearsal" for *Ran*. What is this film?
6. Who does Kyoami believe to be the only sane people in a mad world?
7. What is the name of Hidetora's counselor?
8. How many guards escort Hidetora after he has relinquished his power?
9. Tara says he often prays to the god of war. What does he ask for?
10. The storyboards used to shoot the film were quite different than the average storyboards. How so?
11. What is Kyoami's occupation?
12. Who does Lady Kaede refer to as a "two-headed monster"?
13. What type of animal does Kurogane say can take human form?
14. After Taro banishes his father, he issues a decree regarding the peasants. What is this?
15. It took nearly three years to make the costumes used in the film. Why did it take so long?
16. What instrument does Tsurumaru play for his guests?
17. To whom does Hidetora cede total authority over his dominion?
18. What is Hidetora's title?
19. Hidetora banishes two men at the beginning of the film. Who are they?
20. What does Hidetora say are not easily broken?
21. Who murdered Lady Kaede's father and brother?
22. Who does Hidetora observe to be "unschooled in manners"?

23. Akira Kurosawa received a Best Director Oscar nomination for *Ran.* How many career Best Director nominations did he receive?

24. How does Hidetora ask Lady Sue to look at him?

25. *Ran* is one of six films directed by Akira Kurosawa that feature actor Tatsuya Nakadai. What was the first film on which they worked together?

Quiz No. 69:

THE RED BADGE OF COURAGE
(1951)

Screenplay by Albert Band and John Huston (based on a novella by Stephen Crane)
Directed by John Huston
Starring Audie Murphy, Andy Devine, and Bill Mauldin
Metro-Goldwyn-Mayer
Available on VHS, DVD

> *Move back into the shadows, Yank, unless ya want one of them little red badges. I couldn't miss ya standin' there in the moonlight. I don't see much point in us sentries shootin' each other; especially when we ain't fightin' no battle. So if you'll just get out of the moonlight, I'll be much obliged to ya.* —ANONYMOUS CONFEDERATE SOLDIER

The Red Badge of Courage is an interesting film that is often overshadowed by tales of its troubled production. (Metro-Goldwyn-Mayer chief Louis B. Mayer and production vice president Dory Schary battled over the film from its conception to postproduction, leading to a heavily excised film with which none of the primaries involved were completely happy. Much of this conflict was the result of the film being crafted during the McCarthy era, a period when antiwar films were seen by some as being un-American.) An examination of the thin line between bravery and cowardice, *The Red Badge of Courage* is fascinating because it has divided critics for more than half a century; some contend the film is a classic, while others refuse to see the film as anything other than the victim of a forced abortion at the hands of studio-directed editors. From the nervous banter and false bravado of the scared soldiers to its fine performances, *The Red Badge of Courage* maintains an air of authenticity that many Civil War films don't have. Perhaps this adaptation of Stephen Crane's novella could have been better. We'll never know. But the film we do have is terrific, and it deserves to be judged based on its own merits, rather than on guesswork as to what it could have been.

The Red Badge of Courage was nominated by the British Academy of Film and Television Awards for Best Film from Any Source.

1. The general says two soldiers "deserve to be major generals." Who are they?

2. Who does the narrator call a "mental outcast"?

3. Who does Bill Porter refer to as a "regular Jim Dandy"?

4. What does Porter say he prefers to do standing up?

5. Jim Conklin says "there's them kind" in every regiment. To what is he referring?

6. Of what three things does Porter conclude "the more you beat 'em the better they be"?

7. For what is Tom Wilson given six hours of extra duty?

8. Who is the "gone goose" who concludes that this will be his "first and last battle"?

9. What actor narrates the film?

10. The narrator says Henry Fleming lost every sense but one. What is this?

11. What, according to the narrator, brought Fleming's comrades victory?

12. Who does Wilson say his grandfather fought beside?

13. What does the narrator say Fleming had performed in the dark?

14. What does Porter say he doesn't understand regarding the orders?

15. What does Conklin worry will run over him if he falls?

16. What does Conklin conclude he's not high-spirited enough to be?

17. From what state is Fleming's regiment?

18. Who does Porter say "knows everything in the world"?

19. Who does the narrator say Fleming looked at with envy?

20. How old does the narrator say novelist Stephen Crane was when *The Red Badge of Courage* was published?

21. When Fleming is separated from his regiment, he has something that belongs to Wilson. What is this?

22. Lillian Ross wrote a book about the making of *The Red Badge of Courage* that was ultimately voted as one of the twentieth century's one hundred best American books. What is the title of this book?

23. Porter says this is the first time he's ever been hunting without something. What is this?

24. What is ironic regarding Audie Murphy's being cast as the cowardly Henry Fleming?

25. Who does Wilson say will lose his money?

Quiz No. 70:

RUN SILENT RUN DEEP

(1958)

Screenplay by John Gay (based on a novel by Edward L. Beach)
Directed by Robert Wise
Starring Clark Gable, Burt Lancaster, and Jack Warden
United Artists
Available on VHS, DVD

> It's thirty-eight days now since we left Pearl Harbor. I know how some
> of us felt then. I think I know how some of us feel now. But let no one
> here—no one aboard this boat—ever say we didn't have a captain.
> —LT. JIM BLEDSOE

While far more realistic submarine warfare films have been made since
Robert Wise's *Run Silent Run Deep* was produced (with much better
special effects), the film remains a staple of the genre because of the
craftsmanship that went into its creation. Under Wise's direction, the
cast turns in impressive performances. The conflict between Cmdr.
Richardson (Clark Gable) and Lt. Bledsoe (Burt Lancaster) can be
seen as the inspiration behind the similar Denzel Washington–Gene
Hackman showdown in *Crimson Tide* (1996). Having already lost one
sub to a Japanese destroyer in the Bungo Straits, Richardson is assigned to another. Although he doesn't inform anyone of the fact,
Richardson has a personal agenda: to find the Japanese destroyer that
sunk his sub and destroy it. Both Gable and Lancaster turn in powerful performances, and Wise makes the most of the (sometimes convo-
luted) script's moments of tension and suspense.

When viewed strictly as an example of escapist cinema, *Run Silent
Run Deep* is an entertaining actioner that provides plenty of thrills.

The film received third-place honors at the Golden Laurel Awards
for Top Cinematography (Russell Harlan).

1. What is the name of the crewman who is left on the deck during a diving drill?

2. How long is Cmdr. Richardson told it will take to repair the torpedo firing circuits?

3. "With all due respect to [his] rank," what does Mueller call Cartright?

4. What is the name of the submarine in which the story takes place?

5. What does Robertson order Hendrix and Mueller to keep to themselves?

6. What does Mueller do after saying "this time words just fail me"?

7. *Run Silent Run Deep* is discussed in a 1995 Cold War submarine drama directed by Tony Scott. What is this film?

8. Who does Richardson say should be the only person to give permission to dump the trash?

9. How many enemy ships does Tokyo Rose say the Japanese fleet has sunk during the month?

10. How often does Richardson say the Japanese dispatch convoys?

11. What does Richardson order Bledsoe to send to the surface to trick the enemy destroyer?

12. *Run Silent Run Deep* was one of two films directed by Robert Wise that were released in 1958. The second film stars Susan Hayward as a woman sentenced to death. What is this film?

13. What does Richardson ask his wife to pour into his lemonade?

14. Bledsoe gives Richardson two options if he wants to return to the Bungo Straits. What are these?

15. A loose torpedo falls on some crew members, crushing them. How many men are killed?

16. What do the crewmen pat for luck on the way to their battle stations?

17. How many Japanese planes show up when the sub first prepares to engage the convoy?

18. What, according to the film's tagline, "make the seas boil"?

19. What is the name of Richardson's wife?

20. What derogatory term does Cartright call Mueller?

21. What does Richardson say he's "never even thought of" doing?

22. What gift does the crew give Bledsoe prior to Richardson's being assigned to the sub?

23. What nickname does Mueller give the enemy ship that sunk Richardson's first sub?

24. What does Bledsoe say the sub hates doing?

25. *Run Silent Run Deep* was one of two films starring Clark Gable that were released in 1958. The second film pairs Gable with Doris Day and was directed by George Seaton. What is this film?

Quiz No. 71:

SAHARA

(1943)

Screenplay by Zoltan Korda, John Howard Lawson, and James O'Hanlon
  (based on a novel by Philip MacDonald)
Directed by Zoltan Korda
Starring Humphrey Bogart, Bruce Bennett, and J. Carol Naish
Columbia Pictures
Available on VHS, DVD

> *Italians are not like Germans. Only the body wears the uniform. Not the soul. Mussolini is not so clever like Hitler. He can dress his Italians up only to look like thieves, cheats, murderers. . . . He cannot, like Hitler, make them feel like that. He cannot, like Hitler, scrape from the conscience the knowledge that right is right and wrong is wrong or dig holes in their heads to plant his own ten commandments: steal from thy neighbor, cheat thy neighbor, kill thy neighbor.* —GIUSEPPE

Former Hungarian cavalry officer Zoltan Korda is known for crafting high-flying adventure films such as *The Four Feathers* (1939), and *Sahara* is no different. Despite its being created as wartime propaganda, *Sahara* is a thoroughly entertaining "road" film. After an unlikely group of passengers find themselves crammed together inside a Sherman tank in the middle of the desert, they are forced to unite and hold off the enemy in a one-sided battle reminiscent of the final conflict in *Beau Geste* (1939). *Sahara* is an outstanding film that doesn't strive to be much more than light escapism. One of the most realistic depictions of lost-in-the-desert desperation, Korda's film stands up to repeated viewings.

Sahara received three Academy Award nominations for Best Supporting Actor (J. Carol Naish), Best Black-and-White Cinematography (Rudolph Mat) Mat), and Best Sound Recording (John P. Livadary). Unfortunately these nominations failed to yield a single Oscar.

1. For whom does Giuseppe say God created Hell?
2. Who does Sgt. Gunn say believes he's a god?
3. Who is wounded when the tank is attacked by a German plane?
4. What was Marty Williams's profession before the war?
5. Jimmy Doyle says there are two things on the radio. What are these?
6. By what nickname does Gunn refer to Capt. Halliday?
7. According to Sgt. Tambul, how many wives does the Prophet say are sufficient?
8. What does Gunn offer the Germans for each rifle they hand over?
9. What is the name of Gunn's tank?
10. By what name do the men refer to Jean Leroux?
11. How many people from his village does Leroux say he saw executed?
12. Which member of the infamous "Rat Pack" appears in an uncredited bit part?
13. Which of the men climbs down into the well to catch the dripping water?
14. How many men does Halliday say he'd had in his charge?
15. What does Tambul give Waco "for the road"?
16. What is Gunn's first name?
17. How long has Tambul been in the army?
18. What is the nationality of Tambul's prisoner?
19. Gunn offers the German soldier something in exchange for information regarding his battalion. What is this?
20. A screenwriter who had contributed previously to *The Awful Truth* (1937), *Lost Horizon* (1937), and *Mr. Smith Goes to Washington* (1939) worked on *Sahara* but received no credit. Who is this?
21. What does Halliday say one cannot "scientifically" call the well?
22. After obtaining water from the well, how much does Gunn allow each of the men?
23. Who is the tank named after?
24. How many men take on the German battalion at the end of the film?
25. What does Leroux say it's "stupid to have" in war?

Quiz No. 72:

THE SAND PEBBLES

(1966)

Screenplay by Robert Anderson
Directed by Robert Wise
Starring Steve McQueen, Richard Crenna, and Richard Attenborough
Twentieth Century-Fox
Available on VHS, DVD

> *At home in America when today reaches them it'll be Flag Day. For us who wear the uniform, every day is Flag Day. It is said there will be no more wars. We must pretend to believe that. But when war comes, it is we who will take the first shots and bide our time with our lives. It is we who will keep the faith. We serve the flag. The trade we all follow is the give and take of death. It is for that purpose that the people of America maintain us. And any one of us who believes he has a job like any other for which he draws a money wage is a thief of the food he eats and a trespasser in the bunk in which he lies down.*
> —CAPT. COLLINS

Robert Wise's *The Sand Pebbles* is a thinly veiled statement on the United States' involvement in Vietnam. The story, which takes place in 1926, on the eve of the Chinese revolution, focuses on naval engineer Jake Holman (Steve McQueen), who has just been assigned to serve on a gunboat on the Yangtze River. Holman quickly establishes himself as a loner with few people skills. As a result, he is alienated from the rest of the crew. When the gunboat is attacked by locals, the turmoil on-board comes to a head. Unlike many war movies, *The Sand Pebbles* is a character-driven film. Because of this, its pacing will seem a bit slow for cineastes seeking an action-packed film with lots of fireworks. The acting is exemplary, and McQueen gives a performance that is equalled only by his turn in *Papillon* (1973). Richard Crenna also gives a solid performance as the gunboat's no-nonsense captain. By this point in his career, Wise's name had become a brand name for quality no matter what genre he worked in, and *The Sand Pebbles* is one of his finest efforts.

Although the Academy of Motion Picture Arts and Sciences snubbed Wise for a Best Director nomination, the film received eight nominations in the categories of Best Picture (Wise), Best Actor (McQueen), Best Supporting Actor (Mako), Best Color Cinematography (Joseph MacDonald), Best Film Editing (William Reynolds), Best Sound (James Corcoran), Best Original Score (Jerry Goldsmith), and Best Color Art Direction–Set Decoraton (Boris Leven, Walter M. Scott, John Sturtevant, and William Kiernan). However, these nominations failed to yield a single Oscar. Other honors include eight Golden Globe nominations (resulting in a single win for Richard Attenborough), an American Cinema Editors nomination, a Writers Guild nomination, and three Laurel Award nominations.

1. Steve McQueen had made his film debut a decade before in another film directed by Robert Wise. This film, which stars Paul Newman, featured McQueen in an uncredited turn as a character named Fidel. What is this film?

2. What is the name of the man who replaces Chien as top coolie?

3. Capt. Collins says he'll overlook Jake's insubordination if he'll do something. What is this?

4. Of whom does Jake say "by God I can't get along without him"?

5. How much money does Frenchy promise to raise for Maily?

6. For what does Jameson say "it's too late in the world"?

7. What does Shirley say "makes you feel marvelous"?

8. Steve McQueen received a Best Actor Oscar nomination for his work on this film. How many nominations did McQueen receive during his career?

9. Who does Jake say "nice American girls" don't talk to?

10. What does Jake do with his rifle after shooting Po-Han?

11. Who alone does Jameson say endangers the missionaries?

12. What is Shanahan's nickname?

13. Which cast member later directed the films *A Bridge Too Far* (1977), *Gandhi* (1982), and *Chaplin* (1992)?

14. What does Jake say killed Chien?

15. What is the name of the bar where Maily works?

16. Jake is told that American gunboats in China are a "painful joke." What is he then told is the most painful of these jokes?

17. What is the name of Maily's pimp?

18. Jake says the judge offered him three choices after he was convicted for gouging out the principal's eyes. What were they?

19. What day of the week, according to Frenchy, is the only day the gunboat crew doesn't turn the hose on the locals?

20. How much does Jake bet Stawski that Po-Han will beat him?

21. Steve McQueen served in the military in real life. In what branch?

22. Jameson says the navy takes care of a sailor as long as he does one thing. What is this?

23. What actor appears in the role of Crosley?

24. What, according to Shirley, did officials find growing on a remote part of the mission property?

25. From what state is Jake?

Quiz No. 73:

SANDS OF IWO JIMA

(1949)

Screenplay by Harry Brown and James Edward Grant
Directed by Allan Dwan
Starring John Wayne, John Agar, and Adele Mara
Republic Pictures
Available on VHS, DVD

> *That's war. Trading real estate for men.*　　　　—PFC. AL THOMAS

Like the characters he played on screen, John Wayne was larger than life. A man of ideals with an enormous sense of patriotism and pride in his country, Wayne carefully selected the films in which he appeared, always seeking characters and stories that represented those beliefs. With that in mind, it is no surprise that Wayne chose to appear in Allan Dwan's *Sands of Iwo Jima*. Released only five years after the end of World War II, the film follows the exploits of one rifle squad at the Battle of Iwo Jima. Wayne is tough and confident as Sgt. John Stryker and gives one of his most memorable performances. The film's jingoism is never too heavyhanded, and Dwan maneuvers through the battle scenes quickly without glorifying the violence. *Sands of Iwo Jima* laid the groundwork for numerous war films and is remembered today as Wayne's quintessential war picture.

The film received four Academy Award nominations for Best Actor (Wayne), Best Story (Harry Brown), Best Film Editing (Richard Van Enger), and Best Sound. These nominations, however, failed to yield a single statuette. In addition, Wayne received the Photoplay Award for Most Popular Male Star of 1950.

1. Conway says his son won't read regulations. What does he say that he will read?

2. When Dunn says that Stryker "knows his business," what is Conway's memorable response?

3. How far do the men hike the day after their leave?

4. How much time does Bass say elapsed between Thomas's leaving to get ammo and the position being overrun?

5. Who is Stryker's son named after?

6. What, according to the film's tagline, did the soldiers have "in their favor"?

7. What punishment does Stryker give Conway for dropping his rifle?

8. At the beginning of the film, the rifle squad has just come from another battle. Where was this?

9. From what city do the Flynn brothers hail?

10. How many days has the air corps been bombing Suribachi prior to the invasion?

11. Where were Stryker and Thomas stationed together previously?

12. What is Hellenpolis's nickname?

13. Who does Thomas conclude lives "the life of Riley"?

14. What is Shipley's nickname?

15. Josh Becker named his 1985 film *Stryker's War* as an homage to *Sands of Iwo Jima*. However, the distributor changed the film's title. Under what title was this film released?

16. What does Stryker say he'll do to anyone who won't cooperate?

17. Whose "spies" always seem to provide him with the wrong information?

18. What is the name of the character who serves as the narrator?

19. What is the name of the girl Conway marries?

20. In how many films directed by Allan Dwan did John Wayne appear?

21. To whom is this film dedicated?

22. Thomas returns with coffee and ammo to discover that his two comrades have been gunned down. What are their names?

23. What is the name of Stryker's ex-wife?

24. How much does Regazzi jokingly say he would pay someone to shoot him in the foot?

25. How old is Stryker's son?

Quiz No. 74:
SAVING PRIVATE RYAN
(1998)

Screenplay by Robert Rodat
Directed by Steven Spielberg
Starring Tom Hanks, Edward Burns, and Tom Sizemore
Paramount Pictures
Available on VHS, DVD

> *Someday we might look back on this and decide that saving Private Ryan was one decent thing we were able to pull out of this whole god-awful mess. Like you said, Captain, maybe we do that, we all earn the right to go home.*
> —SGT. HORVATH

Only Steven Spielberg could, at this late date, turn the entire genre on its head by crafting what is arguably the finest war film ever made. *Saving Private Ryan* features a stellar ensemble that includes Tom Hanks, Edward Burns, Tom Sizemore, Vin Diesel, Barry Pepper, Giovanni Ribisi, Dennis Farina, Paul Giamatti, Ted Danson, and of course, Matt Damon as the title character. Spielberg pulls convincing performances from every member of the cast, and the carnage of warfare is depicted so realistically that many World War II veterans who saw the film were overcome with trauma. Janusz Kaminski's cinematography is first rate, as is Michael Kahn's editing, and Spielberg uses the handheld camera to great advantage. Also, the film's muted colors lend the film a nostalgic feeling. In short, *Saving Private Ryan* did for the war genre what *Pulp Fiction* (1994) had done four years prior for the gangster genre; after reinventing their respective genres by retooling the time-proven formulas, both films spawned countless imitators that have failed to approach their quality.

Saving Private Ryan received eleven Oscar nominations in 1998, winning five statuettes in the categories of Best Director (Spielberg), Best Cinematography (Kaminski), Best Film Editing (Kahn), Best

Sound (Gary Rydstrom, Gary Summers, Andy Nelson, and Ron Judkins), and Best Sound Effects Editing (Rydstrom and Richard Hymns).

1. What is the first image shown in the film?
2. Just before the final battle of the film, the soldiers discuss the song "Tu Es Partout." Who sings this tune?
3. Cpl. Upham spends much of the film trying to figure out what the term "fubar" means. What does it mean?
4. What kind of German knife does Caparzo brag about finding at Omaha Beach?
5. What substance makes up the sticky coating of a "sticky bomb"?
6. Capt. Miller is a schoolteacher. What subject does he teach?
7. What is Caparzo's first name?
8. What actually kills Wade?
9. What noted screenwriter/director contributed heavily to the screenplay for *Saving Private Ryan* before later directing Tom Hanks in *The Green Mile* (1999)?
10. What are the names of Pvt. Ryan's three dead brothers?
11. How many men are initially assigned to the squad that is dispatched to find Ryan?
12. Actors Giovanni Ribisi and Vin Diesel later reunite in a 2000 film directed by Ben Younger. What is this film?
13. Actors Barry Pepper and Vin Diesel later reunite in a 2002 film directed by Brian Koppelman and David Levien. What is this film?
14. When Reiben asks Sgt. Horvath if he's going to shoot him over Ryan, what is Horvath's memorable response?
15. How many men does Miller tell Horvath he's lost under his command?
16. Which member of the platoon collects soil from each country he's sent to?
17. What is the name of the Boston, Massachusetts, woman Abraham Lincoln wrote to regarding the loss of her five sons?
18. What is Ryan's first name?
19. A retired U.S. Marine captain served as a technical advisor and also appears in the film as a War Department colonel. In addition, this man served as a technical advisor on films such as *Platoon* (1986), *Born on the Fourth of July* (1989), and *Band of Brothers* (2001). Who is this?

20. On what sector is the Omaha Beach landing shown in the film?

21. What is said to be the name of the "friendly neighborhood morale officer" who proclaims that the Statue of Liberty is kaput?

22. What state is Ryan from?

23. Miller recalls a soldier who walked on his hands at Anzio. What was his name?

24. How many prisoners does Miller's company take on Omaha Beach?

25. When Horvath says, "Maybe I should run left," what is Miller's response?

Quiz No. 75:

SAVIOR

(1998)

Screenplay by Robert Orr
Directed by Predrag (Peter) Antonijevic
Starring Dennis Quaid, Stellan Skarsgard, and Nastassja Kinski
Lions Gate Films
Available on VHS, DVD

> *It's easy to kill somebody. Just pull the trigger and it's done. Livin' with it . . . you gotta harden up for that.* —JOSHUA ROSE

One of a handful of fine war films released in 1998 that were over-shadowed by *Saving Private Ryan*, *Savior* tells the story of French Foreign Legionnaire Joshua Rose (Dennis Quaid) and his eye-opening experiences in war-torn Bosnia. Having joined the Legion after aveng-ing the deaths of his wife and son, he develops a numbness to the world around him. However, after he discovers a Serbian woman who became impregnated after being raped by Muslims, his coldness be-gins to melt away. Surrounded by the atrocities of the Bosnian war, Joshua attempts to find refuge for the young woman and the child that not even she wants. Unflinching, *Savior* is one of the most powerful antiwar films ever produced. The film's Bosnian director, Peter Antonijevic, witnessed the horrors of the war firsthand, which lends the film a feeling of authenticity. In addition, the film's screenwriter, Robert Orr, spent nearly three years in Bosnia working as a relief worker. While Dennis Quaid is known for giving effective workman-like performances, here he shines in what is likely the finest turn of his career.

Savior received the 1999 Political Film Society's Peace Award for raising the consciousness "of the need for peaceful ways of resolving conflicts."

1. Joshua Rose sustains a gunshot wound in his side. Who shoots him?

2. Joshua attempts to resuscitate two people in the film. Who are they?

3. Goran wears a T-shirt with a photograph of an American television star on the front of it. Who is this?

4. Who does Vera's brother refer to as a "madman"?

5. Joshua wears a gold necklace with a pendant. What kind of pendant?

6. One of the film's producers is a Vietnam War veteran who also wrote and directed *Platoon* (1986), *Born on the Fourth of July* (1989), and *Heaven and Earth* (1993). Who is this?

7. Joshua helps Vera deliver her baby. What sex is the baby?

8. What is Joshua's response when asked if he's American?

9. Joshua enlists into the Foreign Legion using a pseudonym. What is this?

10. *Savior* is one of two films released in 1998 that feature both Dennis Quaid and Nastassja Kinski. What is the other film?

1. What is the significance of the song the woman from the bus sings to the baby at the end of the film?

12. Goran says Vera has disgraced her family. What did she do?

13. What is the name of Joshua's wife?

14. What, according to the film's tagline, is worth fighting for?

15. Nastassja Kinski's name is misspelled in the film's credits. How is it spelled?

16. What does Vera's father say he wishes she had done in prison?

17. What type of music does Joshua say he likes?

18. What does Joshua use as a makeshift nipple when feeding the baby?

19. In what two countries was *Savior* filmed?

20. What does the old Serbian woman give Vera "for the road"?

21. What does Joshua advise Vera to do if she hears an automobile approaching on her journey to town?

22. Where does Joshua promise to take Christian before being called away?

23. Dennis Quaid made his directorial debut with a telefilm that was aired the same year *Savior* was released. The telefilm stars

Quaid, Mare Winningham, and rock star Meat Loaf. What is this film?

24. What is Vera's response when Joshua tells her he's sorry that her brother and father have been captured?

25. What primary member of the film's crew appears in a cameo as a passenger on the bus to Split?

Quiz No. 76:

SERGEANT YORK

(1941)

Screenplay by Harry Chandlee, Abem Finkel, John Huston, and Howard
   Koch (based on a book by Alvin C. York and Tom Skeyhill)
Directed by Howard Hawks
Starring Gary Cooper, Walter Brennan, and Joan Leslie
Warner Bros.
Available on VHS

> *I ain't a-goin' to war. War is killin', and the Book's agin' killin', so war's
> agin' the Book.*   —SGT. ALVIN C. YORK

This re-creation of real-life Congressional Medal of Honor–winner
Alvin York's World War I heroics plays like a prequel to *The Grapes of
Wrath* (1940). Gary Cooper portrays York with the same affable
naivety and hokey hillbilly accent as Henry Fonda had given Tom Joad
the year before. Cooper's dim-witted God-fearing York is presented as
a good-hearted teddy bear who only becomes a hero when he's forced
to do so. While this depiction of York as a reluctant hero is an accurate
one, he's presented as a man so naive and saintly that he doesn't seem
like a real person. Instead, he seems like a Hollywood creation. Director
Howard Hawks admitted that he and Cooper took a number of artistic liberties with York's story, and this unbelievable purity would seem
to be one of them. (After seeing the film for the first time, York said, "I
supplied the tree and Hawks put the leaves on it.") In fact, this extreme
purity can be found throughout the film; because World War II was
just around the corner at the time *Sergeant York* was made, the military
is presented in an overly sympathetic light, and nearly every character
in the film has the ideals of a Frank Capra protagonist. Because of the
film's oversimplification in its depictions of human character, it's difficult to take it too seriously. As light escapism, however, *Sergeant York*
ranks among the best of them.

The film received an impressive eleven Academy Award nominations for Best Picture (Hal B. Wallis and Jesse L. Lasky), Best Director (Hawks), Best Original Screenplay (Harry Chandlee, Abem Finkel, John Huston, and Howard Koch), Best Actor (Cooper), Best Supporting Actor (Walter Brennan), Best Supporting Actress (Margaret Wycherly), Best Film Editing (William Holmes), Best Black-and-White Cinematography (Sol Polito), Best Black-and-White Art Direction–Set Decoration (John Hughes and Fred M. MacLean), Best Sound (Nathan Levinson), and Best Original Score (Max Steiner). These nominations resulted in two statuettes for Cooper's performance and the film's editing. In addition, Cooper won the New York Film Critics Circle Award for Best Actor.

1. *Sergeant York* is one of two films directed by Howard Hawks and starring Gary Cooper that was released in 1941. The other film was released with the title *The Professor and the Burlesque Queen.* What is this film's alternate title?

2. To what city is Alvin C. York presented the key?

3. Who does Pastor Pile believe holds York by his shirttail?

4. By what name do the Crossville residents refer to Jamestown?

5. What is Michael T. Ross's nickname?

6. What is the subject of the book Maj. Buxton shows York?

7. Alvin C. York sold the rights to his life story to Warner Bros., allowing the film to be made with only one condition. What was this?

8. What, according to York, did the "folks back home" say he was doing before he was weaned?

9. Who is the first man to call on Gracie?

10. What are Pusher's last words?

11. Who presides over York and Gracie's wedding?

12. What famed Warner Bros. contract player appears in an uncredited cameo as a piano player?

13. Who writes York's appeals to the draft board?

14. What's the one thing York says he wants to do in New York City?

15. How many days does York have to raise the $70 he needs to pay off the land?

16. How many men assist York in capturing the 132 Germans?

17. Howard Hawks received an Oscar nomination for Best Director

for his work on *Sergeant York*. How many nominations had Hawks received prior to this?

18. York is shown in the film shooting a line of Germans with a Luger. What type of handgun did Alvin C. York use to accomplish this in real life?

19. Who is the first member of York's platoon to be killed in action?

20. What is the name of the mule York trades to Mr. Thompkins?

21. What city is Pusher from?

22. How many studios ask York to appear in motion pictures?

23. *Sergeant York* is one of two 1941 films featuring both Gary Cooper and Walter Brennan. The other film was directed by Frank Capra and also stars Barbara Stanwyck. What is this film?

24. What actress appears as York's sister Rosie?

25. Who, according to York, was the first man to enter the Valley of the Three Forks?

Quiz No. 77:

THE SIEGE OF FIREBASE GLORIA

(1989)

Screenplay by Tony Johnston and William L. Nagle
Directed by Brian Trenchard-Smith
Starring Wings Hauser, R. Lee Ermey, and Robert Arevalo
Metro-Goldwyn-Mayer
Available on VHS

> *Headquarters still didn't buy my analysis of the situation. Hell, they had experts sitting in air-conditioned offices in Saigon who understood the war a whole lot better than anyone on the front line. We had asked for ammunition and reinforcements. What we got was the mail run, a few cases of beer, and a VD pill.* —SGT. MAJ. BILL HAFNER

The Siege of Firebase Gloria may not be as well known as other films in this book, but it easily ranks among the finest films ever produced within the genre. Based on a true story, the film depicts the Marines who defended Firebase Gloria against overwhelming odds during the Vietnam War's grisly Tet Offensive. When Sgt. Hafner (R. Lee Ermey) and Cpl. DiNardo (Wings Hauser) arrive at Firebase Gloria, they find it in a state of disrepair. They immediately relieve the post's crazed commander (John Calvin). Although the military brass refuse to believe the understaffed post is about to be the target of a Vietcong attack, Hafner and DiNardo struggle to get Firebase Gloria and the men assigned there into combat-ready shape. *The Siege of Firebase Gloria* lacks the big budget of its more well-known counterparts, yet director Brian Trenchard-Smith does a terrific job making it look realistic. The film also deserves kudos for its evenhanded treatment of both the Vietcong and the Americans.

1. When A. J. Moran learns that there will be no escort chopper, he quotes the Kenny Rogers tune "Lucille." What is significant regarding this?

2. What is Sgt. Hafner carrying as he says he no longer respects Cpl. Miller?

3. What does Cpl. DiNardo say "even the girls have" in Vietnam?

4. What is Moran's nickname?

5. What does the combat photographer say he paid for the Cambodian Red?

6. What does the sign hanging over the CO bunker read?

7. R. Lee Ermey also appears in a Chevy Chase comedy released the same year as *The Siege of Firebase Gloria*. What is this film?

8. What does DiNardo say was the "only thing I ever loved"?

9. A poster of an American actor who died in 1955 is visible hanging inside the CO bunker. Who is this?

10. How old was Hafner when he enlisted in the U.S. Marine Corps?

11. What is the name of Firebase Gloria's commanding officer Hafner relieves?

12. How many years has Jones been in the military?

13. *The Siege of Firebase Gloria* is one of two 1989 films directed by Brian Trenchard-Smith. The other is a thriller starring Mark Hembrow and Tessa Humphries. What is this film?

14. What does Hafner say was the closest Murphy had ever been to death?

15. What does Sgt. Jones suggest DiNardo may have been before the war?

16. Actor Wings Hauser received his first production credit for a 1983 war film directed by Ted Kotcheff. What is this film?

17. Short Wave says he wasn't trained to be a radio operator. What does he say he was trained for?

18. What is DiNardo's response when he is asked for the password when entering Firebase Gloria?

19. What name does DiNardo give the Vietnamese child he finds in the village?

20. From what city does Short Wave hail?

21. What does Hafner say it was time to sprinkle in Charlie's rice?

22. Who does Hafner describe as being "the kind of gung-ho fighting machine the marines were famous for"?

23. What is referred to as "death detail"?

24. One of the NVA says "a man like that could make it difficult." To whom is he referring?

25. Hafner frees an American prisoner of war. What nickname is given to him?

Quiz No. 78:

SINK THE BISMARCK!

(1960)

Screenplay by Edmund H. North (based on a book by C. S. Forester)
Directed by Lewis Gilbert
Starring Kenneth More, Dana Wynter, and Carl Mohner
Twentieth Century-Fox
Available on VHS

> *In this battle, Britain's lifeblood is at stake. This is the battle on which depends the future course of the war, the future course of British history.*   —EDWARD R. MURROW

Lewis Gilbert's depiction of this great Allied naval achievement in World War II, has the detached feeling of a documentary. The film begins with the coldhearted by-the-book Capt. John Shepard taking command of the English War Room. Seeing warfare as a game of carefully calculated maneuvers, Shepard is able to make important decisions without worrying about the number of deaths they will result in. Shepard soon sets his sights on the *Bismarck*, the feared German destroyer. An extremely well-crafted film, *Sink the Bismarck!*'s only significant flaw is that it approaches its subject with the same lack of compassion or sentimentality as its protagonist Shepard. As a result, viewers may find difficulty fully investing themselves.

Sink the Bismarck! received fourth-place honors at the Laurel Awards for Top Action Drama.

1. What does Adm. Lutjens advise the *Bismarck*'s crew to never forget?

2. An agent is killed while sending a telegraph to British intelligence regarding the *Bismarck*. In what country is this agent stationed?

3. The war room is located how many feet underground?

4. The *Bismarck* shoots down two British planes in the film. In real life, how many planes did the *Bismarck* shoot down?

5. What is the name of the ship on which Capt. Shepard's son serves?

6. What does Shepard refer to as a "peace time luxury"?

7. What is Shepard's first name?

8. The *Bismarck* destroys the HMS *Hood*. What is the significance of this?

9. What is the name of Shepard's son?

10. In a "calculated risk," Shepard orders two ships that are protecting a convoy to join the search for the *Bismarck*. How many men is the convoy carrying?

11. What is Shepard's first order as director of operations?

12. The hunt for the *Bismarck* also inspired a popular song, also entitled "Sink the Bismarck." Who sang this?

13. British planes accidentally attack one of their own ships. What is the name of this ship?

14. Lutjens receives a telegram offering him "best wishes." Who is this from?

15. Where has the *Bismarck* recently completed three months of training?

16. Lutjens says he is forced to take orders from Group North. What does he say he does *not* have to take?

17. What is Lutjens' first name?

18. What, according to Shepard, is the "one tremendous weakness" of German fleet commanders?

19. Who, according to the disclaimer at the end of the closing credits, is the character Capt. John Shepard *not* based on?

20. What is the name of the *Bismarck*'s captain?

21. How many of the HMS *Hood*'s fifteen hundred men survive its sinking?

22. *Sink the Bismarck!* was one of two war films directed by Lewis Gilbert that were released in 1960. The second film is about a World War II searchlight squad. What is this film?

23. What is the name of the British cruiser carrying civilian contractors?

24. What does Anne Davis say she would do if she were the *Bismarck!*?

25. Shepard's commanding officer concludes that Shepard cares about only two things. What are these?

Quiz No. 79:

SPARTACUS

(1960)

Screenplay by Dalton Trumbo (based on a novel by Howard Fast)
Directed by Stanley Kubrick
Starring Kirk Douglas, Laurence Olivier, and Jean Simmons
Universal Pictures
Available on VHS, DVD

> *And maybe there's no peace in this world, for us or for anyone else. I don't know. But I do know that, as long as we live, we must remain true to ourselves.*
> —SPARTACUS

Mainstream audiences tend to see the words "epic" and "boring" as being interchangeable. However, the word "boring" can hardly be used to describe *Spartacus.* This three-hour seventy-millimeter tale about a slave who leads a revolt against the Roman Empire is packed with action and scenes of violent bloodletting. While director Stanley Kubrick brought his own artistic flair to the project, most of the credit for the film's success (both artistically and monetarily) clearly belongs to its star and executive producer Kirk Douglas. This film was clearly a labor of love for Douglas, who hired all the primary creative forces involved with its creation, and also spent a reported $12 million out of his own pocket. Kubrick later complained about not having full creative control on *Spartacus,* but that restraint worked in favor of the film. While Kubrick is, without a doubt, one of the most gifted auteurs ever to work within the medium, his films often have a voyeuristic feeling of detachment that confuses the less-savvy viewer. This is not to say filmmakers should pander to the lowest common denominator, but rather to point out that *Spartacus*'s ability to find favor with both the mainstream and arthouse crowds is one of its most impressive strengths.

Spartacus received six Academy Award nominations for Best Supporting Actor (Peter Ustinov), Best Color Cinematography (Russell

Metty), Best Film Editing (Robert Lawrence), Best Original Score (Alex North), Best Color Costume Design (Valles and Bill Thomas), and Best Art Direction–Set Decoration (Alexander Golitzen, Eric Orbom, Russell A. Gausman, and Julia Heron). These nominations led to four Oscars for the film's costume design, cinematography, art direction–set decoration, and Ustinov's performance. Other honors include a Golden Globe Award for Best Dramatic Motion Picture, a British Academy of Film and Television Awards nomination for Best Film, a Writers Guild nomination, and Laurel Award nominations for both Ustinov and Douglas.

1. A screenwriter who also worked with Stanley Kubrick on *Paths of Glory* (1957) and *One-Eyed Jacks* (1961)—a film Kubrick began but was ultimately fired from—made uncredited contributions to *Spartacus*. Who is this?

2. What accomplished actor provided the voice for Marcus Licinius in the 1991 restored version?

3. What, according to Batiatus, is as "cheap as life itself"?

4. Crassus says he's not after glory. What does he say he is after?

5. *Spartacus* executive producer Kirk Douglas hired blacklisted screenwriter Dalton Trumbo to write the film. He also hired a blacklisted actor for the project. Who is this?

6. What does Crassus call a disadvantage of being a patrician?

7. What does Gracchus say is like a wealthy widow?

8. What does Crassus say he would do if there was no Rome?

9. What does Gracchus observe that the "nastiest of tyrants" are?

10. What actor rewrote much of Charles Laughton's dialogue to appease him?

11. Antoninus asks Spartacus if he is afraid to die. What is Spartacus's memorable response?

12. Russell Metty received the Oscar for Best Color Cinematography. However, roughly one-third of the film's cinematography was actually performed by someone else. Who was this?

13. Several scenes in the film were shot at the San Simeon castle. Who was the famous owner of this estate?

14. Who does Batiatus believe he's more of a civilian than?

15. Screenwriter Dalton Trumbo fought to have an actor cast in the role of Tigranes Levantus, which ultimately went to Herbert Lom. Who was this?

16. Batiatus says there's only one man he hates. Who is this?

17. Kirk Douglas and Laurence Olivier had previously appeared together in a film that was released one year before *Spartacus*. This Guy Hamilton–directed film is a comedy. What is this film?

18. One controversial scene was cut from the film in 1960 and was not restored until 1991. What did this scene depict?

19. What does Gracchus say Batiatus has "grown very ambitious" in?

20. Some extras can be seen wearing items of jewelry that were not in existence in the period in which the film depicts. What are these?

21. Crassus suggestively says his taste includes two things. What are these?

22. Executive producer and star Kirk Douglas briefly considered directing *Spartacus* himself, but ultimately decided against this. Douglas would not make his directorial debut until 1973. What is the title of the film Douglas directed?

23. The first actress cast in the role of Varinia was fired and replaced by Jean Simmons. Who was this?

24. Who does Draba say do not make friends?

25. Stanley Kubrick replaced the film's first director. Who was this?

Quiz No. 80:

STALAG 17

(1952)

Screenplay by Billy Wilder and Edwin Blum (based on a play by Donald
Bevan and Edmund Trzcinski)
Directed by Billy Wilder
Starring William Holden, Don Taylor, and Otto Preminger
Paramount Pictures
Available on VHS, DVD

> *I don't know about you, but it always makes me sore when I see those*
> *war pictures . . . all about flying leathernecks and submarine patrols*
> *and frogmen and guerillas in the Philippines. What gets me is that*
> *there never was a movie about POWs—about prisoners of war.*
> —COOKIE

Throughout his career, William Holden was usually at his most effective when playing smarmy cynical characters. Here, Holden was given just such a character in Sgt. J.J. Sefton, and he does outstanding work. A story that runs the gamut from comedy to drama, *Stalag 17* focuses on a group Allied soldiers during World War II who are being held captive at a German concentration camp. After a pair of would-be escapees are gunned down by guards, it becomes apparent that one of the prisoners is a spy. But who? Unsure of who to trust, the prisoners soon find themselves in agreement that Sefton must be the traitor. Now outcast, beaten, and robbed of his belongings, Sefton is determined to unmask the real spy among them. Billy Wilder has a well-deserved reputation as being one of the finest screenwriter/directors in the history of cinema, and *Stalag 17* serves as a good example of why this is so. The performances are great, the script is tight, and Wilder's direction is flawless.

Stalag 17 received three Academy Award nominations for Best Director (Wilder), Best Actor (Holden), and Best Supporting Actor

(Robert Strauss). These nominations resulted in a single statuette awarded to Holden. In addition, Wilder and cowriter Edwin Blum received a Writers Guild nomination for Best Written American Comedy.

1. How many sergeants does Cookie say there are at Stalag 17?
2. What does Sefton say he traded the Nazis for an egg?
3. Sefton strikes a match on a man three times in the film. Who is this?
4. Which cast member was nominated for an Oscar twice in the category of Best Director?
5. What is Stosh's nickname?
6. What do the prisoners of barracks four trade the distillery for?
7. What reason does Stosh come up with for Sefton assisting Dunbar's escape?
8. What does Dunbar suggest Col. Von Scherbach try for his insomnia?
9. Who is elected security?
10. What does Cookie say served as the men's alarm clock?
11. *Stalag 17* was one of four films in which Billy Wilder directed William Holden. Can you name the other three films?
12. What city does Price say he's from?
13. How many Ping-Pong balls do the men receive from the Geneva inspector?
14. What does Sefton bet that Manfredy and Johnson don't get out of the forest?
15. Stosh tells a fellow prisoner that he has the "most beautiful legs in the world." Who is this?
16. Who does Sefton joke about being the illegitimate son of?
17. What is the name of the crazed prisoner who plays the flute?
18. Who is Stosh in love with?
19. Sefton says three things were stolen from him during his first week. What were they?
20. Von Scherbach gives each of the prisoners a book for Christmas. What is this book?
21. What does Shultz say he was doing when he visited Milwaukee, St. Louis, and Cincinnati?
22. William Holden won the Best Actor Oscar for his turn in *Stalag*

17. His acceptance speech was the shortest in Academy Awards history. What did he say?

23. At what time is the Christmas midnight mass held?

24. Who is the elected compound chief?

25. Sefton observes the Nazi spy placing notes inside a hollow chess piece. Which one?

Quiz No. 81:

STALINGRAD

(1993)

Screenplay by Jürgen Büscher, Johannes Heide, and Joseph Vilsmaier
Directed by Joseph Vilsmaier
Starring Dominique Horwitz, Thomas Kretschmann, and Jochen Nickel
Royal Film
Available on VHS, DVD

You were good soldiers until you chose to survive at any cost.
—CAPT. HALLER

When it was announced that *Das Boot* (1981) producers Mark Damon and Gunter Rohrbach were reteaming for another war film, expectations soared. Screenwriter/director Joseph Vilsmaier's film—a powerful battle drama so grim that it makes *Saving Private Ryan* (1998) look like a Disney musical in contrast—more than lived up to those expectations. The $20 million German epic follows a squad of tired and hungry German storm troopers through the bloody Battle of Stalingrad in World War II. After watching the majority of their comrades being decimated by snipers, mines, and tanks, a small group of desperate soldiers attempt to desert. "*Stalingrad* is rough yet fascinating viewing," *San Francisco Chronicle* reviewer Peter Stack observes. "Delving into the brutal realities of war with an almost docudrama style, it renders a bitter, almost choking sense of the futility of war through the destruction not only of bodies, but of the human spirit."

Stalingrad won top honors at the Bavarian Film Awards in the categories of Best Cinematography (Vilsmaier), Best Editing (Hannes Nikel), and Best Production (Bob Arnold, Rohrbach, Vilsmaier, and Hanno Huth). In addition, the film was nominated for the prestigious Golden St. George Award at the Moscow International Film Festival.

1. What is the name of the physician whose signature adorns the wounded tags the men steal from dead soldiers?

2. According to Reiser, how many marks does he earn each month?

3. Lt. Von Witzland writes a letter to his love back home. What is her name?

4. What do the remaining soldiers share after destroying the Russian tanks?

5. How old is Rollo's son?

6. What is Von Witzland's first name?

7. For which of his dead comrades does Reiser pour out alcohol in remembrance of?

8. What, according to Reiser, is the best thing about cold weather?

9. The men are ordered to execute Russian civilians. With what crime are the civilians charged?

10. What is the nationality of the man Rollo's wife is living with?

11. What is Emigholz's first name?

12. What battalion are the men assigned to?

13. The soldiers are decorated at the beginning of the film. For what campaign are they awarded?

14. What are Otto's final words before committing suicide?

15. What is Reiser's rank?

16. What is Rollo's real name?

17. When the other men opt to desert, who remains with Rollo?

18. What is the name of the Russian boy?

19. What is the name of the Russian-speaking soldier who suggests a momentary cease-fire to the enemy?

20. Reiser waves farewell to an Italian woman from the train window. What is her name?

21. What is the occupation of the Russian boy's father and grandfather?

22. What does Otto say he has spent the past two years praying for?

23. What does Otto remark that "it's nice spending some time" doing?

24. According to Adolf Hitler, how many tons of oil will be cut off by securing Stalingrad?

25. Otto recalls being awarded a Christmas leave. What had he done to earn the leave?

Quiz No. 82:
THE STEEL HELMET
(1951)

Screenplay by Samuel Fuller
Directed by Samuel Fuller
Starring Gene Evans, Robert Hutton, and Steve Brodie
Lippert Pictures
Available on VHS

If you die, I'll kill you!   —SGT. MIKE ZACK

Filmed in ten days on a single set, Samuel Fuller's *The Steel Helmet* serves as a reminder that budgetary restraints can sometimes lead a filmmaker to make decisions that result in a superior film. At the center of this microbudget Korean War film is the grizzled Sgt. Mike Zack (Gene Evans). After his entire platoon is massacred, Zack befriends a Korean orphan and eventually agrees to assist a ragtag platoon. While the film is one of the finest combat pictures ever produced, the war itself is not Fuller's primary concern. As with many of his films, Fuller is more interested in the bonds that develop between people in extraordinary circumstances. Here, he examines the unlikely bond between the emotionless noncommissioned officer and the young boy. Throughout much of the film, Zack dismisses the boy's attempts to reach out to him. Then, after the boy is gunned down by a North Korean sniper, the normally unaffected Zack explodes with rage. "It was a growing love affair (between Zack and the boy)," Fuller once explained. "It was a love story." Possibly the greatest B movie ever made, *The Steel Helmet* is a gritty, bleak film that holds up after a dozen viewings.

Fuller won a Writers Guild Award in the category of Best Written American Low-Budget Film for his work on *The Steel Helmet*.

1. Who does Sgt. Zack strike for whistling in his sleep?
2. On what part of his body was Zack injured on D day?

3. What does the statement at the end of the film proclaim about its ending?

4. What does Zack say he'd be if he was correct all the time?

5. What does Short Round believe "Auld Lang Syne" is?

6. What, according to the film's tagline, does *The Steel Helmet* "hit hard at"?

7. What does Sgt. Tanaka rub on Baldy's head to make his hair grow?

8. What is Zack's nickname for Tanaka?

9. Short Round served as the inspiration for a character in a 1984 Steven Spielberg film. What is this film?

10. Who asks to trade helmets with Zack?

11. Zack says he will escort the ragtag platoon in exchange for something. What is this?

12. What does Short Round turn for good luck?

13. What does Zack refer to as a "prize package"?

14. What kind of helmet does Cpl. Thompson say it's a shame no one can make?

15. Who does Short Round say his family is with?

16. How does Zack say one can differentiate between North and South Koreans?

17. *The Steel Helmet* is one of two 1951 Samuel Fuller films starring Gene Evans. The other film features an early uncredited appearance by screen icon James Dean. What is this film?

18. To whom is the film dedicated?

19. What is the name of the soldier who never speaks?

20. A prayer is attached to Short Round's helmet when he is killed. For what does Short Round pray?

21. What does Zack refer to as a "conchy"?

22. How does Zack define the term "short round"?

23. Pvt. Bronte is carrying something that belonged to Father Paul. What is this?

24. What does Tanaka say he's going to do after the war?

25. Richard Loo later appears in a second film directed by Samuel Fuller in 1954. What is this film?

Quiz No. 83:
THE STORY OF G.I. JOE
(1945)

Screenplay by Leopold Atlas, Guy Endore, Ernie Pyle, and Philip Stevenson
  (based on books by Ernie Pyle)
Directed by William A. Wellman
Starring Burgess Meredith, Robert Mitchum, and Freddie Steele
United Artists
Available on VHS, DVD

> *It's a world the other never knows. Even the Air Corps. Up there they*
> *approach death differently. When they die, they're clean shaven and*
> *well fed, if that's any comfort. But the GI, he lives so miserably and he*
> *dies so miserably.* —ERNIE PYLE

William Wellman's superb film *The Story of G.I. Joe* belongs on the
short list of elite battle films alongside such classics as *All Quiet on the
Western Front* (1930), *Ran* (1985), and *Saving Private Ryan* (1998).
Noted filmmaker/film historian Francois Truffaut once pondered
whether or not a film can truly be called an antiwar film since so many
combat films glorify battle. The answer is, of course, yes, and *The Story
of G.I. Joe* is one example of a war film that does not glorify warfare.
The film is based on the true story of Pulitzer Prize–winning war correspondent Ernie Pyle and his World War II travels across North
Africa with the Eighteenth Infantry. As one would expect from a
William Wellman picture, the direction is taut and seamless. While
Burgess Meredith is terrific in his turn as Ernie Pyle, Robert Mitchum
steals the film with a magnificently realistic performance as Lt. Bill
Walker. Equally realistic is the appearance of the soldiers and their
habitat. They live in the mud and look as though they have for a very
long time. Their fatigues are filthy, wrinkled, and torn, and the men
are unshaven and unkempt. They look so realistically grungy, you can

almost smell the odor of their bodies through the screen. While films like *Saving Private Ryan* have done this since, this realistic approach was unheard of in 1945, explaining why *Time* magazine labeled *The Story of G.I. Joe* the "least glamorous war picture ever made."

The Story of G.I. Joe received four Oscar nominations for Best Screenplay (Leopold Atlas, Guy Endore, Ernie Pyle, and Philip Stevenson), Best Actor (Mitchum), Best Score (Louis Applebaum and Ann Ronell), and Best Song (Jack Lawrence). These nominations failed to yield a single Oscar.

1. What nickname does Ernie Pyle give Murphy?
2. What does Capt. Walker call the monastery "in military terms"?
3. What is the name of the squad's adopted canine mascot?
4. What is Pyle's age?
5. Robert Mitchum appears in another film directed by William Wellman nine years later. What is this film?
6. Jack Lawrence's song "Linda" was nominated for an Oscar. Lawrence had penned the song for his attorney's five-year-old daughter, who would grow up to be famous. Who was she?
7. When Pyle asks Walker whether he minds that he go "all the way," what is Walker's response?
8. From where does Joe McClosky hail?
9. What is the name of the woman Murphy refers to as his "ever-lovin'"?
10. Walker yells "Lousy Kraut swine!" What do the German soldiers yell back in response?
11. What does Walker say one gets with every third swig of Italian moonshine?
12. What does Axis Sally advise the American soldiers to "be reasonable" and do?
13. What is Henderson's nickname?
14. The soldiers chant "our hero" because of a letter Pyle receives. Of what does the letter inform him?
15. The film is largely based on two books written by Ernie Pyle. What are their titles?
16. The film's assistant director later becomes an accomplished filmmaker himself. Among the films he directs are the war classics *The Dirty Dozen* (1967) and *Too Late the Hero* (1970). Who is this?

17. Pyle says only one thing can "make a soldier." What is this?

18. What, according to a sign hanging inside the makeshift headquarters, "is spoken here"?

19. Ernie Pyle did not attend the film's premiere. Why?

20. What does Pyle say soldiers can always start a fight by arguing?

21. Where does Warnicki call a "funny place" to be killing people?

22. The film has two alternate titles. What are they?

23. What, according to Walker, is "always the worst"?

24. What does Pyle call the "greatest killing machine of all"?

25. What word does Warnicki say his son "couldn't even say" before he went to war?

Quiz No. 84:

THEY DIED WITH THEIR BOOTS ON

(1941)

Screenplay by Wally Kline and Aeneas MacKenzie
Directed by Raoul Walsh
Starring Errol Flynn, Olivia de Havilland, and Sydney Greenstreet
Warner Bros.
Available on VHS

> *I think it was an idea that made them—an idea and a song. You should have seen them the day they were first mustered in—derelicts, outcasts, criminals of every kind who'd just joined up because they couldn't make a living any other way. But wait till you see them now, Mr. Commissioner. Wait till you see what discipline, devotion to duty, and a little human understanding can do. You'll see men who aren't afraid to look death in the face with pride in their eye. And not for any measly $13 a month, but because they have pride in their regiment!*
> —GEN. GEORGE ARMSTRONG CUSTER

Raoul Walsh's Custer biopic *They Died with Their Boots On* doesn't engage in simple hero worship, nor does it attack its subject as a buffoon. Instead, the film depicts the doomed Gen. George Armstrong Custer (Errol Flynn) as a complicated contradiction; Custer is presented as a careless media whore with ideals who stumbles blindly into the massacre for which he's best known. The film's performances are strong, the direction is terrific, and the battle scenes are extremely well handled. Walsh doesn't really concern himself with historical accuracy, but rather sets out to make an entertaining piece of light escapism, and succeeds admirably.

1. Where does Callie say she found Custer?
2. What does Custer say every soldier has?

3. Gen. Scott says he answered only one question on the West Point exam correctly. What is this?

4. What does William Sharp say Custer has an inclination to be?

5. Who does Custer refer to as a "sanctimonious little skinflint"?

6. Custer is said to have had the worst record of any officer at West Point, "including" another famous officer. Who is this?

7. Custer carries a letter of introduction for Elizabeth's father. Who is this letter from?

8. When does Maj. Taipe say Custer will be given his orders?

9. Custer doesn't speak to Elizabeth the first time they meet. Why?

10. Custer says he doesn't want a medal. What does he say he would like to have?

11. Who does Elizabeth refer to as Uncle Phil?

12. What is the one thing Custer says he won't gamble with?

13. Who does Custer refer to as a "face I always like to shake hands with"?

14. Why does Elizabeth tell her father not to speak ill of Custer?

15. Elizabeth says a train won't wait. What does she say will?

16. What does Senator Smith refer to as being a "nest of secessionists"?

17. Custer's commanding officer says he's in charge as long as he can stand. What is Custer's response?

18. Who appears in the film as Chief Crazy Horse?

19. What does California Joe say Indians are "too dumb" to do?

20. Stuntman Jack Budlong died during filming. How was he killed?

21. Custer is told that only two things can result from an officer disobeying a direct order on the battleground. What are these?

22. *They Died with Their Boots On* is one of eleven films Errol Flynn made with Olivia de Havilland, and one of nine films on which he collaborated with director Raoul Walsh. On how many films did Flynn, Havilland, and Walsh all work together?

23. Whose horse does Custer steal to report to his regiment?

24. What does the West Point commandant say is worse than "no officer"?

25. Where does Custer say the general's headquarters will be located?

Quiz No. 85:

THEY WERE EXPENDABLE

(1945)

Screenplay by Frank Wead (based on a novel by William L. White)
Directed by John Ford and Robert Montgomery
Starring Robert Montgomery, John Wayne, and Donna Reed
Metro-Goldwyn-Mayer
Available on VHS, DVD

> *You're a swell bunch. I'm glad to have been able to serve with you. I'd
> like to be able to tell you that we're going out to bring back help, but
> that wouldn't be the truth. We're going down the line to do a job.
> You're going to Bataan with the army. That isn't what you've been
> trained for, but they need your help. You older men with longer service
> records ... take care of the kids. Maybe ... [Pauses.] That's all. God
> bless you.*   —LT. JOHN BRICKLEY

They Were Expendable is director John Ford's tribute to the PT boats
and the men who served on them during World War II. The film's title
gives an indication of the film's slightly melodramatic tone, but isn't
nearly as jingoistic as it might lead one to believe. The film, based on
the real-life heroics of Lieutenants John Bulkeley (Brickley in the film)
and Robert Kelly (Ryan in the film), is everything one would expect in
a naval war film directed by John Ford and starring John Wayne.
Rather than focusing on the battle scenes, Ford chooses to turn his
camera on the human beings engaged in these conflicts. Firsthand
knowledge of the military on the parts of director Ford and screenwriter Frank Wead lend the film an air of authenticity, and both
Wayne and Robert Ryan give memorable performances. If the film has
a flaw (other than its first few minutes, which drag unbearably), it is
the unneeded presence of the love interest subplot involving Donna
Reed. Nevertheless, *They Were Expendable* is an impressive film that
deserves a second look.

The film received two Academy Award nominations for Best Special Effects (A. Arnold Gillespie, Donald Jahraus, R. A. MacDonald, and Michael Steinore) and Best Sound Recording (Douglas Shearer). However, these nominations failed to yield an Oscar.

1. What are Ens. Andrews's final words to Lt. Brickley?
2. Who is portrayed in the film by Robert Barrat?
3. When Lt. Sandy Davys tears Lt. Ryan's sleeve off, he informs her that sleeves are hard to come by. What is her response?
4. *They Were Expendable* was written by Frank Wead, who was a close friend of both John Ford and John Wayne. Twelve years after this film, Ford and Wayne collaborated on a film that chronicles Wead's life in the military. What is this film?
5. What does Davys say Ryan "might use someday" for plowing or cutting out paper dolls?
6. A man who had worked as a screenwriter on films such as *Fearless Fagan* (1952) and *Smilin' Through* (1922), as well as director for *The Barretts of Wimpole Street* (1957), contributed to the screenplay but did not receive credit. Who is this?
7. Because of a shortage of "steel pot" helmets, only select crew members wear them. Which crew members are these?
8. Ryan writes a letter to the navy brass attempting to convince them of something. What is this?
9. What is significant regarding Robert Montgomery's being cast as a PT boat commander?
10. How many degrees above normal does Davys say "navy boys" tend to run?
11. Ward Bond's role was originally planned to be much bigger, but was rewritten to include his being wounded. Why?
12. Ens. Aikens comments on Cookie's soup. What does Cookie then inform him?
13. What ship does Cookie say has the "best cook stoves in the navy"?
14. What does Ryan say the gun flashes look like?
15. Why did director John Ford donate his entire salary from *They Were Expendable?*
16. From what medical condition does Ryan learn he's suffering just before he's supposed to leave on a mission?
17. Who did John Wayne get into a fistfight with during filming?

18. What does Ryan call a "swell diet"?

19. The sailors sing about monkeys who have no tails. What type of creature do they say bit them off?

20. John Ford was injured during filming, and the film was completed by Robert Montgomery. What happened to Ford?

21. Davys says two things are needed to make the "swell party" complete. What are they?

22. There is a quote at the beginning of the film. Who is it from?

23. Where is the hospital where Ryan is admitted?

24. What is Brickley's nickname?

25. What does Ryan say he "can't take time out" to learn?

Quiz No. 86:

THE THIN RED LINE

(1998)

Screenplay by Terrence Malick (based on a novel by James Jones)
Directed by Terrence Malick
Starring Sean Penn, Adrien Brody, and James Caviezel
Twentieth Century-Fox
Available on VHS, DVD

> *What is this great evil? How did it steal into the world? From what seed, what root did it spring? Who's doing this? Who's killing us? Robbing us of light and life. Mocking us with the sight of what we might have known.*
> —PVT. TRAIN

Released just months after *Saving Private Ryan* (1998), this arthouse film about the bloody World War II battle at Guadalcanal wasn't what audiences wanted or expected. Viewers walked into theaters craving carnage and sugary-sweet sentimentalism. Instead, writer/director Terrence Malick gave them a three-hour meditation on war and its effects on humanity. Rather than reciting the familiar grunt-speak that is found in virtually every other war film, Malick's soldiers reflect with beautiful poetic dialogue that's as fine as anything the Bard ever wrote. For many viewers, Malick's groundbreaking film is challenging because it doesn't adhere to the rules of the genre. Malick and cinematographer John Toll look past the chaos and barbarity of combat and find beauty in the nature that surrounds it. When violence does erupt, Malick seems more interested in the suddenness of the conflict than the battle itself; within a span of minutes, the tranquility of nature is shattered by explosions, and then the skirmish ends as quickly as it began. By distancing himself (and the viewer) from the action, Malick is able to show the soldiers as being no different than the other animals fighting for survival. A film with little action, *The Thin Red Line* is the thinking man's war film.

The Thin Red Line received seven Academy Award nominations for Best Picture (Robert Michael Geisler, John Roberdeau, and Grant Hill), Best Director (Malick), Best Adapted Screenplay (Malick), Best Cinematography (Toll), Best Film Editing (Billy Weber, Leslie Jones, and Saar Klein), Best Sound (Andy Nelson, Anna Behlmer, and Paul Brincat), and Best Original Score (Hans Zimmer). These nominations failed to yield a single Oscar. Other honors include the American Society of Cinematographers Award for Outstanding Achievement in Cinematography, the prestigious Golden Berlin Bear at the Berlin International Film Festival, Chicago Film Critics Association Awards for Best Director and Best Cinematography, New York Film Critics Circle Awards for Best Director and Best Cinematography, and Golden Satellite Awards for Best Dramatic Motion Picture, Best Director, Best Cinematography, and Best Score.

1. Actors Adrien Brody and Elias Koteas reunite two years after *The Thin Red Line* in another film that deals with war. This film, which was directed by Elie Chouraqui, also stars Andie MacDowell and David Strathairn. What is this film?

2. The captain's name is Staros in the film. In the original 1964 version of *The Thin Red Line* his name was Stone. What was the name of this captain in the James Jones novel from which the two films were adapted?

3. Pvt. Train says only two things are permanent. What are they?

4. What is Capt. James Staros's nickname?

5. Sean Penn plays Sgt. Welsh, a role that was originated by Jack Warden in the original 1964 version of the film. Penn and Warden appear together in a 1984 film. What is this film?

6. An Oscar-winning screenwriter/director performed narration for the film that was later discarded. Who is this?

7. An actor who appears in the films *Diner* (1982), *The Pope of Greenwich Village* (1984), and *Nine ½ Weeks* (1986) filmed scenes for this film that were eventually cut. Who is this?

8. Witt says he's twice the man someone else is. Who is this?

9. Although several of his novels were adapted to film, James Jones received only one credit as a screenwriter. For what film did Jones write?

10. What is the name of Bell's wife?

11. One actor was signed to appear in the film, but left the production when offered a role in *Saving Private Ryan* (1998). Who is this?

12. An actor who appears in *Sleepless in Seattle* (1993), *While You Were Sleeping* (1995), and *Independence Day* (1996) filmed scenes for *The Thin Red Line* that were cut from the final film. Who is this?

13. Lt. Col. Tall says it's unnecessary for Staros to say he's right. What does he suggest Staros should do instead?

14. *The Thin Red Line* was the second part of a trilogy written by James Jones that focused on some of the same characters. The other two novels have also been adapted to film. Can you name them?

15. Who does Witt refer to as his people?

16. Which cast member later directs *O* (2001)?

17. What does Tall believe nature is?

18. This is the second film in which both Nick Nolte and John Cusack appear. Can you name the first?

19. Who directed the original 1964 version of *The Thin Red Line*?

20. The Japanese soldier who ultimately shoots Witt repeats something over and over in Japanese. What is he saying?

21. One soldier is shown using a toothbrush that has a "wear" stripe in its bristles. What is the significance of this?

22. Two years after appearing together in *The Thin Red Line,* George Clooney and Tim Blake Nelson reunite in a film directed by Joel Coen that received two Oscar nominations. What is this film?

23. This is the second war film in which characters played by Don Harvey and John C. Reilly serve under a sergeant played by Sean Penn. What was the first?

24. An actor who appears in *A Perfect Murder* (1998), *28 Days* (2000), and *Lord of the Rings: The Fellowship of the Ring* (2001) filmed scenes for this film that were ultimately cut. Who is this?

25. What, according to Tall, is the "only time you should start worrying about a soldier"?

Quiz No. 87:
THIRTY SECONDS OVER TOKYO
(1944)

Screenplay by Dalton Trumbo (based on a book by Robert Considine and
 Ted W. Lawson)
Directed by Mervyn LeRoy
Starring Spencer Tracy, Van Johnson, and Tim Murdock
Metro-Goldwyn-Mayer
Available on VHS

> *Here, you suddenly realize you're gonna dump a ton of explosives on*
> *one of the biggest cities in the world. . . .I don't pretend to like the idea*
> *of killing a bunch of people, but it's a case of drop a bomb on them or*
> *pretty soon they'll be dropping one on Ellen.* —LT. TED LAWSON

Mervyn LeRoy's *Thirty Seconds over Tokyo* is based on the true story of
the April 1942 Doolittle Raid. Just after the Japanese attack on Pearl
Harbor, Col. Jimmy Doolittle (Spencer Tracy) began training a
squadron of fliers for a secret mission. Doolittle and his men perfected
a take-off technique that enabled B-25 Mitchell bombers to be deployed from an aircraft carrier. Then, when his men were fully pre-
pared, Doolittle led them on an attack on Yokohama and Tokyo. While
LeRoy and company carefully re-create the details of the squad's training and the attack, the film is hampered by the obligatory romantic
subplot. Nevertheless, *Thirty Seconds over Tokyo* is a classic war film
that stands up to repeated viewings.

The film received two Academy Award nominations for Best Black-
and-White Cinematography (Robert Surtees and Harold Rosson) and
Best Special Effects (A. Arnold Gillespie, Donald Jahraus, Warren
Newcombe, and Douglas Shearer), winning its only Oscar for the latter.

1. A highly respected army general served as the technical advisor
on this film. Who was this?

2. Planes are normally loaded with ten cans of fuel. How many cans of fuel do the planes carry for this mission?

3. Who does Col. Doolittle say "wear pretty tall hats"?

4. Who does Doolittle allow the fliers to tell about their mission?

5. Lt. White says he is a doctor. What does he say he is *not?*

6. How many times per day will the navy provide planes with their bearings?

7. What is significant regarding the Pensacola, Florida, airbase where the training scenes were filmed?

8. What does Lawson say his wife was born to do?

9. The fliers sing about a state throughout the film. What is this state?

10. What is Lt. Cmdr. Jurika's advice when asked how fliers should conduct themselves if forced down over Japan?

11. Spencer Tracy and director Mervyn LeRoy later collaborate on a second film. This 1961 drama also stars Frank Sinatra. What is this film?

12. Passengers onboard the aircraft carrier are told that the smoking lamp is out. What does this mean?

13. Doolittle has something removed from the B-25s in case they fall into enemy hands. What is this?

14. To what barracks are the enlisted men assigned?

15. What is the name of Lawson's plane?

16. What is Lt. Jacob Manch's nickname?

17. The man who later directs *Breakfast at Tiffany's* (1961), *Days of Wine and Roses* (1962), and *The Pink Panther* (1964) appears in an uncredited cameo. Who is this?

18. What does Thatcher say he plans to do when he gets home?

19. Thatcher says there is "no place as pretty" as his hometown. Where is this?

20. Who does Gray say "used to be as graceful as a Texas steer"?

21. Of what news does Lawson's wife write to inform him?

22. Which of the men sleeps in the bedroom of the admiral's quarters?

23. How long does Gray say he intends to sleep if he's given a leave?

24. What, according to Lawson, will take care of his family "for a long time" if he dies?

25. What does Gray say he wants to purchase after the war?

Quiz No. 88:
THREE KINGS
(1999)

Screenplay by David O. Russell and John Ridley
Directed by David O. Russell
Starring George Clooney, Mark Wahlberg, and Ice Cube
Warner Bros.
Available on VHS, DVD

> *The way it works is you do the thing you're scared shitless of and you get the courage after you do it. Not before you do it.*
> —MAJ. ARCHIE GATES

David O. Russell's stylish film *Three Kings* reworks the concept behind *Kelly's Heroes* (1970). As the Gulf War comes to an end, four American soldiers trek through the Iraqi desert to "liberate" millions in stolen Kuwaiti bullion. While *Three Kings* is largely an escapist adventure, it's an important film for a number of reasons. First, the film provides an accurate depiction of the original Iraqi conflict. Second, Russell's film examines the motives behind the governments and soldiers involved in the conflict. Third, Russell doesn't glorify violence and shows the impact and consequences of each bullet in a manner that conveys his message without being preachy. Russell's script deftly combines humor and tension, and his flashy camerawork is brilliantly effective, yet manages to remain unobtrusive. Russell's use of the skip-bleach process, which gives the film a washed-out but vibrant color, lends the film a unique look. The ensemble is terrific, and most of the actors give arguably their finest performances here.

Despite being snubbed by the Academy of Motion Picture Arts and Sciences, *Three Kings* received a Writers Guild Award nomination, the Political Film Society's Award for Peace, a Golden Reel Award nomination, a Blockbuster Entertainment Award for Favorite Action Team

(George Clooney, Mark Wahlberg, and Ice Cube), and Boston Society of Film Critics Awards for Best Director and Best Film.

1. What is Archie Gates's new occupation after the Gulf War?
2. What reason does Chief Elgin give the Iraqis for Conrad Vig's ignorant views?
3. What is Elgin's civilian occupation?
4. What does Gates believe to be the "most important thing in life"?
5. George Clooney also plays a U.S. Army Special Forces officer in a 1997 film directed by Mimi Leder. What is this film?
6. Troy's wife has a nickname for him. What is this?
7. What former professional football player appears briefly as "Action Star"?
8. After witnessing Iraqis brutally murder a civilian woman, Gates is told to leave. What is his response?
9. What city is Elgin from?
10. Which cast member is a former *Saturday Night Live* regular?
11. *Three Kings* is based on a script by John Ridley. What was the original title of Ridley's script?
12. At the end of the film, Gates is shown strangling an actor. Who appears in a cameo as the actor?
13. What are the two racial slurs Elgin says he does not want to hear?
14. Where do Troy and Vig discover the map?
15. What band does Vig call "good music" that will "pump you up"?
16. At the end of the film, we are told that Mark Wahlberg's character relocates to the same city where his *Boogie Nights* (1997) character is from. Where is this?
17. Which of the four main characters dies?
18. The first line of dialogue in the film is spoken by Troy. What does he say?
19. What is the name of Troy's daughter?
20. George Clooney and Mark Wahlberg appear in another film set in 1991. What is the title of this 2000 Wolfgang Petersen film?
21. The Iraqi soldiers guarding the booty stolen from Kuwait are listening to a song that Troy calls "bad music." What is this?

22. The soldiers sing a Lee Greenwood tune in the film. What is this song?

23. What, according to Adrianna Cruse, is the cost of her camera?

24. What brand of vehicle does Elgin insist does not come in a convertible model?

25. Troy's captor asks him "what is the problem" with a troubled American celebrity. Who is this?

Quiz No. 89:

THRONE OF BLOOD

(1957)

Screenplay by Shinobu Hashimoto, Ryuzo Kikushima, Akira Kurosawa, and
  Hideo Oguni (based on a play by William Shakespeare)
Directed by Akira Kurosawa
Starring Toshiro Mifune, Isuzu Yamada, and Minoru Chiaki
Toho Films
Available on VHS, DVD

I will paint this whole forest with blood! —TAKETORI WASHIZU

Throne of Blood is master filmmaker Akira Kurosawa's spectacular retelling of William Shakespeare's *Macbeth* in a feudal Japanese setting. After being informed by an omniscient witch that he will one day rule the kingdom, Taketori Washizu (Toshiro Mifune) begins scheming to make this prophecy a reality—even if it means killing the emperor and his best friend in the process. Unlike Kurosawa's *King Lear* adaptation *Ran* (1985), *Throne of Blood* is not epic in its scope. Instead, it is a grim tale of two friends, a wife, and a son trapped in a nightmare from which they cannot wake. Rarely known as a subtle actor, Mifune is at his flamboyant, brooding best here. Equally impressive is Isuzu Yamada as his evil, manipulating wife. At a brisk 109 minutes in length (extremely short for a Kurosawa film), *Throne of Blood* grabs hold of the viewer and doesn't let go until its brutal final scene.

Kurosawa was nominated for the prestigious Golden Lion Award at the Venice Film Festival, but did not win.

1. Where on his body does the final arrow strike Washizu?
2. How many castles are there in this story?
3. Washizu says Asaji is "bewitched by the evil spirit" when she does something. What is this?
4. Asaji says her husband has only two options. What are these?

5. Who does the guard say always leaves a house before a fire?

6. Who offers to shave his head as a token of apology?

7. Who does Asaji say she did not stain her hands with blood to benefit?

8. For what does Asaji suggest Miki will open the castle's gates?

9. Large piles surround the witch's lair. What are these piles of?

10. What does Asaji believe the crow is saying to her husband?

11. What does the witch say Washizu should do if he decides to build a mountain of dead bodies?

12. Who does Asaji say will enjoy watching her husband die?

13. What does the witch say mortals do when they want something?

14. What does Miki's son believe to be an omen?

15. What does the witch's song say life must end in?

16. What does Asaji say had nothing to do with Miki's recommendation?

17. What happens to the witch after her first proclamation?

18. What did her Ladyship say she did not want to live to see?

19. What is the name of the forest where the witch resides?

20. Washizu has a vision while waiting for Miki. Whose ghost does he believe he sees?

21. Who commits suicide inside the Forbidden Room?

22. What does Asaji say one must do in this world if he does not want to be killed?

23. The witch says Washizu will only lose a battle if something happens. What is this?

24. On whom does Asaji convince Washizu to lay the blame for Tsuzuki's death?

25. What is the name of Miki's son?

Quiz No. 90:
TO BE OR NOT TO BE
(1942)

Screenplay by Edwin Justus Mayer and Melchior Lengyel
Directed by Ernst Lubitsch
Starring Carole Lombard, Jack Benny, and Robert Stack
United Artists
Available on VHS

> *They named a brandy after Napoleon, they made a herring out of Bismarck, and the Fuhrer is going to end up as a piece of cheese!*
> —COL. EHRHARDT

Nazism is hardly the funniest of subjects, yet Ernst Lubitsch consistently mines humor from the Nazis in this Jack Benny–starrer about the Polish resistance. Things begin to heat up when accomplished actress Maria Tura's (Carole Lombard) lover (Robert Stack) learns that a key member of the Polish underground is actually a German spy. This knowledge inadvertently gets Maria involved with the Gestapo. Soon Maria's husband, Joseph Tura (Jack Benny), and the other members of her theater troupe begin scheming to deceive the Nazis in order to protect their homeland. When the film was released in 1942, it was thought to be in bad taste and quickly tanked. Today, however, *To Be or Not to Be* is recognized as one of the finest films produced in its era.

The film received one Academy Award nomination for Best Score (Werner R. Heymann), but lost. *To Be or Not to Be* was listed to the National Film Registry as a classic in 1996.

1. What does Col. Ehrhardt say would be both his duty and his pleasure?
2. Who writes Professor Siletsky's suicide note?
3. Whose fate does Dobosh say he hates to leave in the hands of a ham?

4. Which of the film's primary characters was killed in a plane crash before the film was released?

5. What does the narrator say was the "answer to the Nazi terror"?

6. What happens when Joseph delivers his soliloquy at the end of the film?

7. What actor appears in the lead role of the 1983 remake?

8. What is the name of the play about Adolf Hitler that is cancelled?

9. What is Ehrhardt's nickname?

10. What does Greenberg say is "nothing to be sneezed at"?

11. In what book does Sobinski attach a photograph of Siletsky?

12. Who coconceived the film's plot but did not receive a screenwriting credit?

13. What does Ehrhardt refer to as the "hot-foot department"?

14. What does Ehrhardt say regarding Joseph's performance in *Hamlet*?

15. What does Sobinski say is worth "ten thousand bombs"?

16. What award does Joseph (posing as Siletsky) say the English are liable to present Shultz?

17. What does Siletsky say is the "right" side?

18. Maria tells Sobinski to come to her dressing room when Joseph says something. What is this?

19. What does Joseph say when he believes he's been shot?

20. What kind of air does Siletsky say "it's good to breathe" again?

21. What does Maria say after kissing Siletsky?

22. Maria tells Joseph that she's not sure she'd be in the role of the mother if they were to have a baby. What is Joseph's memorable response?

23. What does the phoney Hitler order the two pilots to do?

24. What does Joseph say "every actor dreads"?

25. Who pretends to be Hitler?

Quiz No. 91:
TORA! TORA! TORA!
(1970)

Screenplay by Larry Forrester, Ryuzo Kikushima, and Hideo Oguni (based
  on books by Ladislas Farago and Gordon W. Prange)
Directed by Richard Fleischer, Kinji Fukasaku, and Toshio Masuda
Starring Martin Balsam, So Yamamura, and Joseph Cotten
Twentieth Century-Fox
Available on VHS, DVD

> *If we fight the Americans we can't stop at Hawaii or San Francisco.
> We'll have to march into Washington and dictate peace terms in the
> White House. Army hotheads who speak so lightly of war should think
> about that.*
> —ADM. YAMAMOTO

Featuring an extraordinary cast, *Tora! Tora! Tora!* is an extremely realistic depiction of the attack on Pearl Harbor. The film is significant because it allows equal screen time to both the American and Japanese
points of view. Interestingly, this unorthodox even-handedness may
be both the film's central strength as well as its primary weakness as
historians have charged the filmmakers with giving the Japanese military too much credit in their attempt to make audiences sympathize
with both sides of the battle. One of Hollywood's most ambitious under-
takings, *Tora! Tora! Tora!*'s points of view were directed by separate
filmmakers, with the Japanese speaking in their native language (with
subtitles). While the film's special effects—incredibly realistic for the
era in which they were produced—cannot hold a candle to those of
Pearl Harbor (2001), *Tora! Tora! Tora!* is a vastly superior film.

In 1971, *Tora! Tora! Tora!* received five Academy Award nominations for Best Cinematography (Charles F. Wheeler, Osau Furuya,
Sinsaku Himeda, and Masamichi Satoh), Best Sound (Murray Spivack
and Herman Lewis), Best Film Editing (James E. Newcom, Pembroke
J. Herring, and Inoue Chikaya), Best Art Direction–Set Decoration

(Jack Martin Smith, Yoshiro Muraki, Richard Day, Taizo Kawashima, Walter M. Scott, Norman Rockett, and Carl Biddiscombe), and Best Special Effects (A. D. Flowers and L. B. Abbott). The film was awarded one Oscar for its special effects. Other honors include Golden Laurel nominations for Best Picture and Best Cinematography, and an American Cinema Editors nomination for Best Edited Feature Film.

1. What does Adm. Isoroku Yamamoto say is "no longer an issue"?

2. What does Yamamoto fear Japan has filled the "sleeping giant" with?

3. The film was adapted from two books. What are these?

4. The man who planned the actual attack on Pearl Harbor served as the Japanese technical advisor on this film. Who is this?

5. What is referred to in the film as a "remarkable scientific achievement"?

6. What director was hired to shoot the Japanese segments of the film, but was later fired when producers feared he might be going insane?

7. A P-40 is shown crashing into the flight line. What is the significance of this?

8. *Tora! Tora! Tora!* was one of two films released in the United States in 1970 that was directed or codirected by Kinji Fukasaku. What is the other film?

9. What model of Japanese Zero features folding wings?

10. *Tora! Tora! Tora!* is one of three films featuring both Jason Robards and Martin Balsam. What are the other two films on which these two actors collaborated?

11. Why were some U.S. citizens angered by the decision to film *Tora! Tora! Tora!*?

12. Who does Vice Adm. William Halsey conclude to be the "one man in this man's navy who hasn't gone nuts"?

13. Richard Fleischer directs Joseph Cotten in a second film three years after *Tora! Tora! Tora!* The film costars Charlton Heston. What is this film?

14. What was the October 4, 1970, headline to Vincent Camby's review of *Tora! Tora! Tora!* in the *New York Times*?

15. Who is Richard Fleischer's father?

16. How many Japanese aircraft carriers were involved in the attack on Pearl Harbor?

17. During his long career, screenwriter Larry Forrester received only one other credit for a theatrically released film. What is this film?

18. Who does Yamamoto call Japan's "last hope"?

19. At what two locations does Yamamoto say the Japanese cannot stop if engaging in war with the United States?

20. What is the title of the operation to decode Japanese interceptions?

21. As the Zeroes approach Pearl Harbor, they fly over the white cross that stands at the Scofield Barracks. Why is this depiction inaccurate?

22. What time do U.S. military experts conclude to be the "most favorable time" for a Japanese attack on Pearl Harbor?

23. Which of the American actors was actually present when Pearl Harbor was attacked on December 7, 1941?

24. There is much discussion in the film regarding the shallowness of Pearl Harbor. What is the depth of the water there?

25. What does Kimmel say Halsey doesn't "keep asking for"?

Quiz No. 92:
THE TRAIN
(1964)

Screenplay by Franklin Coen and Frank Davis (based on a novel by Rose
    Valland)
Directed by John Frankenheimer
Starring Burt Lancaster, Paul Scofield, and Jeanne Moreau
United Artists
Available on VHS, DVD

> *This morning we had four men left in this group. Now we have three.*
> *One. Two. Three. We started with eighteen. Like your paintings,*
> *mademoiselle, we couldn't replace them. For certain things we take*
> *the risk. But I won't waste lives on painting.* —LABICHE

As one of the few war films that aren't retreads of familiar storylines,
John Frankenheimer's *The Train* tells the story of a Nazi colonel (Paul
Scofield) who is appropriating valuable French art and a resistance
fighter (Burt Lancaster) who is trying to stop him from taking it out of
the country. Screenwriters Franklin Coen and Frank Davis add a decep-
tively small twist to the proceedings by crafting the Nazi as an art lover
and the protagonist Labiche as an indifferent man without any real love
or respect for the artwork. In doing this, the screenwriters add a be-
lievable humanity to their characters. Unlike so many war films of the
past, the protagonist isn't a completely good man and the antagonist
isn't a purely evil man, making the audience more sympathetic toward
him. Like *The Manchurian Candidate* (1962), for which Frankenheimer is better known, *The Train* is a clever thriller offering plenty of
suspense, fine direction, and impressive performances from its cast.

   The Train received a single Oscar nomination for Best Original
Screenplay (Coen and Davis). Other honors include a British Academy
of Film and Television Awards nomination for Best Film from Any

Source and a Laurel Awards runner-up prize for Best Action Performance (Lancaster).

1. Who does Christine sarcastically call her "two best customers"?
2. The first director attached to this film resigned during its production. Who is this?
3. What is the name of the engineer Labiche assigns to commandeer the train carrying the art?
4. Whose sense of survival does Col. Von Waldheim say he admires?
5. For what does Miss Villard say she has long wanted to thank Von Waldheim?
6. What does Von Waldheim refer to as an opportunity for Labiche to "broaden [his] horizons"?
7. Who performed Burt Lancaster's stunts for this film?
8. What does Christine say "goes with the room"?
9. How is the German soldier on the train fooled into believing Pont a Mousson is Remilly?
10. What does Christine say it's a sin to waste?
11. What screenwriter worked on *Fail-Safe* and *The Train,* both of which were released in 1964, but received no credit for his contributions on the latter?
12. With what weapon does Labiche attack the German soldier riding with him inside the engine?
13. The filmmakers thank two groups in the film's opening statement. Who are they?
14. What is the name of the German soldier assigned to travel inside the cab of the engine with Labiche?
15. What is Labiche's first name?
16. Christine says she runs a hotel. What does she say she does *not* operate?
17. How does Labiche protect the engine from the attacking Spitfire?
18. *The Train* is one of five films in which John Frankenheimer directed Burt Lancaster. Their first collaboration was in 1961. What is this film?
19. What, according to the film's tagline, did the train carry?
20. Who does Miss Villard say the paintings belong to?
21. Boule says he knew a girl who modeled for a painter. Who is the painter? (Hint: This artist's son directed *Grand Illusion* [1937].)

22. What is the name of the stationmaster played by Jacques Marin?

23. Burt Lancaster and Paul Scofield later appear in a second film together. This film is directed by Michael Winner and stars Alain Delon as the title character. What is this film?

24. Labiche says he's a railroad man. What does he say he is *not*?

25. *The Train* was one of two 1964 films dealing with war that was directed by John Frankenheimer and starred Burt Lancaster. Can you name the other film?

Quiz No. 93:

THE TUSKEGEE AIRMEN
(1995)

Screenplay by Paris Qualles, Trey Ellis, and Ron Hutchinson (based on a
  novel by Robert Williams and T. S. Cook)
Directed by Robert Markowitz
Starring Laurence Fishburne, Cuba Gooding Jr., and Andre Braugher
Metro-Goldwyn-Mayer
Available on VHS, DVD

> *Why would you wanna fight for a country that thanks you by lynch-*
> *ing you?*
> —BILLY ROBERTS

The strengths of *The Tuskegee Airmen* lie in its subject matter, its message, and its extraordinary cast. A noble endeavor, *The Tuskegee
Airmen* chronicles the struggles of black pilots who served during
World War II. It is the struggle within the struggle—the war the
United States waged against them as they battled for the right to fight
for the freedom of the very people who persecuted them—that makes
this story so fascinating.

The script is filled with war movie clichés and the battle scenes look
as unrealistic as those found in aerial war pictures of the 1940s.
Despite these flaws, *The Tuskegee Airmen* is an important story that
needs to be told and an important film that needs to be seen. The talented actors who portray the pilots turn in magnificent performances,
and the chemistry between them gives the bonds between their characters a feel of authenticity. Especially impressive are Laurence
Fishburne and Courtney B. Vance. While their styles of acting share no
aesthetic, both give incredibly well-articulated performances that
bring their characters to life. In fact, the only lackluster performance
to be found here is that of John Lithgow, who gives his racist senator
the same cartoonish poorly acted Iago approach that made his *Raising
Cain* (1992) character Carter Nix so laughable only three years earlier.

The Tuskegee Airmen stands in opposition to the adage that a chain is only as strong as its weakest link. It may not be a classic, but *The Tuskegee Airmen* is both entertaining and enlightening.

The film received ten Emmy nominations for Outstanding Made for Television Movie (Frank Price, Robert Williams, Bill Carraro, and Carol Bahoric), Outstanding Individual Achievement (Paris Qualles, Trey Ellis, Ron Hutchinson, Williams, and T. S. Cook), Outstanding Lead Actor (Fishburne), Outstanding Supporting Actor (Andre Braugher), Outstanding Individual Achievement in Casting (Robi Reed-Humes), Outstanding Individual Achievement in Editing (David Beatty), Outstanding Individual Achievement in Sound Editing (too many to list), Outstanding Individual Achievement in Music Composition (Lee Holdridge), Outstanding Individual Achievement in Sound Mixing (Veda Campbell, Wayne Artman, Robert L. Harman, and Nick Alphin), and Outstanding Individual Achievement in Special Visual Effects (Michael Muscal, Fred Cramer, Ray McIntyre Jr., and David Fiske). These nominations led to three Emmys for the film's casting, editing, and sound editing. Other honors include a Golden Globe nomination for Best Actor (Fishburne), Image Awards for Outstanding Actor (Fishburne) and Outstanding Television Movie, a Screen Actors Guild nomination for Outstanding Performance by a Male Actor in a Television Movie (Fishburne), and an American Cinema Editors nomination for Best Edited Motion Picture for Non-commercial Television.

1. What does Roberts conclude to be the "worst thing you can do to a pilot"?

2. Senator Conyers says that all points of view are one thing when they're not to your liking. What is this?

3. Legendary director Stanley Kramer nearly made a similar film in the late 1980s that would have depicted the struggles of black soldiers serving in the 761st Tank Battalion during World War II. Unfortunately, that film was never made. The title of its screenplay contained the name of a person who appears as a character in *The Tuskegee Airmen*. What was the title of this unproduced script?

4. Which of the pilots destroys a German warship?

5. Laurence Fishburne had played Cuba Gooding Jr.'s father in a film released only four years before *The Tuskegee Airmen*. What is this film?

6. What state is Lee from?

7. What is the title of the book Peoples is reading when Roberts and Lee first meet him on the train?

8. Who carries Lee's death letter?

9. Allen Payne and Malcolm-Jamal Warner both appeared as regulars on *The Cosby Show*. What were the names of the characters they played?

10. What is William Roberts's nickname?

11. Who does Cappy call a "class act"?

12. What, according to Davis, is the number of missions flown by white pilots before being sent home?

13. *The Tuskegee Airmen* was one of two 1995 war films in which Allen Payne appeared. In the other film, which was about the Vietnam War, Payne received top billing. What is this film?

14. Where does Roberts say there "ain't no gorillas"?

15. Lt. Glenn says there is only one way for a pilot to protect himself against losing friends. What is this?

16. The squadron paints the tails of their planes as a signature. What color are they painted?

17. Which flier does Eleanor Roosevelt choose to take her on a flight?

18. Andre Braugher made his film debut in a 1989 war film directed by Edward Zwick. What is this film?

19. What does Lewis Johns say "turn into strange fruit" where he's from?

20. Which of the pilots is awarded the Distinguished Flying Cross?

21. *The Tuskegee Airmen* is one of two films featuring both Vivica A. Fox and Mekhi Phifer. The other is a 1997 film directed by George Tillman Jr. What is this film?

22. What, according to Maj. Joy, is the pilots' destiny?

23. What is the target city of the final mission shown in the film?

24. Mekhi Phifer reunites with Andre Braugher the following year, appearing with him on an episode of a television series. What is this series?

25. Which of the men commits suicide during training?

Quiz No. 94:

TWELVE O'CLOCK HIGH

(1949)

Screenplay by Sy Bartlett and Beirne Lay Jr.
Directed by Henry King
Starring Gregory Peck, Hugh Marlowe, and Gary Merrill
Twentieth Century-Fox
Available on VHS, DVD

> *I don't have a lot of patience with this "What are we fighting for?"*
> *stuff. We're in a war, a shooting war. We've got to fight. And some of us*
> *have got to die.* —BRIG. GEN. FRANK SAVAGE

One of the finest war films ever produced, *Twelve O'Clock High* tells the story of the "hard luck" 918th Bomber Group based in Archbury, England. After several planes are shot down and the morale of the men reaches an all-time low, Brig. Gen. Frank Savage (Gregory Peck) is assigned to the 918th in the hopes he can turn the group around. The film, which focuses largely on the decisions a commanding officer must make and the effects his choices can have, is still used today as a training tool at a number of U.S. military officer training schools. Peck, who landed the leading role after John Wayne passed on it, turns in one of his finest performances as a strict by-the-book leader who attempts to gain the trust and loyalty of his men. The film later served as the basis for a Golden Globe–nominated television series of the same title, which aired from 1964 to 1967.

Twelve O'Clock High was nominated for four Oscars: Best Picture (Darryl F. Zanuck), Best Actor (Peck), Best Supporting Actor (Dean Jagger), and Best Sound, winning statuettes for the two latter nominations. In addition, Peck was awarded Best Actor honors from the New York Film Critics Circle.

1. What does Savage say is the "one thing" the 918th is not short on?

2. According to the proclamation stenciled on the side of the plane Bishop lands at the beginning of the film, two types of individuals fear treading on board. Who are these?

3. What is the name of the navigator who commits suicide?

4. Who does Savage assign as Col. Gately's replacement as air executive?

5. According to Savage, a formation's defensive power is reduced when one B-17 pulls out. By how many guns does he say the formation's defensive power is reduced?

6. What is Maj. Stovall's civilian occupation?

7. What is the "one thing" Savage believes can fix the problems of the 918th?

8. What name does Savage instruct Gately to paint on the nose of his bomber?

9. Who is assigned to be Savage's personal driver?

10. What is Maj. Cobb's drink of preference?

11. Twenty-eight men request off duty in one day. According to Maj. Kaiser, how many men request off duty on an average day?

12. How many men make up a B-17 flight crew?

13. When at full strength, how many bombers are assigned to the 918th?

14. What does Maj. Kaiser believe Col. Davenport's diet consists of?

15. While talking with Col. Davenport, where does Savage suggest the "real problem" with the 918th lies?

16. What does Maj. Gen. Prichard say he does not believe in?

17. What is Bishop's first name?

18. Who does Savage say "could have done more than anybody to take the load off Col. Davenport"?

19. Who is the 918th group adjutant?

20. Maj. Gen. Prichard says there is only one hope of shortening the war. What is this?

21. How many of the men assigned to the 918th request a transfer after Savage's arrival?

22. When ordered to fly over a target at nine thousand feet, Davenport believes this is a mistake. What does he initially believe the order should read?

23. What does Savage say he had to steal from the Royal Air Force?

24. Who does Savage have placed under arrest for leaving the post and being intoxicated?

25. Savage says the 918th is a military post. What does he say it is *not*?

Quiz No. 95:

U-571

(2000)

Screenplay by Jonathan Mostow, Sam Montgomery, and David Ayer
Directed by Jonathan Mostow
Starring Matthew McConaughey, Bill Paxton, and Harvey Keitel
Universal Pictures
Available on VHS, DVD

> *You have to act. If you don't, you put the whole crew at risk. Now that's the job. It's not a science. You have to be able to make hard decisions based on imperfect information. Asking men to carry out orders that may result in their deaths. And if you're wrong, you suffer the consequences. If you're not prepared to make those decisions without pause—without reflection—then you've got no business being a submarine commander.*
> —LT. CMDR. DAHLGREN

A throwback to films like *The Dirty Dozen* (1967) and *Kelly's Heroes* (1970), *U-571* is part of a tradition that filmmaker Quentin Tarantino has given name to as the "bunch of guys on a mission" movie. There are no political messages to be found within *U-571*, nor are there any arthouse pretensions. The story of an American submarine crew who must overtake a damaged German u-boat to capture an onboard device, *U-571* is a fast-paced thrill ride featuring a solid ensemble that includes Matthew McConaughey, Bill Paxton, Harvey Keitel, David Keith, Jon Bon Jovi, T. C. Carson, and Jake Weber. Despite the fact that it breaks no new ground (see *Das Boot* [1981]) and is historically inaccurate (the British Royal Navy actually captured the German device depicted in the film months before the United States entered the war), *U-571* is an entertaining piece of popcorn cinema. *San Francisco Chronicle* reviewer Mick LaSalle raves, "[I]f there's anything wrong with *U-571*, it's that it's too effective—at times unbearable. . . . To compare *U-571* to *Saving Private Ryan* is like comparing a miniature to a mural, but there is one point of similarity: The audience is made to feel the full weight and terror of combat."

U-571 received two Oscar nominations for Best Sound (Steve Maslow, Gregg Landaker, Rick Kline, and Ivan Sharrock) and Best Sound Effects Editing (Jon Johnson), winning for the latter. Other honors include Blockbuster Entertainment Award nominations for McConaughey and Keitel, two Golden Reel Award nominations, and a Las Vegas Film Critics Society Awards nomination for Best Visual Effects.

1. Just after the S-33 is destroyed, the crewmen use the German u-boat to torpedo an attacking submarine. What is the significance of the attacking sub?

2. Matthew McConaughey and Bill Paxton reunite in a film released in 2001 that was directed by Paxton. What is this film?

3. The German u-boat commander says, "The Tommies are crapping all over us." What does this mean?

4. What is Lt. Tyler's first name?

5. Which *U-571* cast member has been nominated for an Oscar as a composer?

6. Who, according to Adm. Duke, has operational control on the mission?

7. The crew overhears a Morse code message, discovering that it's being sent from within the submarine. What is the message?

8. What was the occupation of Tyler's father?

9. The crew of the S-33 must overtake the U-571 to capture a device that is onboard. What is this device?

10. Which S-33 crewmember sees the incoming torpedo just before it slams into the sub?

11. Harvey Keitel appears as Brig. Gen. Warren Black in a war-themed telefilm that aired the same year *U-571* was released. What is this film?

12. The German "mechanic" onboard the U-571 says he apprenticed in his uncle's garage. What does he say he repaired there?

13. What does Wentz ask Tyler to keep secret?

14. To whom is *U-571* dedicated?

15. What is Rabbit's real name?

16. Whose body does Tyler say will save the lives of his crew?

17. The film's executive producer has produced films as diverse as

Barbarella (1968), *Mandingo* (1975), and the classic war film *Anzio* (1968). Who is this?

18. What three words does Klough say "will kill a crew"?

19. Who informs Tyler that his liberty pass has been revoked?

20. Hirsch offers the German sailors a bag. What does he say it contains?

21. What depth does Dahlgren say submarine commanders "try not to" take their subs any deeper than?

22. *U-571* marked the second film on which actors Harvey Keitel and David Keith collaborated. Their first collaboration was on a 1990 film directed by Jack Nicholson. What is this film?

23. What does Hirsch say Tyler must do if he is unsuccessful in his attempt to sink the German destroyer?

24. Which crew member remarks that he is seen "but never seen"?

25. Bill Paxton had portrayed Col. John Paul Vann in a Vietnam War film released two years prior to *U-571*. Can you name this film?

Quiz No. 96:

VON RYAN'S EXPRESS

(1965)

Screenplay by Wendell Mayes and Joseph Landon (based on a novel by
  David Westheimer)
Directed by Mark Robson
Starring Frank Sinatra, Trevor Howard, and Raffaella Carra
Twentieth Century-Fox
Available on VHS, DVD

> *You'll get your Iron Cross now, Von Ryan!*   —MAJ. ERIC FINCHAM

Seeking a sure-fire formula for success, screenwriters Wendell Mayes
and Joseph Landon combined elements of two popular war films, *The
Great Escape* (1963) and *The Train* (1964). Add these ingredients with
star Frank Sinatra, and the end result is *Von Ryan's Express.* While the
film doesn't approach either of the films that inspired it in terms of
artistry or quality, the film is an effective actioner with absolutely no
pretentions.

By 1965, Sinatra had already earned himself a well-deserved reputation as a name player who refused to accept direction. On *Von Ryan's
Express,* Sinatra seemingly went out of his way to be a menace. While
on location in Spain, Sinatra squared off against director Mark
Robson, disrespected him in front of the rest of the cast and crew, and
allowed his entourage to do the same. Indifferent to production costs,
Sinatra threatened to walk off the film and demanded that many
scenes be completed in a single take. Because of this, Sinatra's performance lacks depth and he appears to simply be playing Frank Sinatra
in a prison camp setting. While film historians and members of the arthouse crowd may seek something more substantial, *Von Ryan's Express*
is an example of crowd-pleasing escapism at its most effective.

Von Ryan's Express received one Academy Award nomination for
Best Sound Effects (Walter Rossi), but did not win the Oscar.

1. Frank Sinatra and Brad Dexter were both jailed on the last day of location shooting in Spain. What were the two actors jailed for?

2. What is done with the sick and wounded as the prisoners are loaded onto the train?

3. The previous senior officer of the prisoners had died in the "sweat box." What offense had landed him there?

4. Maj. Fincham suggests tying a knot in the rope before strangling a man. What does this knot do?

5. Frank Sinatra had previously vowed never to return to Spain after filming a 1957 movie there. What is this film?

6. Wolfgang Preiss appears in the film as Maj. Von Klemment. The previous year, Preiss had played another German officer in a World War II film that takes place on a train. What is this film?

7. *Von Ryan's Express* is one of two 1965 war films starring Frank Sinatra. Sinatra directed the other himself. What is this film?

8. When the Brits prepare to stage a summary court-martial for Battaglia, who is to preside over the proceedings?

9. While attempting to seduce him, Gabriella asks Ryan to close the door. What is Ryan's response?

10. When Fincham says "all the comforts of home," he's referring to something he's just found. What is this?

11. What, according to Fincham, constitutes a victory?

12. George Segal was nearly cast in the leading role. Segal wound up starring in another prisoner of war film released the same year as *Von Ryan's Express*. What is this film?

13. *Von Ryan's Express* was the second film to feature both Frank Sinatra and Trevor Howard. What was the first?

14. Who suggests that Ryan wait to break the wood floor of the boxcar until the train hits crosstracks?

15. What, according to Gabriella, do all men say?

16. How much tunnel soil do the prisoners believe the barracks roof will hold "if spread right"?

17. Why does Sgt. Bostick say that only fourteen of the prisoners were able to wear the German uniforms?

18. Why does Ryan's watch attract attention from the Gestapo?

19. What does Ryan say outranks a "bird brain"?

20. After being informed by Battaglia that no new clothes will be issued, what does Ryan do to force his hand?

21. What is the name of the film's theme song performed by Frank Sinatra?

22. What type of medicine is Bostick caught attempting to steal?

23. Why does Ryan and company's attempt to derail the train pursuing them fail?

24. Who strangles the first Nazi guard on top of the train?

25. What type of officer does Bostick say is needed "real bad"?

Quiz No. 97:

WE WERE SOLDIERS

(2002)

Screenplay by Randall Wallace (based on a book by Harold G. Moore and
   Joseph L. Galloway)
Directed by Randall Wallace
Starring Mel Gibson, Madeleine Stowe, and Sam Elliott
Paramount Pictures
Available on VHS, DVD

> *We who have seen war will never stop seeing it.* —JOE GALLOWAY

We Were Soldiers depicts Lt. Col. Hal Moore (Mel Gibson) leading the
Seventh Cavalry in the Battle of Drang Valley, significant because it
was the first battle in Vietnam involving U.S. troops. Completed in the
wake of the September 11, 2001, attack on the World Trade Center and
the Pentagon, the resulting film is one of the most patriotic American
war features ever produced. Director/screenwriter Randall Wallace's
script is tight (save for a few clichés and predictable turns à la *Pearl
Harbor,* [2001]). With a cast featuring Mel Gibson and a host of under-
rated performers including Sam Elliott, Barry Pepper, and Greg Kinnear,
the acting is extraordinary; Gibson especially shines in his portrayal of
Moore. With the exception of a cheesy montage showing Barry Pepper's
character snapping pictures, Wallace's direction is flawless.

Real-life Drang Valley survivors Hal Moore and Joe Galloway
served as technical advisors, lending the film credibility. Also, one particularly gruesome scene depicting a soldier burned by napalm gives
Saving Private Ryan (1998) a run for its money in terms of realistic
graphic violence in a war film.

   1. What, according to Sgt. Maj. Plumley, is the difference between
Lt. Col. Hal Moore and Gen. George Armstrong Custer?

2. At what university did Moore receive a master's in international relations?

3. What 1992 book is this film based on?

4. Plumley made four jumps in World War II. How many did he make in the Korean War?

5. Actor Barry Pepper portrays Joe Galloway in the film. In 1998, he appeared in another war film playing a character named Pvt. Daniel Jackson. What is this film?

6. Moore receives orders that he says do not make sense. What are these?

7. In the film, Maj. Bruce Campbell sings the song "Hold On! I'm A Comin'." What group made this song popular?

8. What term does the radio man use in the film to indicate that the Americans' position has been overrun?

9. What tagline was used to promote the film at the time of its release?

10. Just after arriving in Vietnam, how many "battle ready" soldiers does Plumley say he has?

11. What is Jack Geoghegan's rank?

12. What is the name of Moore's wife?

13. The term "LZ" is used throughout the film. What does this term mean?

14. When Sgt. Savage announces that it's a "beautiful morning," what is Plumley's response?

15. What does Plumley inform Galloway that there "ain't no such thing today"?

16. Who does the army hire to deliver the Western Union telegrams informing the families that their loved ones have been killed?

17. As his children sing "Bear Went over the Mountain," Moore suggests they sing a different song. What is this?

18. Moore is a Catholic. His wife is not. What is her religious preference?

19. *We Were Soldiers* was the fourth screenplay written by Randall Wallace to be produced theatrically. Two of the other three scripts were also for war films. Which one was *not*?

20. Moore shares a story with his soldiers about a Sioux warrior. Who was this?

21. In the trailer for the film, Moore's wife observes that most

dying men's final words are "Tell my wife I love her." What is the significance of this?

22. What is the name of the ill-fated soldier who announces "I got a baby being born today"?

23. What nickname is Maj. Crandall given by his men?

24. What name does Plumley advise the soldiers not to call him by unless they want to die?

25. For what does Moore say he will never forgive himself?

Quiz No. 98:
WHEN TRUMPETS FADE
(1998)

Screenplay by William W. Vought
Directed by John Irvin
Starring Ron Eldard, Zak Orth, and Frank Whaley
HBO
Available on VHS, DVD

> *Last time I had a hot meal was five days ago. Since then, my entire platoon has been wiped out. That's why you're here. You're just a bunch of guys in line to get shot so you can bring in a bunch of other guys. See how that works? Now once you get that through your fuckin' head, maybe you'll realize how important a hot meal could be.*
> —SGT. MANNING

This made-for-cable film was a victim of bad timing. Released the same year as *Saving Private Ryan* and *The Thin Red Line* (both 1998), John Irvin's powerful film was overshadowed by those larger, flashier films. *When Trumpets Fade,* written by William W. Vought, examines the actions of ordinary men placed in extraordinary situations. The film is set during one of World War II's most shocking and unforgettable battles: the battle of Hurtgen Forest in 1944. Irvin and Vought update the World War II scenario by mixing in elements of the Vietnam War film: dominant attitudes of antiauthority, adult language, and horrifically gory battle scenes. The film offers an unflinching look at the senselessness of war. Ron Eldard gives a rich, multilayered performance, and the rest of the ensemble is equally impressive. *When Trumpets Fade* may not be as effects-laden as *Saving Private Ryan,* nor does it feature a big-name cast, but it does manage to be every bit as effective in its antiwar message without resorting to blatant sentimentalism.

Honors for *When Trumpets Fade* include the Seattle International

Film Festival's third-place prize for Best Actor (Eldard), two Motion Picture Sound Editors nominations, an American Society of Cinematographers nomination (Thomas Burstyn), and a silver award in the category of Fiction Film at the Biarritz International Festival of Audiovisual Programming.

1. *When Trumpets Fade* was released in Australia as the sequel to another war film directed by John Irvin. What is this film?
2. What is Capt. Pritchett's first name?
3. Who shoots Baxter?
4. Who is this film dedicated to?
5. What battle began only days after the Battle of Hurtgen Forest, thus overshadowing it?
6. What is the two-word mantra the soldiers recite before going into battle?
7. Manning commits an act of euthanasia at the beginning of the film. What is the name of the soldier he kills?
8. What is Despin's first name?
9. The central storyline to *When Trumpets Fade* was borrowed from a 1962 war film directed by Don Siegel and starring Steve McQueen. What is this film?
10. What does Pritchett say he'll do if Manning smiles at him again?
11. Director John Irvin's first war film was released in 1980. The film stars Christopher Walken and Tom Berenger. What is this film?
12. What is the name of the officer who suffers a breakdown at the Kall Trail bridge?
13. Six years prior to his turn in *When Trumpets Fade,* Frank Whaley played a character known as "Father" in a World War II film directed by Keith Gordon. What is this film?
14. What is Sanderson's nickname?
15. One of the film's cast members dated actress Sharon Stone, who later likened kissing him to "eating a dirt sandwich." Who is this?
16. What, according to Manning, "doesn't really matter"?
17. How many men does the film's postscript say were killed at the Battle of Hurtgen Forest?
18. Sanderson tells Manning, "You're gonna owe me big." What is Manning's response?

19. What does Pritchett promise to give Manning if he can take out the guns on the Kall Trail bridge?

20. The challenge for entry into the perimeter is "Hershey." What is the password?

21. Which cast member is a former golden gloves boxer?

22. How many men does Manning lead on his "renegade mission" behind enemy lines?

23. What does Manning tell Sanderson it's his "first big chance" to do?

24. Nine years prior to his appearance in *When Trumpets Fade*, Frank Whaley played a soldier named Timmie in a film directed by Oliver Stone. What is this film?

25. Two years before working on *When Trumpets Fade*, cinematographer Thomas Burstyn was presented a Genie Award for Best Achievement in Cinematography. What film was Burstyn awarded for?

Quiz No. 99:

WHERE EAGLES DARE

(1968)

Screenplay by Alistair MacLean (based on a novel by Alistair MacLean)
Directed by Brian G. Hutton
Starring Richard Burton, Clint Eastwood, and Mary Ure
Metro-Goldwyn-Mayer
Available on VHS

> *Do me a favor, will ya? The next time you have one of these things, try
> to keep it an all-British operation.* —LT. MORRIS SCHAFFER

Screenwriter Alistair MacLean's *Where Eagles Dare* aspires to be a combination of the James Bond adventure-thriller and his own *The Guns of Navarone* (1961). While the film never manages to be quite as effective as either, it's a thoroughly enjoyable yarn. MacLean's screenplay doesn't break much new ground, but he crafts interesting characters for stars Clint Eastwood and Richard Burton. As in the Sergio Leone–directed *Man with No Name* films from which he'd just come, Eastwood chews through enough scenery to fill two studio backlots, but still manages to conjure up enough charisma to hold his own with classically trained English stage actor Burton. MacLean's commandos-on-a-suicide-mission tale owes an obvious debt to his earlier film *The Guns of Navarone,* and the storyline follows that film's footsteps closely. But this isn't a bad thing. *Where Eagles Dare* is a thrilling actioner that stands up to repeated viewings.

Where Eagles Dare received fourth-place honors at the Laurel Awards in the categories of Best Action Drama and Best Action Performance (Eastwood).

1. While disguised as a German officer, Maj. Smith gives a fake name in the bar. What is this?

2. What does Lt. Schaffer comment that Smith has a lot of "stashed around this country"?

3. A novel written by Alistair MacLean was adapted the same year *Where Eagles Dare* was released. The adaptation was directed by John Sturges and stars Rock Hudson, Ernest Borgnine, and Patrick McGoohan. What is this film?

4. The name of the castle the film's plot revolves around is *Schloss Adler*. What does this mean?

5. Where does Maj. Von Hapen say he was educated?

6. Maj. Vilmer asks the Germans to inspect Smith's right arm. What does he say they will see?

7. Why does Smith say Schaffer was chosen for the mission?

8. What is Schaffer's first name?

9. Who does Smith conclude to be the top German agent in Britain?

10. What is Smith's radio handle?

11. Who does Smith trick to get into the radio shack where Schaffer kills him?

12. Smith tells Von Hapen that he has just uncovered a plot to do something. What is this?

13. What does Smith consider an advantage to drinking cold coffee?

14. Two key figures involved with this production were badly burned during filming. Who are they?

15. What rank is the actor posing as Gen. Carnaby?

16. Smith says, "In the next fifteen minutes we have to create enough confusion to get out of here alive." What is Schaffer's memorable response?

17. What does Smith tell Heidi "there's no more important work" than?

18. Prior to *Where Eagles Dare*, Alistair MacLean's work had already been adapted into a 1961 war film starring Gregory Peck. What is this film?

19. Who helps Smith and Schaffer get into the castle?

20. What is Mary's pseudonym?

21. What is the name of the man posing as Gen. Carnaby?

22. What does Vice Adm. Rolland say the word "security" has become?

23. Smith tells the Germans that Schaffer is an assassin. What organization does he say Schaffer works for?

24. Which of the commandos speak fluent German?

25. What does Schaffer say "fear lent" the pilot he's just killed?

Quiz No. 100:

WINDTALKERS
(2002)

Screenplay by John Rice and Joe Batteer
Directed by John Woo
Starring Nicolas Cage, Adam Beach, and Peter Stormare
Metro-Goldwyn-Mayer
Available on VHS, DVD

> *You and me and every other mother's son want out. But as long as there's a Tojo and a Hitler out there, we have to keep on fighting.*
> —CAPT. HJELMSTAD

John Woo's superb World War II drama *Windtalkers* is based on the little-known true story about the Navajo Indians who assisted the U.S. Marines in the Pacific theater. After having had their codes repeatedly broken by the Japanese, the marines began utilizing an obscure dialect of the Navajo language. Told to protect the code "at all costs," distraught Sgt. Joe Enders (Nicolas Cage) finds himself questioning his orders. Should Ben Yahzee (Adam Beach), the Navajo he's been assigned to escort, come close to falling into enemy hands, Enders' orders are to kill him. However, things become complicated when the two men become unlikely friends.

Although *Windtalkers* is a fine, well-crafted film, it never quite measures up to the genre's elite entries like *Saving Private Ryan* (1998) and *The Story of G.I. Joe* (1945). The problem is that beyond the story of the Navajos and their work in the war, the film offers little that audiences haven't already seen. *Village Voice* critic J. Hoberman observes, "*Windtalkers* is at once chintzy and grandiose, awash in battlefield sentimentality and platoon clichés." In all fairness, it should be noted that *Windtalkers* reportedly underwent substantial cuts before release in the wake of the September 11, 2001, terrorist attacks on New York City and Washington, D.C. While the film is still quite entertaining, those who saw the film in its earlier prerelease form claim it ranked with Woo's finest pre-Hollywood films: *The Killer* (1989) and *Bullet in the Head* (1990). Let's all keep our fingers crossed in the hopes that a director's cut will be released sometime down the road.

1. *Windtalkers* was the second collaboration between director John Woo and actor Nicolas Cage. What was their first?

2. *Windtalkers* was the second collaboration between director John Woo and actor Christian Slater. What was their first?

3. What is the name of the California-based camp where the Navajos are trained to be code talkers?

4. What is the name of Yahzee's son?

5. What, according to Chick, is the only difference between Yahzee and a "Jap"?

6. What is Whitehorse's first name?

7. Where does Enders reside?

8. Enders is shown a photograph of a Navajo GI who was tortured by the Japanese. Why didn't the GI break and tell the Japanese the code?

9. Enders shares a bottle of liquor with Yahzee. What kind of liquor is this?

10. Nicolas Cage's uncle is a filmmaker responsible for several fine war films. He served as a screenwriter on both *Is Paris Burning?* (1966) and *Patton* (1970). He also directed *Apocalypse Now* (1979) and *Gardens of Stone* (1987). Who is this?

11. Which ear does Enders injure?

12. The soldiers joke about Chick's girlfriend being an animal. What kind of animal?

13. How many men died under Enders' command on the Solomon Islands?

14. Why does Enders say he was awarded his first Silver Star?

15. Who kills Whitehorse?

16. What is the name of the nurse who writes Enders throughout the film?

17. How much does Chick say his grandfather was paid for each Comanche ear?

18. Why does Enders shoot Harrigan?

19. Nicolas Cage appeared in another World War II film the year before *Windtalkers* was released. In the film, Cage played an Italian of-

ficer stationed in Greece during the war. What is this film?

20. What does Enders say his family's surname was "before some asshole at Ellis Island got ahold of it"?

21. How does Anderson die?

22. How old was Enders for his Catholic confirmation?

23. What is Anderson's nickname?

24. There are fifty stars on the U.S. flag at Yahzee's enlistment ceremony. This is a mistake. How many stars should there have been at that time?

25. When Whitehorse asks Yahzee how his white man is, what is Yahzee's response?

War Film Master Quiz #1:
NAME THE ACTOR

Twenty-five actors who have regularly appeared in war films are described below. Can you name them?

1. This actor plays Gunner's Mate Tyrone Miller in *Apocalypse Now* (1979), Lightbulb in *A Rumor of War* (1980), and Hannibal Lee in *The Tuskegee Airmen* (1995). Who is this?

2. This actor plays Frank Dunne in *Gallipoli* (1981), Capt. Kelly in *Attack Force Z* (1982), and Col. Benjamin Martin in *The Patriot* (2000). Who is this?

3. This actor plays Capt. Jim Gordon in *Flying Tigers* (1942), Col. Joseph Madden in *Back to Bataan* (1945), and Maj. Dan Kirby in *Flying Leathernecks* (1951). Who is this?

4. This actor plays Sgt. Kinnie in *Battleground* (1949), narrates *The Red Badge of Courage* (1951), and appears as Sgt. Mac in *Battle Cry* (1955). Who is this?

5. This actor plays Cpl. Colin Spence in *Immortal Sergeant* (1943), Lt. Roberts in *Mister Roberts* (1955), and Adm. Chester W. Nimitz in both *In Harm's Way* (1965) and *Midway* (1976). Who is this?

6. This actor plays Col. Dax in *Paths of Glory* (1957), Col. Marcus in *Cast a Giant Shadow* (1966), and Gen. George S. Patton Jr. in *Is Paris Burning?* (1966). Who is this?

7. This actor plays Sgt. Loyce in *The Boys in Company C* (1978), Gunnery Sgt. Hartman in *Full Metal Jacket* (1987), and Sgt. Hafner in *The Siege of Firebase Gloria* (1989). Who is this?

8. This actor plays Cpl. Bowman in *The Glory Brigade* (1953),

Meatball in *The Caine Mutiny* (1954), and Lt. Col. Clyde Bartlett in *Attack* (1956). Who is this?

9. This actor plays Sgt. Dhom in *From Here to Eternity* (1953), Sgt. Kolowicz in *Merrill's Marauders* (1962), and Pvt. Rockwell Rockman in *The Devil's Brigade* (1968). Who is this?

10. This actor plays Capt. Courtney in *The Dawn Patrol* (1938), Lt. Douglas Lee in *Dive Bomber* (1941), and Capt. Nelson in *Objective, Burma!* (1945). Who is this?

11. This actor plays Pvt. Flanagan in *The Longest Day* (1962), Trooper Joe Roberts in *The Hill* (1965), and Maj. Gen. Urquhart in *A Bridge Too Far* (1977). Who is this?

12. This actor plays Lt. Flynn in *The Wild Geese* (1978), Maj. Hecht in *Escape to Athena* (1979), and Capt. Stewart in *The Sea Wolves* (1980). Who is this?

13. This actor plays Ens. Bandover in *Assault on the Wayne* (1971), Brig. Gen. Buford in *Gettysburg* (1993), and Sgt. Maj. Plumley in *We Were Soldiers* (2002). Who is this?

14. This actor appears as Peter Moss in *Home of the Brave* (1949), Cpl. Thompson in *The Steel Helmet* (1951), and Sgt. Meeks in *Patton* (1970). Who is this?

15. This actor plays Maj. Burns in *M*A*S*H* (1970), Lt. Col. Kilgore in *Apocalypse Now* (1979), and Gen. Robert E. Lee in *Gods and Generals* (2003). Who is this?

16. This actor plays Lt. Campbell in *Red Ball Express* (1952), Capt. Hawks in *Away All Boats* (1956), and Brig. Gen. Frank Merrill in *Merrill's Marauders* (1962). Who is this?

17. This actor plays Lt. McGregor in *The Lives of a Bengal Lancer* (1935), Michael Geste in *Beau Geste* (1939), and Alvin C. York in *Sergeant York* (1941). Who is this?

18. This actor plays Lt. Schaffer in *Where Eagles Dare* (1968), Lt. Kelly in *Kelly's Heroes* (1970), and Gunnery Sgt. Highway in *Heartbreak Ridge* (1986). Who is this?

19. This actor plays Lt. Lawson in *Thirty Seconds over Tokyo* (1944), Sgt. Evans in *Command Decision* (1948), and Pfc. Holly in *Battleground* (1949). Who is this?

20. This actor plays Cpl. Frank Henshaw in *Hell Is for Heroes* (1962), Louis Sedgwick in *The Great Escape* (1963), and Sgt. Steiner in *Cross of Iron* (1977). Who is this?

21. This actor plays Shan in *Genghis Khan* (1965), Sgt. Guffy in *Battle of the Bulge* (1965), and Sgt. Maj. Dagineau in the 1966 version of *Beau Geste*. Who is this?

22. This actor plays Lt. Cmdr. Conway in *Battle of the Coral Sea* (1959), Wing Cmdr. Grant in *633 Squadron* (1964), and Lt. Lawson in *Too Late the Hero* (1970). Who is this?

23. This actor plays Cmdr. White in *Submarine Command* (1952), Lt. Brubaker in *The Bridges at Toko-Ri* (1955), and *The Bridge on the River Kwai* (1957). Who is this?

24. This actor plays Lt. Walker in *The Story of G.I. Joe* (1945), Col. Janowski in *One Minute to Zero* (1952), and Dick Ennis in *Anzio* (1968). Who is this?

25. This actor plays Capt. MacRoberts in *The Desert Rats* (1953), Capt. Foster in *Raid on Rommel* (1971), and Sgt. Steiner in *Sergeant Steiner* (1978). Who is this?

War Film Master Quiz #2:
NAME THE DIRECTOR

Twenty-five directors who have worked extensively within the war film genre are described below. Can you name them?

1. This filmmaker directed *The Alamo* (1960) and *The Green Berets* (1968). Who is this?

2. This filmmaker directed *A Midnight Clear* (1992) and *Mother Night* (1996). Who is this?

3. This filmmaker directed *They Were Expendable* (1945) and *Mister Roberts* (1955). Who is this?

4. This filmmaker directed *The Dirty Dozen* (1967) and *Too Late the Hero* (1970). Who is this?

5. This filmmaker directed *The Longest Day* (1962) and *The Battle of the Bulge* (1965). Who is this?

6. This filmmaker directed *Empire of the Sun* (1987) and *Saving Private Ryan* (1998). Who is this?

7. This filmmaker directed *The Caine Mutiny* (1954) and *The Young Lions* (1958). Who is this?

8. This filmmaker directed *Apocalypse Now* (1979) and *Gardens of Stone* (1987). Who is this?

9. This filmmaker directed *The Charge of the Light Brigade* (1936) and *Dive Bomber* (1941). Who is this?

10. This filmmaker directed *China Gate* (1957) and *The Big Red One* (1980). Who is this?

11. This filmmaker directed *Sergeant York* (1941) and *Air Force* (1943). Who is this?

12. This filmmaker directed *The Manchurian Candidate* (1962) and *The Train* (1965). Who is this?

13. This filmmaker directed *Paths of Glory* (1957) and *Full Metal Jacket* (1987). Who is this?

14. This filmmaker directed *The Red Badge of Courage* (1951) and *The Battle of San Pietro* (1944). Who is this?

15. This filmmaker directed *Where Eagles Dare* (1968) and *Kelly's Heroes* (1970). Who is this?

16. This filmmaker directed *Hamburger Hill* (1987) and *When Trumpets Fade* (1998). Who is this?

17. This filmmaker directed *The Four Feathers* (1939) and *Sahara* (1943). Who is this?

18. This filmmaker directed *Bataan* (1943) and *One Minute to Zero* (1952). Who is this?

19. This filmmaker directed *In Which We Serve* (1943) and *The Bridge on the River Kwai* (1957). Who is this?

20. This filmmaker directed *Thirty Seconds over Tokyo* (1944) and codirected *Mister Roberts* (1955). Who is this?

21. This filmmaker directed *All Quiet on the Western Front* (1930) and *Pork Chop Hill* (1959). Who is this?

22. This filmmaker directed *Home of the Brave* (1949) and *The Bridges at Toko-Ri* (1955). Who is this?

23. This filmmaker directed *Platoon* (1986) and *Born on the Fourth of July* (1989). Who is this?

24. This filmmaker directed *Objective, Burma!* (1945) and *Battle Cry* (1955). Who is this?

25. This filmmaker directed *The Story of G.I. Joe* (1945) and *Battleground* (1949). Who is this?

War Film Master Quiz #3:
NAME THE WAR

Twenty-five well-known war films are listed below. Read each one and see if you know what conflict each film is about.

1. *The Red Badge of Courage* (1951).
2. *The Big Parade* (1925).
3. *The Charge of the Light Brigade* (1936).
4. *Glory* (1989).
5. *The Blue Max* (1966).
6. *Mother Night* (1996).
7. *Paths of Glory* (1957).
8. *Courage Under Fire* (1996).
9. *The Siege of Firebase Gloria* (1989).
10. *The Last of the Mohicans* (1992).
11. *The General* (1927).
12. *Pork Chop Hill* (1959).
13. *Lifeboat* (1944).
14. *Grand Illusion* (1937).
15. *The Steel Helmet* (1951).
16. *Three Kings* (1999).
17. *Hell's Angels* (1930).
18. *A Rumor of War* (1980).
19. *The Immortal Sergeant* (1943).
20. *The Horse Soldiers* (1959).
21. *The Tuskegee Airmen* (1995).

22. *Gods and Generals* (2003).
23. *M*A*S*H* (1970).
24. *Lawrence of Arabia* (1962).
25. *Gallipoli* (1981).

War Film Master Quiz #4:
NAME THE FILM

Below are twenty-five descriptions of films covered in this book. How many of them do you know?

1. Jürgen Prochnow appears in this film as a grizzled u-boat commander. What is this film?

2. Burgess Meredith plays a war correspondent assigned to Robert Mitchum's platoon. What is this film?

3. Henry Fonda tries to convince his superiors that the Germans are up to no good after he spots a Nazi officer played by Robert Shaw during a reconnaissance flight. What is this film?

4. Clint Eastwood leads a renegade mission to steal enemy gold. What is this film?

5. George Clooney leads a renegade mission to steal enemy gold. What is this film?

6. A fighter pilot played by William Holden has a hunch he's about to die on an upcoming mission. What is this film?

7. Steve McQueen plays an escaped prisoner of war on a motorcycle. What is this film?

8. Lee Marvin finds himself stranded on a desert island with Toshiro Mifune. What is this film?

9. This biopic begins with Vladimir Roudenko's character engaging in a snowball fight. What is this film?

10. Members of Ethan Hawke's platoon engage in a snowball fight against enemy soldiers. What is this film?

11. Stanley Kubrick shot the Vietnam War scenes for this film in England. What is this film?

12. Dennis Quaid is a member of the French Foreign Legion. What is this film?

13. John Wayne plays a character named Sgt. John Stryker who says "saddle up" throughout the film. What is this film?

14. Charlton Heston's son dates a Japanese woman during World War II. What is this film?

15. Frank Sinatra and other prisoners of war take to the rails. What is this film?

16. Burt Lancaster battles Nazis on the rails. What is this film?

17. Buster Keaton battles Union soldiers on the rails. What is this film?

18. Nicolas Cage is told to protect the code at all costs. What is this film?

19. Toshiro Mifune orders Slim Pickens to defecate a compass. What is this film?

20. Charlie Sheen is the protagonist and narrator. What is this film?

21. Martin Sheen is the protagonist and narrator. What is this film?

22. Gary Cooper plays a hillbilly who becomes a highly decorated war hero. What is this film?

23. Screenwriter Buck Henry also appears in this Mike Nichols film. What is this film?

24. Alec Baldwin gives several patriotic speeches that are unintentionally funny. What is this film?

25. Humphrey Bogart's crazed naval captain embarks on the "great key hunt." What is this film?

War Film Master Quiz #5:
PORTRAYALS

Each of the twenty-five questions in this quiz are about the actors who have portrayed famous leaders and warriors in war films. How many do you know?

1. Who portrays John F. Kennedy in *PT 109* (1963)?
2. Who portrays Franklin D. Roosevelt in *Pearl Harbor* (2001)?
3. Who portrays Theodore Roosevelt in *Rough Riders* (1997)?
4. Who portrays Gen. Dwight D. Eisenhower in *Ike: The War Years* (1978)?
5. Who portrays Gen. Dwight D. Eisenhower in *The Longest Day* (1962)?
6. Who portrays Gen. Douglas MacArthur in *They Were Expendable* (1945)?
7. Who portrays Gen. Douglas MacArthur in *MacArthur* (1977)?
8. Who portrays Gen. George S. Patton Jr. in *Is Paris Burning?* (1966)?
9. Who portrays Gen. George S. Patton Jr. in *Patton* (1970)?
10. Who portrays Gen. Omar Bradley in *Is Paris Burning?*
11. Who portrays Gen. Omar Bradley in *Patton*?
12. Who portrays Audie Murphy in *To Hell and Back* (1955)?
13. Who portrays Alvin C. York in *Sergeant York* (1941)?
14. Who portrays Field Marshal Erwin Rommel in *The Desert Fox* (1951)?
15. Who portrays Field Marshal Erwin Rommel in *Patton*?
16. Who portrays Field Marshal Erwin Rommel in *Raid on Rommel* (1971)?

17. Who portrays Field Marshal Erwin Rommel in *The Longest Day*?

18. Who portrays Field Marshal Erwin Rommel in *The Night of the Generals* (1966)?

19. Who portrays Field Marshal Erwin Rommel in *The Desert Rats* (1953)?

20. Who portrays Gen. George Armstrong Custer in *They Died with Their Boots On* (1941)?

21. Who portrays Gen. George Armstrong Custer in *Custer of the West* (1967)?

22. Who portrays Gen. George Armstrong Custer in *Little Big Man* (1970)?

23. Who portrays Gen. James Doolittle in *Thirty Seconds over Tokyo* (1944)?

24. Who portrays Gen. James Doolittle in *Pearl Harbor?*

25. Who portrays T. E. Lawrence in *A Dangerous Man: Lawrence After Arabia* (1990)?

ANSWERS

Quiz No. 1: All Quiet on the Western Front

1. Personal ambition. 2. He knocks him unconscious. 3. A confession. 4. James Whale. 5. Yellow Rat. 6. Behm. 7. George Cukor. 8. *Two Arabian Knights* (1927), *Tempest* (1928), and *The Racket* (1929). 9. Because he can't run away. 10. His leg, which has been amputated. 11. *New York Nights* (1929) and *The Captain Hates the Sea* (1934). 12. Being alive or dead. 13. Everything they've ever learned. 14. Zasu Pitts. 15. *The Front Page* (1931). 16. He is a postal worker. 17. Burning books. 18. Fred Zinneman. 19. Director Lewis Milestone's. 20. Women. 21. One war. 22. Behm. 23. Die. 24. Paul Baumer's. 25. He believes the Frenchman is better off because he is dead.

Quiz No. 2: Apocalypse Now

1. Zero. Brando refused to set foot on the same set as Hopper. Therefore, the scenes in which they were to appear together had to be filmed separately with the actors speaking to stand-ins. 2. Sheen's brother, Joe Estevez. 3. Roger Corman. 4. Because he's still alive. 5. New Orleans. 6. Francis Ford Coppola. 7. R. Lee Ermey. 8. *Hearts of Darkness: A Filmmaker's Apocalypse.* 9. The plan was to actually film the movie in Vietnam. Filming actors involved in real battles would have made the film look very realistic and also save money on special effects. 10. Vittorio Storaro. 11. *Eagle's Wing* (1979). 12. The mission to kill Kurtz. 13. *Apocalypse Now Redux.* 14. Lt. Col. Kilgore. 15. George Lucas. 16. Fourteen. 17. The edge of a razor blade. 18. Mr. Clean. 19. Cold rice and rat meat. 20. Human heads. 21. A puppy. 22. If. 23. *Gardens of Stone.* 24. *Free Money.* 25. *Reflections in a Golden Eye.*

Quiz No. 3: Band of Brothers

1. *Catch Me If You Can.* 2. Shifty. 3. *Saving Private Ryan.* 4. *A Tree Grows in Brooklyn.* 5. "It appears the Germans are bad. Very bad." 6. *Henry V.* 7. The Niagra. 8. Dale Dye. 9. Camp Toccoa. 10. Take from his men. 11. Nine. 12. Jimmy Fallon. 13. Because he was suffering a horrible hangover on the morning of his audition. 14. Capt. Lewis Nixon. 15. Urinate in his coffee. 16. Phil Alden Robinson. 17. "No. But I served in a company of heroes." 18. Roosevelt will change Thanksgiving to Joe Toye Day, and the government will pay him $10,000 annually for the rest of his life. 19. His left ankle. 20. Capt. Ronald Speirs. 21. The world. 22. *From the Earth to the Moon* (1998). 23. "[Y]ourself and the fella next to you." 24. Malarkey. 25. Nazi prisoners.

Quiz No. 4: Battleground

1. Denise. 2. At the art galleries. 3. He was a columnist for the *Sedalia News.* 4. *It's a Big Country* (1951). 5. Snow. 6. "That's fer sure, that's fer dang sure!" 7. Texas leaguer. 8. Holly. 9. The lieutenant is wearing his bars while on patrol in the woods. 10. Ernest "Pop" Stazak. 11. Albert Einstein's theory of relativity. 12. "The Battered Bastards of Bastogne." 13. Cognac. 14. Richard Jaeckel. 15. Stazak. 16. "[W]hen I climbed out in the morning I got the bends." 17. James Whitmore. 18. His false teeth. 19. "[Y]ou try to figure out why you acted the way you did." 20. Rodriguez. 21. "A good clean flesh wound." 22. *Across the Wide Missouri* (1951). 23. The feet must be discolored. 24. 102 degrees. 25. "Welcome to the 101st Airborne Division."

Quiz No. 5: The Battle of Algiers

1. *The Wide Blue Road* (1957) and *Kapo* (1959). 2. Philippe. 3. All three. 4. The reunification of Korea, disarmament, and the Algerian question. 5. Insurrection. 6. Medjebri. 7. Engineering. 8. Producer Yacef Saadi. 9. Because the bartender is Algerian. 10. Chopin Street. 11. Midnight. 12. Terrorism. 13. Front de Liberation Nationale. 14. Eighty thousand. 15. Eight. 16. Operation Champagne. 17. "Long live Algeria!" 18. *A Man and a Woman* (1966). 19. Three. 20. That they recognize the right of the people to self-government. 21. A gun. 22. "[I]ndependence was obtained." 23. Omar Ali. 24. "[O]ne that laughs and one that cries." 25. Corruption and brutality.

Quiz No. 6: Battle of the Bulge

1. Two. 2. A single tiger. 3. Dwight D. Eisenhower. 4. Philip Yordan. 5. Petrol. 6. *In Harm's Way* (1965). 7. William Conrad. 8. Karl-Otto Alberty. 9. Having been a police inspector. 10. Bargain basement. 11. They were all military police. 12. *Kelly's Heroes*. 13. *The Dirty Dozen* (1967). 14. At home in his bed. 15. Toys. 16. *Those Magnificent Men in Their Flying Machines* and *The Informers*. 17. Poor. 18. Delinquents. 19. To disrupt enemy communications. 20. "[T]he genius of the German people." 21. Serve under brilliant men. 22. "[W]hat you see." 23. Fifty. 24. His reputation with the ladies. 25. "[S]ittin' on your butt tryin' to keep warm."

Quiz No. 7: Beau Geste

1. *The Last Remake of Beau Geste*. 2. Beautiful gesture. 3. Michael. 4. Buttercup Valley. 5. The Blue Water. 6. *Beau Sabreur*. 7. Sgt. Markoff's. 8. A wooden jewel box. 9. Wellman had himself served in the French Foreign Legion. 10. Donald O'Connor. 11. Isobel. 12. Digby. 13. The sentry. 14. Sgt. Markoff. 15. One thousand. 16. "Escape" back into the desert. 17. Henry Hathaway. 18. *Variety Girl*. 19. That it "isn't good to plan them at the top of your voice." 20. For cruelty. 21. Beau and John. 22. A slit in his belly. 23. *The Legion of the Condemned*. 24. A mouse. 25. The men in his charge.

Quiz No. 8: The Big Parade

1. *His Hour* (1924) and *The Wife of the Centaur* (1924). 2. Jensen. 3. His hat. 4. Twenty miles. 5. Melisande. 6. *Proud Flesh*. 7. Bartender. 8. "[A] social success." 9. Shovel. 10. Slim. 11. Cake. 12. Jim Apperson. 13. A frog. 14. Flying Fritzie. 15. Idlers. 16. A barrel. 17. Justyn. 18. French. 19. Harry. 20. Saps. 21. Rivets. 22. Rookies. 23. The "fragrance of beautiful flowers." 24. "The goo and the muck." 25. Berlin.

Quiz No. 9: The Big Red One

1. Kaiser. 2. The Bangalore Torpedo. 3. Edward G. Robinson and Humphrey Bogart. 4. They were all played by Jews. 5. Four hours. 6. West Point. 7. Wetnoses. 8. Griff. 9. Tunis. 10. "[Y]ou always feel alone." 11. Six. 12. Bob Fosse's *All That Jazz* (1979) and Akira Kurosawa's *Kagemusha* (1980). 13. Zab. 14. Seven. 15. Waves, engines, the occasional muffled

prayer, and the sound of fifty guys heaving their guts out. 16. Marvin is the only Oscar-winning actor to be buried there. 17. Griff, Zab, Vinci, and Johnson. 18. Kill. 19. A bagel shop. 20. Horses. 21. *Sam Fuller and the Big Red One*. 22. *Shark!* (1970). 23. The USS *Savanna*. 24. The St. George Hotel. 25. *The Meanest Men in the West* (1967).

Quiz No. 10: Black Hawk Down

1. Director Ridley Scott's mother, who died while the film was in post-production. 2. "Suspicious Minds." 3. A photograph of his wife and child. 4. Nineteen. 5. Josh Hartnett, Tom Sizemore, Ewen Bremner, William Fichtner, and Kim Coates. 6. "Help, or we can sit back and watch a country destroy itself on CNN." 7. *The Client*. 8. Killing. 9. Nothing. 10. Simon West. 11. Dependable. 12. Limo. 13. Coffee. 14. The Mog. 15. Taping his blood type to his boot and writing a "death letter." 16. Peace. 17. Steven Zaillian. 18. *Money for Nothing*. 19. That he fought well and that he fought hard. 20. "[S]hit and French fries." 21. *Hannibal* (2001). 22. "Fragile." 23. *Gladiator* (2000). 24. Genocide. 25. A United Nations tank.

Quiz No. 11: The Boys in Company C

1. R. Lee Ermey. 2. An AK-47 Assault Rifle. 3. James Whitmore Jr., whose father is, of course, James Whitmore. 4. "Cause navy nurses suck our cocks." 5. Washington. 6. Body bags. 7. Soccer. 8. Washington. 9. Yale. 10. Pike. 11. Fabrizio. 12. All of them. 13. Sea duty. 14. *Purple Hearts*. 15. Be smart enough to pull the trigger. 16. Murder another human being. 17. Listen to their drill sergeants. 18. Bisbee. 19. Basic infantryman. 20. "[B]ecause your ass is mine." 21. A body bag. 22. Because Fazio attempted to sleep with his daughter. 23. Two. 24. Toilet paper. 25. A baby.

Quiz No. 12: Braveheart

1. The French and the Romans. 2. Seventeen. 3. "Those who have hanged heroes." 4. Malcolm. 5. True. 6. Isabelle. 7. "[H]e's pretty sure you're fucked." 8. Uncompromising men. 9. Talk to God. 10. Murron. 11. *Prima nocta*. 12. *The Man Without a Face* (1993). 13. The nobles. 14. In his arm. 15. A man. 16. Face him in person. 17. McGoohan won Emmys in 1975 and 1990 for his appearances in *Columbo: By Dawn's Early Light* (1974) and *Columbo: Agenda for Murder* (1990). 18. The bridge. 19. Terry

Gilliam. 20. Philip. 21. It's filled with Scots. 22. It was in Latin. 23. Seven feet tall. 24. His head. 25. Their freedom.

Quiz No. 13: Breaker Morant

1. The sacrifice of the three Australians. 2. His wife and son. 3. Eight. 4. *King David* and *Mister Johnson*. 5. "And a man's foes shall be they of his own household." 6. Lord Byron. 7. The execution of his murderers. 8. Lie straight. 9. Sunday. 10. He was a horse breaker prior to joining the military. 11. Life imprisonment. 12. *Tender Mercies* (1983). 13. Immortality. 14. He shot a Boer in self-defense. 15. "[T]o kill as many of the enemy as possible." 16. *The Equalizer.* 17. Zero. 18. "[T]hey tell the story of Breaker Morant." 19. "Shoot straight, you bastards! Don't make a mess of it!" 20. It was April Fool's Day. 21. Zero. 22. Hadcock. 23. Because "one day you're sure to be right." 24. Alvin Sargent for *Ordinary People* (1980). 25. Civilian rules.

Quiz No. 14: The Bridge at Remagen

1. Only one; Robert Vaughn is the only American cast as a Nazi. 2. "About two hundred." 3. Sgt. Angelo. 4. *The Wild Bunch.* 5. Cecil E. Roberts. 6. The Obercassel Bridge. 7. Maj. Barnes. 8. Capt. Colt. 9. While the crew was on location filming in Czechoslovakia, the Soviet army invaded the country. 10. He's approximately twelve years old. 11. His gold cigarette case. 12. This was the first American film to be shot in the country. 13. Loose tongues. 14. Ben Gazzara. 15. *The Young Doctors* (1961). 16. For leaving his post. 17. Two panzer battalions. 18. A deathtrap. 19. Angel. 20. Female companionship. 21. *Sheena.* 22. Hartman looking back at him through binoculars. 23. The East German press. 24. Inside a railway tunnel. 25. Italy.

Quiz No. 15: The Bridge on the River Kwai

1. *The Prince and the Showgirl* (1957), which he directed. 2. To attempt an escape. 3. Living like a human being. 4. Michael Wilson and Carl Foreman were blacklisted at the time, and producer Sam Spiegel simply chose not to credit David Lean. 5. Kim Novak. 6. Kill himself. 7. Philip John Denton Tootsey. 8. Ceylon. 9. *Return from the River Kwai* (1988). 10. Because officers are entitled to better treatment than enlisted men as prisoners of war. 11. "Guiness." 12. *King Rat.* 13. *Lawrence of Arabia* (1962). 14. Major. 15. A

grave marker. 16. Approximately ten months. 17. Demoralization and chaos. 18. He died. 19. Red Buttons for *Sayonara* (1957). 20. Zero. 21. Charles Laughton. 22. Saito. 23. He didn't believe he would win. 24. Calder Willingham. 25. *The Wind Cannot Read*, which was later directed by Ralph Thomas.

Quiz No. 16: The Bridges at Toko-Ri

1. *Men of the Fighting Lady.* 2. To back down quickly when arguing for something he believes is right. 3. Women. 4. Dennis Weaver. 5. $80. 6. Nancy. 7. To the U.S. Navy and "especially to the men of the Naval Air and Surface Forces of the Pacific fleet." 8. *Citizen Kane* (1941). 9. "[P]ut'sir' at the end of it." 10. Twenty. 11. Denver, Colorado. 12. Cathy and Susie. 13. Four. 14. Nestor Gamidge. 15. His pistol. 16. George. 17. "Where do we get such men?" 18. Because it gets caught on his seat. 19. *The Country Girl.* 20. Because his doctor won't let him. 21. His green leprechaun hat. 22. An irrigation ditch. 23. He's a lawyer. 24. That his wife and children are waiting for him in Tokyo. 25. *Executive Suite.*

Quiz No. 17: A Bridge Too Far

1. "Tell them to go to hell." 2. "I got divorced twice. Does that count?" 3. The bridges. 4. Mental patients from a nearby asylum. 5. Berets. 6. Operation Market Garden. 7. An umbrella. 8. Polish. 9. Liv Ullman. 10. Four. 11. *Butch Cassidy and the Sundance Kid* (1969), *The Hot Rock* (1972), *The Great Waldo Pepper* (1975), and *All the President's Men* (1976). 12. Their rifles. 13. *Magic* (1978) and *Chaplin* (1992). 14. Yugoslavia. 15. They are too lightly equipped to do so. 16. Air sickness. 17. George Washington. 18. Living and dying. 19. John Ratzenberger. 20. Capture him. 21. "God bless Field Marshal Montgomery." 22. *Young Winston* (1972), *Magic, Chaplin,* and *Shadowlands* (1993). 23. Just under eight. 24. *Cross of Iron.* 25. Because they were delivered with the wrong crystals.

Quiz No. 18: The Caine Mutiny

1. "As big as the ocean." 2. Lt. Steve Maryk, Lt. Tom Keefer, and Ens. Willis Keith. 3. Maryk. 4. "The right way, the wrong way, the navy way, and my way." 5. "Yeah, so was Captain Bligh." 6. A wristwatch. 7. "The Yellow Stain Blues." 8. Richard Widmark. 9. "[S]he was designed by geniuses to be run by idiots." 10. Brad Davis. 11. Keefer. 12. Princeton. 13. Hickey later changed

her name to that of her character, May Wynn. 14. His mother. 15. Strawberries. 16. *On the Waterfront* (1954). 17. There has never been a mutiny aboard a U.S. Navy vessel. 18. Military orders. 19. Keefer. 20. *Broken Lance.* 21. Clues. 22. Never losing an argument onboard his ship. 23. One. 24. Horrible. 25. "[S]weep a single mine."

Quiz No. 19: Casualties of War

1. Methodist. 2. Eriksson. 3. *The New Yorker.* 4. Meserve. 5. His tour of duty is almost finished. 6. A Vietnamese girl. 7. Rest and relaxation. 8. Cherry. 9. Clark. 10. *Reservoir Dogs.* 11. Two Creeks, Texas. 12. He is twenty years old. 13. "[A] sack of monkey shit." 14. "I'm sorry." 15. *Carlito's Way* (1993). 16. Thirty. 17. Meserve. 18. *The Thin Red Line* (1998). 19. Corporal. 20. Diaz. 21. She coughs. 22. Clark. 23. Brownie. 24. Soldiers don't care about anything. 25. Eriksson.

Quiz No. 20: Catch-22

1. Aetheism. 2. Hungry Joe. 3. Snowden. 4. Col. Cathcart. 5. Malta. 6. Sweden. 7. A head cold. 8. M&M Enterprises. 9. "I don't wanna." 10. *The Graduate* (1967) and *The Day of the Dolphin* (1973). 11. He must agree to like them. 12. Supernatural episodes. 13. George C. Scott. 14. Nately. 15. Chocolate-covered cotton. 16. Milo. 17. *Dirty Dingus Magee* (1970). 18. Because it's after curfew. 19. For moaning. 20. Nately. 21. He was sucked out of the airplane during the bombing scene. 22. Dying on your feet. 23. *Hell Is for Heroes.* 24. Because she's not a virgin. 25. Orr.

Quiz No. 21: The Charge of the Light Brigade

1. He was a member of a British commando unit during World War II. 2. Disagreements. 3. Benji. 4. 150 pounds. 5. Another pill. 6. *Anthony Adverse.* 7. His brother Perry. 8. "[G]iving me pills and scandalous intrigue." 9. A small man. 10. Other people. 11. "[A]bout the first forty years." 12. The Chukoti massacre. 13. *The Adventures of Robin Hood, Four's a Crowd,* and *The Sisters.* 14. Friends and foes. 15. The entire British army. 16. *Bring on the Empty Horses.* 17. *The Roots of Heaven* (1958). 18. Geoffrey. 19. Geoffrey. 20. His life. 21. Reptiles. 22. *The Dawn Patrol* (1938). 23. A handshake. 24. Silence. 25. "They show you a brief glimpse of paradise and then they take it away."

Quiz No. 22: Cross of Iron

1. "You shoot him, Sir." 2. Engaging in homosexual activity. 3. 65 percent. 4. "[T]he myth of Russian invincibility." 5. Richard Burton. 6. "Long live Germany." 7. Paris. 8. Stealing the laurels of a man who has been killed in battle. 9. *The Desert Fox* (1951) and *The Desert Rats* (1953). 10. Orson Welles. 11. Steiner and Triebig. 12. Waterproof. 13. The Iron Cross. 14. Rays of sunlight. 15. "[T]hat God is a sadist . . . and he probably doesn't even know it." 16. Demarcation. 17. Steiner. 18. Her waist. 19. Six. 20. His harmonica. 21. His health. 22. *Casablanca* (1942). 23. "Prepare for the next one." 24. The war. 25. Running.

Quiz No. 23: Das Boot

1. Thirty thousand. 2. Johann. 3. Don Siegel. 4. It is destroyed by an air raid. 5. Winston Churchill. 6. 280. 7. *Air Force One*. 8. Sex. 9. Thomsen's being awarded the Iron Cross. 10. That it would be impossible to break through. 11. 230 meters. 12. *Stalingrad*. 13. *The Perfect Storm*. 14. A belief in the Fuhrer. 15. Johann. 16. Chief. 17. Naval war correspondent Lt. Werner. 18. *The Boat*. 19. French. 20. They will have beards. 21. They urinated on him. 22. In the casino. 23. A submarine. 24. The Weser. 25. One.

Quiz No. 24: The Devil's Brigade

1. *Picnic* (1955). 2. *Hogan's Heroes* and *Stalag 17* (1952). 3. "We keep it." 4. Thirty-five. 5. One version provides subtitles and the other does not. 6. Snakes. 7. Rope burns. 8. *Charly* (1968). 9. Rockman. 10. They were members of the Utah National Guard. 11. Treason. 12. The Devil's Brigade. 13. Not to assume the "role of almighty God." 14. Ft. William Henry Harrison. 15. Troublemakers. 16. The piano. 17. Frederick. 18. Fifty. 19. Nine. 20. Two weeks. 21. Pvt. Greco. 22. Remove the cigar from his mouth. 23. The real-life Devil's Brigade. 24. Pvt. Billy "Bronc" Guthrie. 25. Capt. Quill.

Quiz No. 25: The Dirty Dozen

1. *Kelly's Heroes* (1970). 2. Discipline. 3. Maggott. 4. *The Dirty Dozen: The Next Mission*. 5. Drill. 6. Wladislaw and Jefferson. 7. Project Amnesty. 8. A bottle of ink. 9. D-12. 10. Take care of himself. 11. The Visiting Forces Act.

12. John Wayne. 13. The world. 14. *Attack* (1956). 15. Jimenez. 16. Thirty. 17. Cold water. 18. "Just act mean and grunt." 19. Wladislaw. 20. *Faces* (1968). 21. The Marston-Tyne Military Prison. 22. "You let somebody see you do it." 23. Maggott. 24. He is hanged. 25. Archer.

Quiz No. 26: Enemy at the Gates

1. Time. 2. A piece of glass. 3. *Enemy at the Gates: The Battle for Stalingrad.* 4. His cap. 5. "I'll fix it so that he's the one who finds me." 6. "[T]hat the Germans are starting to shit their pants!" 7. Sacha. 8. A wolf. 9. Because Khruschev has ordered him to make sure nothing happens to him. 10. His son. 11. "[B]alls." 12. Heroes. 13. Potatoes and bacon. 14. The hunter. 15. "Because I haven't killed him yet." 16. She is shot in the head by Konig. 17. Joseph Stalin. 18. *Nixon.* 19. Konig. 20. To a factory. 21. German. 22. *Pollock* (2000), which he also directed. 23. *Stealing Beauty* (1996). 24. To survive. 25. Stalin.

Quiz No. 27: The Fighting Seabees

1. "I love you." 2. Water. 3. The Civil Engineer Corps and the Construction Battalions. 4. That she's Robert Yarrow's girlfriend. 5. Three. 6. A gentleman. 7. Cannibals. 8. "Yeah, your lipstick's on crooked." 9. Donovan. 10. Friday. 11. William Frawley. 12. Hopes, dreams, and illusions. 13. Going home wearing nothing but a hat. 14. *Reap the Wild Wind* (1942) and *The Conqueror* (1956). 15. Brooklyn. 16. Fifty-fifty. 17. *Wake of the Red Witch* (1948) and *Big Jim McLain* (1952). 18. Not drinking. 19. Denny Ryan. 20. Thirty. 21. Animals. 22. Cigarettes. 23. Made at least one mistake and lived. 24. Waiting. 25. A "user of big words."

Quiz No. 28: Flying Tigers

1. $500. 2. Termites. 3. Rice cakes. 4. The belongings of dead pilots. 5. That Dale's dead. 6. *Pittsburgh.* 7. Blackie. 8. Pappy. 9. Nowhere. 10. Hap. 11. Woody. 12. A chicken ranch. 13. Gin Rummy. 14. "Sorry, I never get quite *that* hungry." 15. Zero; he has no ammunition. 16. Headquarters. 17. *Flying Leathernecks* (1951). 18. The Hotel Continental. 19. Return it to the factory. 20. Bales. 21. A pilot's not being able to fly any longer. 22. He dies on December 7, 1941, which is the day Pearl Harbor was bombed. 23. Confucius. 24. Thursday. 25. Jason.

Quiz No. 29: Full Metal Jacket

1. Pvt. J.T. Davis. 2. *The Short Timers*. 3. *Dispatches*. 4. Anthony Michael Hall. 5. Chaplain services. 6. Lawrence. 7. Texas. 8. Stanley Kubrick's daughter, Vivian Kubrick. 9. *The Boys in Company C.* 10. *Memphis Belle* (1990). 11. Sir. 12. A jelly doughnut. 13. Pvt. Joker. 14. "[N]ot having anyone around that's worth shooting." 15. Pvt. Snowball. 16. *The Salton Sea* (2002). 17. That it's better to be alive. 18. A marine and his rifle. 19. "[B]ecause we kill everything we see." 20. His BDU cap. 21. "Me So Horny." 22. Thirty seconds. 23. That he had stolen hundreds of library books. 24. "[I]t sucks." 25. "Full Metal Jacket."

Quiz No. 30: Gallipoli

1. Waste a bullet on Frank. 2. *The Year of Living Dangerously* (1982). 3. "Life is cheap here and the women have no respect for themselves." 4. Eighteen. 5. Hamilton. 6. Three. 7. Friends ("mates") splitting up. 8. Twenty quid. 9. *Attack Force Z* (1982). 10. Box. 11. Doc Morgan. 12. A cookbook. 13. That he's always cheerful. 14. The pyramids. 15. *The Jungle Book*. 16. The Melbourne Horse Cadets. 17. "[T]hat you and I are different." 18. A leopard. 19. *The Road Warrior* (1981). 20. *The Chain Reaction*. 21. "[A]bout an hour before every battle." 22. 9.5 seconds. 23. His diary. 24. Shark attack. 25. "See ya when I see ya."

Quiz No. 31: The General

1. Oregon. 2. Nine a.m. 3. Annabelle's father, Mr. Lee. 4. Because Johnnie is still wearing the uniform of a Union soldier. 5. Rock River Bridge. 6. *The Great Locomotive Chase*. 7. A rifle. 8. Big Shanty. 9. Ten. 10. His engine and Annabelle. 11. As he had done throughout his career, Keaton performed all of his own stunts. 12. The baggage car. 13. His saber. 14. Johnnie standing beside his engine. 15. Love, locomotives, and laughs. 16. A chain. 17. Gen. Thatcher. 18. William Brown. 19. These troops were comprised of members of the Oregon National Guard. 20. Telegraph lines. 21. By getting caught in a bear trap. 22. Joe was Buster's father. 23. *The General* was their only collaboration. 24. Five. 25. Because it's decided that he's more valuable to the South as an engineer.

Quiz No. 32: Gettysburg

1. Charles Darwin's theory of evolution. 2. Gen. Ewell. 3. Maj. Gen. Hancock. 4. *Apocalypse Now*. 5. Ken Burns. 6. Thespian. 7. *The Killer*

Angels. 8. Laurence. 9. The fat man. 10. To conduct a defensive campaign wherever possible. 11. Elmira Hancock. 12. The term refers to a runaway slave. 13. Retreat. 14. Ted Turner. 15. Pettigrew's book. 16. George Lazenby. 17. A race. 18. He was a college instructor. 19. Maine. 20. Victory. 21. Longstreet. 22. *Rough Riders.* 23. Being outnumbered. 24. Justice. 25. "See you in hell."

Quiz No. 33: Glory

1. Thomas Searles. 2. He was looking for new shoes. 3. $10. 4. Trip. 5. The quartermaster. 6. Searles. 7. Rawlins. 8. *Courage Under Fire* (1996). 9. Screenwriter Kevin Jarre. 10. Searles. 11. Fort Wagner. 12. Trip. 13. He is originally from Kentucky, but later relocated to Kansas. 14. Jupiter. 15. "Stripes on a nigger." 16. That he won't send him home. 17. *The True Story of Glory Continues* (1991). 18. The Irish. 19. Morgan Freeman. 20. Matthew Broderick's character, Shaw, is the only one based on a real soldier. 21. He is beaten with a whip. 22. Slaves. 23. Searles. 24. Snowflake. 25. A "negro."

Quiz No. 34: Good Morning, Vietnam

1. Robin Williams improvised them in their entirety. 2. *Good Morning, Chicago.* 3. *Beach Blanket Bingo* (1965). 4. Guam. 5. Large, medium, and Caucasian. 6. Queens. 7. *Readers Digest.* 8. Capt. Noel. 9. Dan "the Man" Levitan. 10. Scenes featuring Adrian Cronauer in fatigues were shot especially for the trailer to give the film more military appeal. 11. Walter Brennan. 12. Tonto. 13. The U.S. Air Force. 14. Pat Boone. 15. Frank Sinatra. 16. Wisconsin. 17. His buttocks. 18. Hauk. 19. Monday. 20. Pope-on-a-rope. 21. Receive fan mail. 22. Forest Whitaker. 23. Richard Nixon. 24. Zorba the Greek. 25. "They are full of shit."

Quiz No. 35: Grand Illusion

1. He might never leave. 2. An armchair, playing cards, books, and English cigarettes. 3. Crawling. 4. Fifi. 5. The soldiers play like children. 6. The flute. 7. Twelve. 8. It was the first foreign language film to be nominated. 9. Because they smell. 10. Outside the window in a gutter. 11. Hide their valuables. 12. *The Lower Depths* (1936). 13. "[S]hit." 14. Boldieu. 15. "Let's not talk about it." 16. That the man is suffocating. 17. Because much of his

body—including his hands—was badly burned. 18. Erich von Stroheim. 19. Their skirts and their hair. 20. Pride. 21. Cognac. 22. French regulations. 23. Cancer and gout. 24. Sentiment. 25. Von Rauffenstein.

Quiz No. 36: The Great Escape

1. *King Rat* (1965). 2. Bartlett. 3. *The Great Escape II: The Untold Story.* 4. *The Magnificent Seven* (1960). 5. The woods. 6. He had been held in a German camp during World War II. 7. Danny Willenski. 8. Chemical engineering. 9. Sedgewick. 10. Hilts. 11. Tom, Dick, and Harry. 12. Zero. 13. Wally Floody. 14. *Hard Times.* 15. Hendley. 16. Spain. 17. The Cooler King. 18. *The Satan Bug* (1965). 19. Uncivilized. 20. Richard Attenborough. 21. So the guards won't want to move it. 22. Steve McQueen. 23. Hendley and Blythe. 24. Fifty. 25. "I'm a lifeguard."

Quiz No. 37: Guadalcanal Diary

1. Chicken. 2. Half tobacco and half stinkweed. 3. Fullback. 4. "Marguerita." 5. Aloysius Potts. 6. *Roger Touhy, Gangster* (1944). 7. *Sergeant York.* 8. Jesus Alvarez. 9. His helmet. 10. The high grass of the Solomon Islands. 11. A photograph of his wife and children. 12. Richard Jaeckel. 13. "The Jap." 14. Cross was Davis's teacher. 15. Grenades. 16. Brooklyn. 17. The memory of death. 18. He was a taxi cab driver. 19. *The Ox-Bow Incident* (1943). 20. "[S]hooting the breeze." 21. A samurai sword. 22. *The Milky Way.* 23. Reed Hadley. 24. A single whisker. 25. "I'm starting right now."

Quiz No. 38: The Guns of Navarone

1. Euthanasia. 2. *Force 10 from Navarone.* 3. James Robertson Justice, who also appears in the film as Commo. Jensen. 4. Capt. Keith Mallory. 5. David Niven. 6. The Butcher of Barcelona. 7. *West Side Story* (1961), which was directed by Robert Wise. 8. The gangrene in his leg. 9. That the landing will be the following night. 10. Maria Pappadimos. 11. A soldier. 12. *The Sea Wolves.* 13. The Human Fly. 14. Franklin. 15. Miller's. 16. "[A] well-organized setup." 17. Because they are not in uniform. 18. Stavros. 19. Brandy. 20. Maj. Franklin. 21. Zero. 22. Maria. 23. Cpl. Miller. 24. David Niven. 25. Spyro Pappadimos.

Quiz No. 39: Hamburger Hill

1. Eleven. 2. Area of operations. 3. Taking the hill. 4. Fuckin' new guy. 5. The American soldiers serving in Vietnam. 6. Gaigin. 7. Kick his ass. 8. "[P]ut a poncho over your head." 9. Motown. 10. *When Trumpets Fade.* 11. Infantrymen. 12. Maj. Michael Davis O'Donnell. 13. *Heartbreak Ridge* (1986). 14. Alphabet. 15. May 20, 1969. 16. A "hair-head." 17. A "round-eye" is an American woman. 18. Frantz's. 19. Armored underwear. 20. "Niggers." 21. "Welcome to Hamburger Hill." 22. Claire. 23. *The Tuskegee Airmen.* 24. Fry it. 25. "[A]nother nigger with a limp."

Quiz No. 40: Heartbreak Ridge

1. Nothing. 2. Pass through a metal detector. 3. Johanson. 4. "Handful of pussy and a mouth full of ass." 5. The Palace. 6. It was actually taken by U.S. Army Rangers, not by marines. 7. The AK-47 Assault Rifle. 8. The Congressional Medal of Honor. 9. Mario Van Peebles. 10. "[A] good case of hemorrhoids." 11. "[T]o assure he does it in an orderly proficient military manner." 12. A stereo. 13. "It's a clusterfuck." 14. Joseph Stinson. 15. Bo Svenson. 16. Live forever. 17. *The Road Warrior.* 18. Three. 19. "Heartbreak Ridge." 20. Making love and music. 21. In jail. 22. Faggetti. 23. "Break only in the event of war." 24. Marriage. 25. His beer.

Quiz No. 41: Hell in the Pacific

1. At the end of the Japanese version, the two men walk off the screen in separate directions. 2. Fresh water. 3. The American pilot's life raft. 4. *Enemy Mine.* 5. The American. 6. Japan's. 7. So the American can no longer stare at him. 8. God. 9. Live rounds of ammunition. 10. He discovers his flight cap and goggles. 11. A knife. 12. A butterfly. 13. A dog. 14. Sake. 15. *Life* magazine. 16. The Palau Islands. 17. Destroy them immediately. 18. His fishing basket. 19. First his knife and then his cup. 20. The flute. 21. "My log!" 22. Photographs of dead Japanese soldiers in the magazine. 23. Tennessee. 24. Fishing. 25. The American pilot is urinating on him.

Quiz No. 42: Hell Is for Heroes

1. J.J. 2. North Africa. 3. Cobbler. 4. *The Magnificent Seven* (1960) and *The Great Escape* (1963). 5. Two. 6. *Road to Morocco* (1942). 7. One hundred. 8. Bob Newhart. 9. $8.50. 10. Three. 11. "[H]is basic nature." 12. James. 13. *Battle Cry.* 14. Because he gets seasick. 15. Squaring off against Reese. 16. Driscoll. 17. Ten. 18. Type. 19. Forty minutes. 20. Brandy. 21. Being observant. 22. "I'll blow your head off." 23. Nick Adams. 24. Trouble. 25. Take his head off.

Quiz No. 43: The Horse Soldiers

1. Hoppy. 2. The death of stuntman Fred Kennedy. 3. Martin Rackin. 4. Pride. 5. To write his mother a letter. 6. "[W]here only the great ones dare to go." 7. Andersonville. 8. That he's an "official" taster. 9. *The Alamo* (1960). 10. The reputation of his profession. 11. He was a railroad engineer. 12. Althea Gibson. 13. *Rio Bravo.* 14. To sober him up. 15. Doctors had misdiagnosed his wife, leading to her death. 16. Digging the latrines downstream. 17. Spies. 18. Female. 19. "[T]o get as many of these men back alive as I can." 20. Tree moss. 21. Col. Benjamin Grierson. 22. "[S]pank him." 23. Insubordination. 24. *How the West Was Won.* 25. Salt.

Quiz No. 44: In Harm's Way

1. Ens. Jeremiah Torrey. 2. Lt. Cmdr. William McConnell. 3. *Operation Pacific* (1951). 4. Marrying actresses. 5. Naval aviation. 6. Journalism. 7. CPO Culpepper. 8. Thirty. 9. *Cast a Giant Shadow* (1966) and *The War Wagon* (1967). 10. Operation Skyhook. 11. *Midway.* 12. Liz. 13. McConnell. 14. His right arm is broken. 15. Rockwell Torrey. 16. Nine. 17. Just after filming wrapped, Wayne learned that the cough was caused by cancer. 18. Six. 19. "[A] bunch of pig tracks." 20. Screenwriter. 21. Four. 22. She broke her ankle when she accidentally kicked it. 23. She is killed in a head-on collision with a truck. 24. John Paul Jones. 25. Powell.

Quiz No. 45: Is Paris Burning?

1. One. 2. "They are announcing our funeral." 3. Because they don't want to give their position away. 4. The entire block where the shot was fired is to be destroyed. 5. *A Man for All Seasons.* 6. Von Cholitz. 7. Brandy. 8. Gen.

Leclerc, Maj. Gallois, and himself. 9. To destroy the German army. 10. He was arrested. 11. A giant mortar capable of destroying an entire city block. 12. *Fanny* (1961) and *A Very Special Favor* (1965). 13. Trout. 14. Swedish consul. 15. "[F]eeding four million Parisians." 16. *Patton* (1970). 17. The people of Paris. 18. Leclerc. 19. "Because he is insane." 20. Time. 21. Traitors. 22. If the resistance is able to convince Gen. DeGault to come to their aid. 23. They will all be executed. 24. Tourists. 25. They are arrested by the Gestapo and executed.

Quiz No. 46: Kelly's Heroes

1. Paris. 2. Yugoslavia. 3. Because "their husbands carry guns." 4. Donald Sutherland. 5. A medal. 6. *Space Cowboys* (2000). 7. Mike Curb. 8. "[T]hreats against the captain's life, or any more rumors about going down to headquarters and assassinating the general, or raping the nurses at the field hospital." 9. "[D]amn near won a war." 10. Letting them shoot holes in him. 11. "Never stick your neck out for nobody." 12. Claremont. 13. Communicate. 14. Terry Savalas's brother, George Savalas. 15. Three. 16. *The Warriors.* 17. Crapgame. 18. John Landis. 19. Hank Williams Jr. 20. *Where Eagles Dare* (1968). 21. Moriarty. 22. Because he attacked the wrong hill and wiped out "half a company of GIs." 23. It's American. 24. Moriarty's. 25. A Sherman tank.

Quiz No. 47: King Rat

1. A chicken. 2. Squadron Leader Vexley. 3. Novelist James Clavell's. 4. Max. 5. Survival. 6. *Doctor Zhivago* (1965). 7. He's greedy. 8. "He can heal." 9. A fallen tree is rolled over it. 10. "Well, you could say I'm a genius." 11. His dog. 12. Marlowe's gangrene-infected arm. 13. "When do I have to kiss thee on the ass?" 14. Bury them. 15. Stealing rations. 16. A wireless radio. 17. Officers. 18. Grey. 19. The "Changi Blues." 20. One of the Japanese guards (Torasumi). 21. Existed. 22. Dog. 23. "Ceremonial death." 24. Richard Dawson. 25. His first offer is $20, but he then offers $30.

Quiz No. 48: The Last of the Mohicans

1. Chingachgook. 2. Respect and friendship. 3. Duncan. 4. "Only when it's covered in blood." 5. Sedition. 6. Randolph Scott. 7. Dale Dye. 8. Col. Munro. 9. Chingachgook. 10. War. 11. Himself. 12. Nathaniel "Natty"

Bumpo. 13. His own. 14. Alice Munro. 15. "The whole world." 16. Pete Postlethwaite. 17. Dunne was responsible for writing the original 1962 script, which inspired the screenplay for this film. 18. Fort William Henry. 19. Poison. 20. She leaps from a cliff to her death. 21. "A British officer afraid to support another." 22. His women. 23. Because she has become infatuated with him. 24. North Carolina. 25. To spare him the agony of being burned alive.

Quiz No. 49: Lawrence of Arabia

1. Fred. 2. Desolate places. 3. Michael Wilson. 4. Marlon Brando. 5. Cary Grant. 6. Passionate. 7. Lewis Milestone. 8. His nose. 9. Noel Howard and Andre De Toth. 10. Explosives and machines. 11. Director David Lean. 12. A miracle. 13. Katharine Hepburn. 14. Ralph Fiennes. 15. In Damascus. 16. Zero. 17. In Cairo. 18. Not minding that it hurts. 19. That they are one in the same. 20. Lion tamers. 21. Gregory Peck for *To Kill a Mockingbird* (1962). 22. The compassionate. 23. Big things. 24. Seventy-five. 25. "He was the most extraordinary man I ever knew."

Quiz No. 50: The Longest Day

1. Hell. 2. "[T]hose that are already dead and those that are gonna die." 3. *How the West Was Won*. 4. Rubber dummmies. 5. At Calais. 6. *El Dorado* (1967). 7. Champagne. 8. Sean Connery, of course, played James Bond in a string of films beginning with *Dr. No* (1962). Frobe and Jurgens played Bond villains. Frobe appears as Auric Goldfinger in *Goldfinger* (1964) and Jurgens appears as Karl Stromberg in *The Spy Who Loved Me* (1977). 9. Because his father was president of the United States. 10. His shoes are on the wrong feet. 11. "Anything mechanical, give it a good bash." 12. "[T]he way we keep on getting fewer." 13. Zero. 14. Millin is the man who actually did this during the invasion at Normandy. 15. The "final victory." 16. His "communion set." 17. They've always attacked in perfect weather conditions and they've always attacked at dawn. 18. Gerd Oswald. 19. They felt he looked too old to appear as himself circa World War II. 20. A clicking device known as a "cricket" that is to be used to distinguish enemy soldiers from Allied soldiers in the darkness. 21. Winston. 22. A bottle of cognac. 23. Peter Lawford. 24. Fire on their homeland. 25. Paul Anka, who also appears in the film.

Quiz No. 51: M*A*S*H

1. *The Glory Brigade* was released in 1953. *M*A*S*H* takes place in 1952. 2. Zero. 3. Jawbreaker and Painless. 4. Walter O'Reilly. 5. "M-U-S-H." 6. "He was drafted." 7. "[A] damn." 8. Three. 9. O'Reilly, who was played by Gary Burghoff. 10. Brig. Gen. Charlie Hammond. 11. The army. 12. The men showing disrespect to Frank Burns. 13. Andy Sidaris. 14. Benjamin Franklin Pierce. 15. Army morale. 16. Carl Gottlieb. 17. *M*A*S*H, Trapper John, M.D., After M*A*S*H,* and *W*A*L*T*E*R.* 18. Generals. 19. Actor McLean Stevenson, who played Lt. Col. Henry Blake on the television series, died from a heart attack. Roger Bowen, the actor who appears as Blake in the film, died from a heart attack the following day. 20. Dago Red. 21. Having no olives for his martini. 22. Augustus Bedford Forrest. 23. The Kansas City Chiefs. 24. Blondes. 25. Sex.

Quiz No. 52: Merrill's Marauders

1. Blood poisoning. 2. Quarterback. 3. In Quebec. 4. The aptly named Chowhound. 5. Fight. 6. The enemy. 7. "One million Japanese joining forces with the German army." 8. Taggy. 9. Wilson was a member of the real-life Merrill's Marauders. 10. Sneaking three thousand men through the jungle. 11. Eleanor. 12. It is never given in the film. 13. January 4, 1944. 14. Make one foot move out in front of the other. 15. O'Brien's father. 16. Hungry. 17. The Philippines. 18. His chow. 19. The men in his charge. 20. Tokyo. 21. Stockton punches him in the face. 22. No one. 23. A general. 24. Frank. 25. Kolowicz.

Quiz No. 53: A Midnight Clear

1. Mother. 2. Kill Germans. 3. Camp Shelby. 4. Twelve. 5. Janice. 6. Shutzer. 7. Eddie. 8. John C. McGinley. 9. "Fuck Hitler!" 10. The death of his child. 11. An asshole. 12. Because he's Jewish. 13. He was a mortician. 14. He hangs it on the Christmas tree. 15. *Birdy.* 16. Love. 17. Vance Wilkins. 18. That there is to be no cursing. 19. *Dad* (1989). 20. A snowball fight. 21. Trenchfoot. 22. Dancing. 23. The scope and the map. 24. *Platoon* (1986). 25. Bronowski.

Quiz No. 54: Midway

1. "Were we better than the Japanese, or just luckier?" 2. *In Harm's Way.* 3. *Away All Boats.* 4. William Wellman Jr. 5. Identifying the enemy. 6. RAdm. Raymond Spruance. 7. *The Longest Day.* 8. Winston Churchill. 9. Capt. Maddox. 10. Turning around and heading home. 11. Zero. 12. *The Battle of Midway.* 13. Because they're armed with torpedoes, not bombs. 14. Paul Frees. 15. Bull. 16. Doolittle's raid on Tokyo. 17. The *Yamamato.* 18. "Sweating it out." 19. *Tora! Tora! Tora!* 20. In the Coral Sea. 21. *Returning Home* (1975). 22. Chili Bean. 23. A birthday. 24. Strawberries. 25. Haruko.

Quiz No. 55: Mister Roberts

1. "That's the day I'll have some respect for you." 2. He ruptured his gall bladder and had to be hospitalized. 3. Roberts. 4. The line had Roberts commenting that Pulver had managed to get the "clap" despite having been at sea with no women around for well over a year. 5. Opportunity. 6. This was his final film. 7. Sleep. 8. Pulver. 9. Six. 10. Roberts's telling the men to take off their shirts. 11. Iodine. 12. That Roberts is dead. 13. Marlon Brando or William Holden. 14. The USS *Reluctant.* 15. Starch. 16. Ward Bond. 17. Doc. 18. They're nurses. 19. *What Price Glory.* 20. Twenty-eight. 21. *How the West Was Won* (1962). 22. A navy captain. 23. Because his palm tree has been destroyed. 24. A quart of scotch. 25. Thirty-eight.

Quiz No. 56: Mother Night

1. The Soviet Union. 2. "I don't need credit for all of them. I'm sure I could spare you a few." 3. Berlin. 4. Because he doesn't want to put her in danger. 5. "To create the most challenging role I could imagine, and then play the part myself." 6. The Brotherhood of the Walking Wounded. 7. Wirtanen. 8. Franklin Delano Rosenfeld. 9. Helga Noth. 10. Three. 11. The Black Fuhrer of Harlem. 12. *Christ Was Not a Jew.* 13. *Breakfast of Champions.* 14. "White Christmas" by Bing Crosby. 15. He is the chief of police. 16. Three. 17. Henry Gibson. 18. *Slaughterhouse-Five.* 19. His wife's. 20. Because he gets to type his memoirs. 21. "Pure hearts and heroism." 22. *I Love Trouble.* 23. "Heil Hitler!" 24. Novelist Kurt Vonnegut Jr. 25. *The White Christian Minuteman.*

Quiz No. 57: Napoleon

1. *Bonaparte et la Revolution.* 2. Brienne College. 3. Screenwriter/director Abel Gance. 4. His Uncle Paraviccini. 5. The falling hail. 6. Five hundred livres. 7. "Either I command or I say nothing." 8. Six. 9. Lucien and Joseph. 10. Danton and Marat. 11. Phelipeaux. 12. Francis Ford Coppola's father, Carmine Coppola. 13. A drum. 14. The sea. 15. Corsica. 16. Josephine de Beauharnais. 17. Filmmaker Abel Gance's wife, Marguerite Gance. 18. Danton, Marat, and Robespierre. 19. Sixty. 20. Swords and bayonets. 21. Nothing. 22. The ocean. 23. "[M]ost unpleasant." 24. Santo-Ricci. 25. Filmmaker Abel Gance died.

Quiz No. 58: 1941

1. Ocean Park. 2. Lander and McKean played the not-so-dynamic duo Lennie and Squiggy on *Laverne and Shirley.* 3. Wally. 4. Al's Grocery and Market. 5. The Serenaders. 6. Polar Bear Club. 7. Eggs. 8. Raoul. 9. *The Blues Brothers* (1980) and *Neighbors* (1981). 10. *The Night the Japs Attacked.* 11. Ninja assassins. 12. *Jaws* (1975). 13. John Wayne's. 14. A compass. 15. Their names are Ward and June; this is a reference to the television series *Leave It to Beaver.* 16. "Anybody got a light?" 17. Five. 18. Kelso. 19. Bombs. 20. RKO Pictures. 21. Airplanes. 22. His boots. 23. Tennessee. 24. Toshiro Mifune. 25. John Wayne.

Quiz No. 59: No Man's Land

1. "Dream on." 2. Two thousand. 3. The Rolling Stones. 4. Press cards, helmets, and flak jackets. 5. Cancer. 6. Tom. 7. "A pessimist thinks things can get worse. An optimist knows they can." 8. "Because I have a gun and you don't." 9. "Because I have a gun and you don't." 10. Neil. 11. A cigarette. 12. Sanja. 13. Media relations. 14. Nine thousand. 15. Germany. 16. He flips her off. 17. Because it might be booby-trapped. 18. The Global News Channel. 19. French and English. 20. Choosing his occupation. 21. A photograph of a nude man. 22. In the right leg. 23. Murder. 24. Load his weapon. 25. A cigarette lighter.

Quiz No. 60: Objective, Burma!

1. Wrenches. 2. John Barrymore's. 3. Hugh Beaumont. 4. History. 5. Himself. 6. Thirty-four. 7. *San Antonio.* 8. At a football game. 9. Fire their weapons. 10. Eleven hours. 11. Gen. Joseph W. Stilwell. 12. Because they have to know the exact location of the target. 13. Lt. Jacobs. 14. "The jeep to carry it in." 15. They were blacklisted. 16. "You'll be the first one on the ground." 17. Five. 18. A bullet. 19. *Distant Drums.* 20. Just outside Pasadena, California. 21. "You'll be all right." 22. Nervous men who need to vomit. 23. *Thank Your Lucky Stars* (1943). 24. His age. 25. New Guinea.

Quiz No. 61: Operation Petticoat

1. "It'd ruin your manicure." 2. Ninety. 3. *Some Like It Hot* (1959). 4. USS *Sea Tiger.* 5. Lt. Crandall. 6. Because he's a pig. 7. In Milwaukee. 8. Pink. 9. At Saks Fifth Avenue. 10. Poor children. 11. *The Perfect Furlough.* 12. A maternity ward. 13. Perspiration. 14. That Holden may be caught stealing and shot. 15. Ramon Gillardo. 16. Nature. 17. Encouragement. 18. The supply depot. 19. "Because I needed an officer's uniform." 20. "That way I can worry without it showing." 21. A typewriter. 22. Jamie Lee Curtis. 23. Gertie. 24. Get back into the war. 25. "She owns the tracks."

Quiz No. 62: Paths of Glory

1. Zero. 2. For not telling him sooner that he is a "degenerate, sadistic old man." 3. "[T]o hell and back." 4. Pvt. Lejeune. 5. His rifle. 6. *Spartacus* (1960). 7. The Ant Hill. 8. Cowardice in the face of the enemy. 9. Whether or not an order is "possible." 10. The human race. 11. Thomas Grey. 12. Maj. Vigdon's. 13. Personally shoot each man in the head to ensure his death. 14. Shell shock. 15. A streak of spit. 16. Sitting down. 17. Timothy Carey. 18. "Now you've got the edge on him." 19. Switzerland and France. 20. Samuel Johnson. 21. They'll face French ones. 22. Burt Lancaster. 23. Schleissheim Castle. 24. Blackmail. 25. She and director Stanley Kubrick later married, and she ultimately changed her name to Christiane Kubrick.

Quiz No. 63: The Patriot

1. Eighteen. 2. Edward. 3. *Saving Private Ryan* (1998). 4. The Ghost. 5. Green. 6. Jupiter and Mars. 7. Seven. 8. Harrison Ford. 9. Ink. 10. Eight thousand.

11. Fifteen. 12. His family's esteem. 13. The shooting of enemy officers at the outset of every battle. 14. *What Women Want, Chicken Run,* and *The Million Dollar Hotel.* 15. Susan. 16. An elected legislature. 17. Pride. 18. Brutal tactics. 19. *The Four Feathers* (2002). 20. Because British soldiers kill his wife and son. 21. Red. 22. Principles. 23. Dog. 24. Seventeen. 25. Peter Cuppin.

Quiz No. 64: Patton

1. Fleeting. 2. *Is Paris Burning?*. 3. Omar Bradley. 4. A swastika. 5. *The Last Days of Patton.* 6. Richard M. Nixon. 7. Field Marshal Erwin Rommel. 8. The Bible and Hollywood. 9. *Patton: Ordeal in Triumph* (1970) by Ladislas Farago and *A Soldier's Story* (1951) by Omar Bradley. 10. By the last bullet of the last battle of the last war. 11. Carry a pearl-handled pistol. 12. Give them a medal. 13. Read the Bible. 14. Willie. 15. *Patton: Salute to a Rebel.* 16. *Anatomy of a Murder* (1959) and *The Hustler* (1961). 17. "[A] hoot in hell." 18. *Patton: Lust for Glory* and *Blood and Guts.* 19. Because he's been trained to do so. 20. Self-inflicted wounds. 21. These tanks had not yet been introduced at the time in which the film takes place. 22. The Nazis. 23. Rod Steiger. 24. Because George C. Scott insisted the scene appear at the end of the film. Knowing he would use it at the beginning of the film anyway, director Franklin J. Schaffner opted to humor him and shoot it last. 25. His dog.

Quiz No. 65: Pearl Harbor

1. Gene Hackman. 2. Jack Ryan. 3. *Boiler Room.* 4. *Tennessee.* 5. "[B]ullshit." 6. Master Chief Carl Brashear. 7. Another sunset. 8. Friendship medals. 9. "[E]xactly where you think you are safe." 10. A sleeping giant. 11. Sunday. 12. Returning from the dead. 13. California. 14. "Not anxious to die, just anxious to matter." 15. *Black Hawk Down.* 16. Top secret. 17. Director Michael Bay's. 18. "No, you are." 19. "Well, you're a lousy friend. That's a new development." 20. Four. 21. Respect. 22. Find a way not to fight a war. 23. Ashton Kutcher. 24. The heart of a volunteer. 25. Charlize Theron.

Quiz No. 66: Platoon

1. Capt. Dale Dye, U.S. Marine Corps, who also served as the film's technical advisor. 2. Two years later, Dafoe portrayed Jesus Christ in *The Last*

Temptation of Christ (1988). 3. Three. 4. *Spin City.* 5. His grandmother. 6. *Wall Street* (1987). 7. "[G]o around a village cuttin' off heads." 8. Excuses. 9. *Cry-Baby.* 10. This was a tribute to then-girlfriend Sherilyn Fenn. 11. Kyle MacLachlan. 12. Elias and Barnes. 13. That his tour of duty is nearly completed. 14. Sidney Lumet. 15. "[S]o the world can kiss my ass." 16. The next person who falls asleep during guard duty. 17. *Born on the Fourth of July.* 18. Taylor. 19. Director Oliver Stone. 20. Himself. 21. The Indy 500. 22. *Article 99.* 23. Living Colour. 24. Red. 25. The world will turn.

Quiz No. 67: Pork Chop Hill

1. Pvt. Velie. 2. Harry Dean Stanton. 3. Lt. Suki Ohashi. 4. Love Company. 5. Thirty-one. 6. *Hamburger Hill.* 7. Lt. Joseph Clemons, whom Gregory Peck portrays in the film. 8. "[T]he more ground you take, the more you have to defend." 9. *Ocean's Eleven.* 10. One. 11. Woody Strode. 12. Robert Blake. 13. Losing his leg. 14. Their teeth. 15. The hill. 16. King Company. 17. Norman Fell. 18. Equal. 19. 135. 20. *Cape Fear* (1962). 21. "[W]e're not gonna give up any more chips." 22. Gavin MacLeod. 23. They're being bombarded with American shells. 24. Because it "always means something's coming." 25. A Cadillac convertible.

Quiz No. 68: Ran

1. The birds and the beasts. 2. Seventeen. 3. Words. 4. Ogura. 5. *Kagemusha* (1980). 6. Those who are mad. 7. Ikoma. 8. Thirty. 9. That his father should live to be one hundred years old. 10. Akira Kurosawa painted each of them by hand. 11. He is Hidetora's entertainer. 12. Kurogane. 13. The fox. 14. That anyone who assists him will be executed. 15. Because they were made by hand. 16. The flute. 17. Taro. 18. The Great Lord. 19. Tango and Saburo. 20. Three arrows held together. 21. Hidetora. 22. Warriors. 23. This was his only one. 24. With hatred. 25. *The Seven Samurai* (1954).

Quiz No. 69: The Red Badge of Courage

1. Henry Fleming and Tom Wilson. 2. Fleming. 3. Jim Conklin. 4. His fighting. 5. Cowards. 6. A woman, a dog, and a walnut tree. 7. Speaking in formation. 8. Wilson. 9. James Whitmore. 10. Hate. 11. Their ignorance. 12. George Washington. 13. His mistakes. 14. Why they're traveling up the river rather than down. 15. The artillery wagons. 16. A good soldier. 17. Ohio. 18. Wilson.

19. The wounded soldiers. 20. Twenty-two. 21. His pocket watch. 22. *Picture.* 23. His dog. 24. In real life, Murphy was the most decorated American soldier in World War II. 25. Any man who bets on him running from battle.

Quiz No. 70: Run Silent Run Deep

1. Russo. 2. Twenty-four hours. 3. An ass. 4. USS *Nerka.* 5. His medical condition. 6. He punches Cartright. 7. *Crimson Tide.* 8. The captain. 9. Sixteen. 10. Every forty-eight hours. 11. The bodies of dead crewmen. 12. *I Want to Live!* 13. Gin. 14. Swim or use a lifeboat. 15. Three. 16. The derriere of a pin-up girl whose picture hangs on the wall. 17. Five. 18. Gable and Lancaster. 19. Laura. 20. Kraut. 21. Failing. 22. A captain's jacket. 23. Bungo Pete. 24. "[S]howing her backside to Japanese submarines." 25. *Teacher's Pet.*

Quiz No. 71: Sahara

1. Men like Adolf Hitler. 2. Benito Mussolini. 3. Fred Clarkson. 4. He was a typesetter. 5. "[S]tatic and heil Hitler." 6. Doc. 7. Four. 8. A pint of water. 9. Lulubelle. 10. Frenchy. 11. Twelve. 12. Peter Lawford. 13. Tambul. 14. Forty-two. 15. A full canteen. 16. Joe. 17. Twenty years. 18. Italian. 19. Water. 20. Sidney Buchman. 21. An oasis. 22. Three swallows. 23. A horse Gunn had in the cavalry. 24. Nine. 25. Pity.

Quiz No. 72: The Sand Pebbles

1. *Somebody up There Likes Me* (1956). 2. Po-Han. 3. Request a transfer. 4. Chien. 5. $200. 6. Flags. 7. Setting a bird free. 8. This was his only nomination. 9. Chinese sailors. 10. He tosses it overboard. 11. The American gunboat. 12. Red Dog. 13. Richard Attenborough. 14. "The system you got on this ship." 15. Red Kettle Bar. 16. The San Pablo. 17. Victor Shu. 18. Army, navy, or reform school. 19. Sunday. 20. $100. 21. The U.S. Marine Corps. 22. Obey orders. 23. Gavin MacLeod. 24. Opium. 25. Utah.

Quiz No. 73: Sands of Iwo Jima

1. William Shakespeare. 3. "So did Jack the Ripper." 3. Twenty-two miles. 4. Forty minutes. 5. Conway's father, Lt. Sam Conway. 6. The American

dream. 7. He makes him sleep with it. 8. Guadalcanal. 9. Philadelphia, Pennsylvania. 10. Sixty-two days. 11. China. 12. Greek. 13. The mortar crew. 14. Handsome Dan. 15. *Thou Shalt Not Kill . . . Except.* 16. Make them wish they'd never been born. 17. Scuttlebutt. 18. Cpl. Robert Dunne. 19. Allison. 20. *Sands of Iwo Jima* is the only film on which the two collaborated. 21. The U.S. Marine Corps. 22. Helenopolis and Bass. 23. Mary. 24. $5. 25. Ten years old.

Quiz No. 74: Saving Private Ryan

1. The American flag. 2. Edith Piaf. 3. Fucked up beyond all recognition. 4. A Hitler Youth knife. 5. Axle grease. 6. English composition. 7. Adrian. 8. A morphine overdose. 9. Frank Darabont. 10. Sean, Peter, and Daniel. 11. Eight. 12. *Boiler Room.* 13. *Knockaround Guys.* 14. "No, I'm gonna shoot you because I don't like you." 15. Ninety-four. 16. Horvath. 17. Mrs. Bix. 18. James. 19. Dale Dye. 20. Dog Green Sector. 21. Daniel Dusseldorf. 22. Iowa. 23. Vecchio. 24. Twenty-three. 25. "Maybe you should shut up."

Quiz No. 75: Savior

1. Vera's father. 2. His son, Christian, and Vera's baby. 3. Luke Perry. 4. Goran. 5. It's a crucifix. 6. Oliver Stone. 7. Female. 8. "I used to be." 9. Guy. 10. *Playing by Heart.* 11. It's the same song Vera sang when she was killed. 12. She was raped by Muslims. 13. Maria. 14. Hope. 15. Nastassia Kinski. 16. Kill herself. 17. Blues. 18. A condom. 19. Yugoslavia and Canada. 20. Sugar. 21. Get off the road. 22. The movie theater. 23. *Everything That Rises.* 24. "It's war." 25. Director Peter Antonijevic.

Quiz No. 76: Sergeant York

1. *Ball of Fire.* 2. New York City. 3. Satan. 4. Jimtown. 5. Pusher. 6. American history. 7. That Gary Cooper portray him. 8. Shooting a rifle. 9. Zeb Andrews. 10. "The end of the line." 11. The governor of Tennessee. 12. Elisha Cook Jr. 13. Pastor Rosier Pile. 14. Ride the subway. 15. Sixty. 16. Seven. 17. Zero. 18. A .45 Colt automatic. 19. Bert Thompson. 20. Abraham. 21. New York City. 22. Two. 23. *Meet John Doe.* 24. June Lockhart. 25. Daniel Boone.

Quiz No. 77: The Siege of Firebase Gloria

1. Moran could not have quoted "Lucille" as it had not been released yet. This film takes place in 1968 and the song was not released until 1977. 2. Miller's head. 3. "[B]alls." 4. Bugs. 5. Two cases of peaches. 6. "Congbusters." 7. *Fletch Lives* (1989). 8. His son, Jimmy. 9. James Dean. 10. Seventeen. 11. Williams. 12. Twenty-three. 13. *Out of the Body*. 14. His grandfather's funeral. 15. A rapist. 16. *Uncommon Valor*. 17. Recon. 18. "Fuck your password." 19. Pee Wee. 20. Detroit, Michigan. 21. "[S]ome shit." 22. DiNardo. 23. The killing of the wounded enemy soldiers after the conclusion of a battle. 24. Hafner. 25. Ghost.

Quiz No. 78: Sink the Bismarck!

1. "Never forget that you are Germans. Never forget that you are Nazis." 2. Norway. 3. Two hundred. 4. Zero. 5. HMS *Ark Royal*. 6. Emotion. 7. Jonathan. 8. The *Hood* is Britain's largest warship. 9. Tom. 10. Twenty thousand. 11. "Everyone will be properly dressed at all times." 12. Johnny Horton. 13. HMS *Sheffield*. 14. Adolf Hitler. 15. In the Baltic Sea. 16. Suggestions. 17. Gunther. 18. Their having to "prove their superiority every day." 19. Capt. R.A.B. Edwards, the real-life director of operations who led the hunt for the *Bismarck*. 20. Capt. Lindemann. 21. Three. 22. *Light up the Sky!* 23. HMS *Prince of Wales*. 24. Return home. 25. His family and the sea.

Quiz No. 79: Spartacus

1. Calder Willingham. 2. Anthony Hopkins. 3. "A good body with a dull brain." 4. Spartacus. 5. Peter Brocco. 6. That he is "occasionally" obliged to act like one. 7. The republic. 8. "[D]ream of her." 9. "[I]nvariably thin." 10. Peter Ustinov. 11. "No more than I was to be born." 12. Stanley Kubrick. 13. William Randolph Hearst. 14. "[M]ost civilians." 15. Orson Welles. 16. Crassus. 17. *The Devil's Disciple* (1959). 18. Crassus attempting to seduce Antonius. 19. His hatred. 20. Wrist watches. 21. Snails and oysters. 22. *Scalawag*. 23. Sabine Bethmann. 24. Gladiators. 25. Anthony Mann.

Quiz No. 80: Stalag 17

1. 630. 2. Forty-five cigarettes. 3. Duke. 4. Otto Preminger. 5. Animal. 6. A record player. 7. "Maybe he just wanted to steal our wire cutters." 8. Forty sleeping pills. 9. Price. 10. Von Scherbach. 11. *Sunset Blvd.* (1950), *Sabrina* (1954), and *Fedora* (1978). 12. Cleveland, Ohio. 13. Two thousand. 14. Two packs of cigarettes. 15. Harry Shapiro. 16. Adolf Hitler. 17. Joey. 18. Betty Grable. 19. A Red Cross package, a blanket, and his left shoe. 20. *Mein Kampf* by Adolf Hitler. 21. Wrestling. 22. "Thank you." 23. Seven a.m. 24. Sgt. Hoffman. 25. The black queen.

Quiz No. 81: Stalingrad

1. Dr. Heider. 2. Thirty-six. 3. Clara. 4. A cigar. 5. Three years old. 6. Hans. 7. Gege. 8. Not having to worry about getting a sunburn. 9. Sabotage. 10. French. 11. Edgar. 12. Battalion 336. 13. El Alamein. 14. "Heil Hitler." 15. Corporal. 16. Manfred Rohleder. 17. Otto. 18. Kolya. 19. Wolk. 20. Viola. 21. They are cobblers. 22. Death. 23. Dying together. 24. Nine million. 25. He had destroyed three enemy tanks.

Quiz No. 82: The Steel Helmet

1. Baldy. 2. His face. 3. "There is no end to this story." 4. An officer. 5. The Korean national anthem. 6. "[Y]our heart." 7. Dirt. 8. Buddha Head. 9. *Indiana Jones and the Temple of Doom.* 10. Lt. Driscoll. 11. A box of cigars. 12. The prayer wheel. 13. The prisoner. 14. A bulletproof helmet. 15. Buddha. 16. "He's a South Korean when he's runnin' with ya, and he's a North Korean when he's runnin' after ya." 17. *Fixed Bayonets.* 18. The U.S. Infantry. 19. Joe. 20. For Zack to like him. 21. A conscientious objector. 22. "A bullet that don't go all the way." 23. A portable organ. 24. Join the U.S. Air Force. 25. *Hell and High Water.*

Quiz No. 83: The Story of G.I. Joe

1. Wingless. 2. An observation post. 3. Arab. 4. He is forty-three years old. 5. *Track of the Cat* (1954). 6. Linda Eastman, who would later become Linda McCartney (wife of Beatle Paul). 7. "It's your funeral." 8. Cleveland. 9. Elizabeth. 10. "Lousy American swine!" 11. The Purple Heart. 12. Surrender. 13. Cookie. 14. That he's won the Pulitzer Prize. 15. *Here Is Your*

War and *Brave Men*. 16. Robert Aldrich. 17. Battle experience. 18. Broken English. 19. Pyle, as well as a number of the soldiers who appear in the film, were killed in battle before the film was completed. 20. Which is the best outfit. 21. Inside the church. 22. *Ernie Pyle's Story of G.I. Joe* and *War Correspondent*. 23. The first death. 24. "The infantry soldier." 25. Mama.

Quiz No. 84: They Died with Their Boots On

1. In a teacup. 2. A bad day. 3. "Name the present commander in chief of the United States Army." 4. "[A] romantic fool." 5. Elizabeth's father, Samuel Bacon. 6. Ulysses S. Grant. 7. Gen. Sheridan. 8. After every "competent officer" has been assigned duty. 9. Because he's under orders not to speak. 10. A beefsteak and a bottle of bourbon. 11. Col. Sheridan. 12. His name. 13. Sharp. 14. "Because he's the man I'm going to marry." 15. A woman. 16. West Point. 17. He knocks him off his horse. 18. Anthony Quinn. 19. "[F]ight right." 20. He fell on his sword after being thrown from his horse. 21. A firing squad or a medal. 22. This is the only film on which all three of them worked. 23. Taipe's. 24. "A half-baked officer." 25. "[I]n front of the attacking regiment."

Quiz No. 85: They Were Expendable

1. "Sorry I couldn't do more for the squadron." 2. Gen. Douglas MacArthur. 3. "So are artificial arms." 4. *The Wings of Eagles* (1957). 5. His arm. 6. Sidney Franklin. 7. Gunners and torpedo men. 8. That he should be reassigned to a destroyer. 9. In real life, he commanded a PT boat during World War II. 10. Two. 11. Because Bond was injured in an automobile accident early in the production. 12. That it's not soup—it's dishwater. 13. The USS *Arizona*. 14. Fireflies. 15. Because he was still officially on military active duty. 16. Blood poisoning. 17. Director John Ford. 18. Razor blades and toothpaste. 19. Whales. 20. Ford slipped on a scaffold and fell twenty feet onto concrete, suffering a compound fracture to his left leg. 21. "[A]n orchestra and a floorshow." 22. Gen. Douglas MacArthur. 23. Corregidor. 24. Brick. 25. Dancing.

Quiz No. 86: The Thin Red Line

1. *Harrison's Flowers*. 2. Stein. 3. Death and the Lord. 4. Bugger. 5. *Crackers*. 6. Billy Bob Thornton. 7. Mickey Rourke. 8. Welsh. 9. *The Longest Day*

(1962). 10. Marty. 11. Tom Sizemore. 12. Bill Pullman. 13. Assume he's correct. 14. *From Here to Eternity* (1953) and *Whistle* (2003). 15. Charlie Company. 16. Tim Blake Nelson. 17. Cruel. 18. *The Player* (1992). 19. Andrew Marton. 20. "I don't want to kill you. Don't move." 21. The "wear" stripe had not yet been invented at the time in which the film takes place. 22. *O, Brother Where Art Thou?* (2000). 23. *Casualties of War* (1989). 24. Viggo Mortensen. 25. When he stops bitching.

Quiz No. 87: Thirty Seconds over Tokyo

1. Gen. James Doolittle, who led the bombing raid on Tokyo. 2. Fifteen. 3. Cowboys. 4. No one. 5. A jitterbug. 6. Two times. 7. This is the airbase where Doolittle's men actually trained. 8. Marry a flier. 9. Texas. 10. "See that you're not forced down over Japan." 11. *The Devil at Four O'Clock*. 12. That all cigarettes must be extinguished. 13. The Norton bomb sights. 14. Barracks twelve. 15. The Ruptured Duck. 16. Shorty. 17. Blake Edwards. 18. Get married. 19. Billings, Montana. 20. Lawson. 21. That she's pregnant. 22. Lt. Jacob Manch. 23. For six days. 24. Military insurance. 25. A ranch.

Quiz No. 88: Three Kings

1. He becomes a military consultant in Hollywood. 2. "No high school." 3. Airport baggage handler. 4. Necessity. 5. *The Peacemaker*. 6. Gooneybird. 7. Brian Bosworth. 8. "I don't think so." 9. Detroit, Michigan. 10. Nora Dunn. 11. *Spoils of War*. 12. Director David O. Russell. 13. "Dune coon" or "sand nigger." 14. In the buttocks of a prisoner. 15. Judas Priest. 16. Torrance, California. 17. Vig. 18. "Are we shooting?" 19. Crystal. 20. *The Perfect Storm*. 21. "Party All the Time" by Eddie Murphy. 22. "God Bless the USA." 23. $70,000. 24. Lexus. 25. Michael Jackson.

Quiz No. 89: Throne of Blood

1. In the throat. 2. Three. 3. Doubt Miki. 4. Stay and wait to be killed or take command of Lord Tsuzuki's castle. 5. The rat. 6. Fujimaki. 7. Miki's son. 8. Tsuzuki's coffin. 9. Human skeletons. 10. "The throne is yours." 11. Build it to the sky. 12. Miki. 13. Pretend as though they do not. 14. Miki's horse becoming upset. 15. Fear. 16. Friendship. 17. She disappears. 18. Hear enemies taking the castle. 19. The Cobweb Forest. 20. Miki's. 21. Fujimaki.

22. Strike first. 23. The forest moves. 24. Noriyasu and his men. 25. Yoshi-teru.

Quiz No. 90: To Be or Not to Be

1. Getting to know Maria Tura better. 2. Maria. 3. Poland's. 4. Carole Lombard. 5. "Hate and more hate." 6. A different man stands up. 7. Mel Brooks. 8. *Gestapo*. 9. "Concentration Camp Ehrhardt." 10. A laugh. 11. Leo Tolstoy's *Anna Karenina*. 12. Ernst Lubitsch. 13. The Gestapo. 14. "What he did to Shakespeare we are doing to Poland." 15. One of Siletsky's speeches. 16. The Victorian Cross. 17. The winning side. 18. "To be or not to be." 19. "Long live Poland!" 20. "[T]he air of the Gestapo." 21. "Heil, Hitler!" 22. "I'm satisfied to be the father." 23. Jump to their deaths. 24. A member of the audience walking out on them. 25. Bronski.

Quiz No. 91: Tora! Tora! Tora!

1. Whether or not to adopt the plan to attack Pearl Harbor. 2. "[A] terrible resolve." 3. *The Broken Seal* by Ladislas Farago and *Tora! Tora! Tora!* by Gordon W. Prange. 4. Minoru Ganda. 5. Radar. 6. Akira Kurosawa. 7. This was a real, unplanned accident that occurred during filming. 8. *If You Were Young: Rage* a.k.a. *Kimi ga wakamono nara*. 9. Type 21. 10. *A Thousand Clowns* (1965) and *All the President's Men* (1976). 11. They believed the film would glorify the Japanese attack while making the United States look foolish and ill-prepared. 12. Adm. Kimmel. 13. *Soylent Green* (1973). 14. "Tora-ble, Tora-ble, Tora-ble." 15. Animator Max Fleischer, famous for such characters as Popeye and Betty Boop. 16. Six. 17. *Fathom* (1967), which was based on his novel. 18. Navy Minister Zengo Yoshida. 19. Hawaii and San Francisco. 20. Operation Magic. 21. Because the cross was not erected until later, as it was built in memory of those killed in the attack on Pearl Harbor. 22. Dawn. 23. Jason Robards. 24. Forty feet. 25. The moon.

Quiz No. 92: The Train

1. Labiche and Gen. DeGaulle. 2. Arthur Penn. 3. "Papa" Boule. 4. Labiche's. 5. Saving the art. 6. His traveling to Germany. 7. Lancaster performed them himself. 8. Coffee. 9. A phoney sign is hung over the sign that reads

"Pont a Mousson." 10. Bread. 11. Walter Bernstein. 12. A shovel. 13. The French National Railway and the French military. 14. Sgt. Schwartz. 15. Paul. 16. A madhouse. 17. He stops the train inside a tunnel. 18. *The Young Savages.* 19. "[T]heir hopes, their nation's honor!" 20. France. 21. Renoir. 22. Jacques. 23. *Scorpio* (1973). 24. A prophet. 25. *Seven Days in May.*

Quiz No. 93: The Tuskegee Airmen

1. Assign him to a desk job. 2. Singular. 3. *Eleanor Roosevelt's Niggers.* 4. Hannibal Lee. 5. *Boyz N the Hood* (1991). 6. Iowa. 7. *Stick and Rudder.* 8. Roberts. 9. Warner played Theo Huxley and Payne played Lance. 10. "Train," or "A-Train." 11. Lt. Col. Benjamin Davis. 12. Fifty. 13. *The Walking Dead.* 14. In Harlem. 15. Not having any. 16. Red. 17. Lee. 18. *Glory.* 19. "Uppity niggers." 20. Lee. 21. *Soul Food.* 22. To die by fire. 23. Berlin. 24. *Homicide: Life on the Street.* 25. Peoples.

Quiz No. 94: Twelve O'Clock High

1. Good navigators. 2. Angels and generals. 3. Zimmerman. 4. Maj. Cobb. 5. Ten. 6. He's a lawyer. 7. Pride. 8. "Leper Colony." 9. Sgt. Ernie McIlhaney. 10. Scotch. 11. Nine. 12. Ten. 13. Twenty-one. 14. Cigarettes and coffee. 15. The formation. 16. Hard luck. 17. Jesse. 18. Gately. 19. Stovall. 20. "Daylight precision bombing." 21. All of them. 22. Nineteen thousand feet. 23. A pair of boots. 24. Gately. 25. A zoo.

Quiz No. 95: U-571

1. It's American. 2. *Frailty.* 3. The British ship is dropping depth charges on the submarine. 4. Andy. 5. Jon Bon Jovi. 6. Hirsch. 7. "I am U-571. Destroy me." 8. He was a fisherman. 9. The Enigma Code Machine. 10. Dahlgren. 11. *Fail Safe* (2000). 12. Scooters. 13. That he's half-German. 14. The British sailors who actually captured the Enigma in World War II. 15. Ronald Parker. 16. Mazzola's. 17. Dino De Laurentiis. 18. "I don't know." 19. A Military Police officer. 20. "Pornography and dirty letters stinking of French perfume." 21. 150 feet. 22. *The Two Jakes.* 23. "[S]ee to it" that every member of his crew dies so that no one can be interrogated by the enemy. 24. Steward Eddie Carson. 25. *A Bright Shining Lie* (1998).

Quiz No. 96: Von Ryan's Express

1. A woman accused them of assault. 2. They are executed. 3. He'd struck Battaglia with a stick. 4. It smashes the victim's larnyx. 5. *The Pride and the Passion*. 6. *The Train* (1964). 7. *None But the Brave*. 8. Fincham. 9. "I will . . . on the way out." 10. Gabriella. 11. The escape of even one prisoner. 12. *King Rat* (1965). 13. *Around the World in Eighty Days* (1956). 14. Capt. Oriani. 15. That they want to help her. 16. Two tons. 17. Because many of the uniforms were too bloody to wear. 18. Because it's an American pilot's watch. 19. "A bird colonel." 20. He burns all of the prisoners' clothing. 21. There is no such song. 22. Mepacrine. 23. Because the engineer spots the missing rail in time to stop the train. 24. Ryan. 25. An American officer.

Quiz No. 97: We Were Soldiers

1. "Custer was a pussy. You ain't." 2. Harvard. 3. *We Were Soldiers Once . . . and Young*. 4. One. 5. *Saving Private Ryan*. 6. To leave his men on the battlefield and return to headquarters for debriefing. 7. Sam and Dave. 8."Broken arrow." 9. "We were fathers, brothers, husbands, sons . . . we were soldiers." 10. 395. 11. Second lieutenant. 12. Julie. 13. Landing zone. 14. "What are you, the fucking weatherman now?" 15. A noncombatant. 16. Cabbies. 17. "Bingo." 18. Methodist. 19. *The Man in the Iron Mask* (1998), which he also directed. 20. Crazy Horse. 21. This scene does not appear in the film (although one dying soldier utters those famous last words). 22. Jimmy Nakayama. 23. "Snake Shit." 24. Grandpa. 25. "That my men died . . .and I didn't."

Quiz No. 98: When Trumpets Fade

1. The film was quite misleadingly sold in Australia as *Hamburger Hill 2*, the sequel to *Hamburger Hill* (1987). 2. Roy. 3. Manning. 4. Joe Lombardi. 5. The Battle of the Bulge. 6. "Nobody dies." 7. Bobby. 8. Doug. 9. *Hell Is for Heroes*. 10. Kick his teeth out. 11. *The Dogs of War*. 12. Lt. Lucas. 13. *A Midnight Clear* (1992). 14. Sandy. 15. Dwight Yoakam. 16. What his men think of him. 17. More than twenty-four thousand. 18. "I'm gonna owe you shit." 19. A Section Eight discharge. 20. Apple. 21. Ron Eldard. 22. Three. 23. Stay alive. 24. *Born on the Fourth of July* (1989). 25. *Magic in the Water* (1995).

Quiz No. 99: Where Eagles Dare

1. Maj. Bernard Himmler. 2. Women. 3. *Ice Station Zebra* (1968). 4. "The Castle of Eagles." 5. Dusseldorf. 6. Two parallel scars. 7. Because he's American. 8. Morris. 9. Col. Turner. 10. Broadsword. 11. The pilot. 12. To kill Adolf Hitler. 13. You can't taste it. 14. Director Brian G. Hutton and producer Elliott Kastner. 15. Corporal. 16. "Major, right now you have me about as confused as I ever hope to be." 17. "[E]ntertaining soldiers of the Fatherland." 18. *The Guns of Navarone.* 19. Mary. 20. Maria Shank. 21. Cartright Jones. 22. A joke. 23. The Office of Strategic Services. 24. All of them. 25. Wings.

Quiz No. 100: Windtalkers

1. *Face/Off* (1997). 2. *Broken Arrow* (1996). 3. Camp Pendleton. 4. George Washington Yahzee. 5. Yahzee's uniform. 6. Charlie. 7. South Philadelphia. 8. Because he didn't know it. 9. Sake. 10. Francis Ford Coppola. 11. His left. 12. A sheep. 13. Fifteen. 14. "For not getting killed." 15. Enders. 16. Rita. 17. $3. 18. To put him out of his misery. (He's on fire.) 19. *Captain Corelli's Mandolin* (2001). 20. Endersini. 21. He is beheaded by a sword. 22. He was eight years old. 23. Ox. 24. Forty-eight. 25. Hungry.

War Film Master Quiz #1: Name the Actor

1. Laurence Fishburne. 2. Mel Gibson. 3. John Wayne. 4. James Whitmore. 5. Henry Fonda. 6. Kirk Douglas. 7. R. Lee Ermey. 8. Lee Marvin. 9. Claude Akins. 10. Errol Flynn. 11. Sean Connery. 12. Roger Moore. 13. Sam Elliott. 14. James Edwards. 15. Robert Duvall. 16. Jeff Chandler. 17. Gary Cooper. 18. Clint Eastwood. 19. Van Johnson. 20. James Coburn. 21. Telly Savalas. 22. Cliff Robertson. 23. William Holden. 24. Robert Mitchum. 25. Richard Burton.

War Film Master Quiz #2: Name the Director

1. John Wayne. 2. Keith Gordon. 3. John Ford. 4. Robert Aldrich. 5. Kenn Annakin. 6. Steven Spielberg. 7. Edward Dmytryk. 8. Francis Ford Coppola. 9. Michael Curtiz. 10. Samuel Fuller. 11. Howard Hawks. 12. John Frankenheimer. 13. Stanley Kubrick. 14. John Huston. 15. Brian G.

Hutton. 16. John Irvin. 17. Zoltan Korda. 18. Tay Garnett. 19. David Lean. 20. Mervyn LeRoy. 21. Lewis Milestone. 22. Mark Robson. 23. Oliver Stone. 24. Raoul Walsh. 25. William A. Wellman.

War Film Master Quiz #3: Name the War

1. Civil War. 2. World War I. 3. Crimean War. 4. Civil War. 5. World War I. 6. World War II. 7. World War I. 8. Operation Desert Storm. 9. Vietnam War. 10. French and Indian War. 11. Civil War. 12. Korean War. 13. World War II. 14. World War I. 15. Korean War. 16. Operation Desert Storm. 17. World War I. 18. Vietnam War. 19. World War II. 20. Civil War. 21. World War II. 22. Civil War. 23. Korean War. 24. World War I. 25. World War I.

War Film Master Quiz #4: Name the Film

1. *Das Boot* (1981). 2. *The Story of G.I. Joe* (1945). 3. *The Battle of the Bulge* (1965). 4. *Kelly's Heroes* (1970). 5. *Three Kings* (1999). 6. *The Bridges at Toko-Ri* (1955). 7. *The Great Escape* (1963). 8. *Hell in the Pacific* (1968). 9. *Napoleon* (1927). 10. *A Midnight Clear* (1992). 11. *Full Metal Jacket* (1987). 12. *Savior* (1998). 13. *Sands of Iwo Jima* (1949). 14. *Midway* (1976). 15. *Von Ryan's Express* (1965). 16. *The Train* (1964). 17. *The General* (1927). 18. *Windtalkers* (2002). 19. *1941* (1979). 20. *Platoon* (1986). 21. *Apocalypse Now* (1979). 22. *Sergeant York* (1941). 23. *Catch-22* (1970). 24. *Pearl Harbor* (2001). 25. *The Caine Mutiny* (1954).

War Film Master Quiz #5: Portrayals

1. Cliff Robertson. 2. John Voight. 3. Tom Berenger. 4. Robert Duvall. 5. David Grace. 6. Robert Barrat. 7. Gregory Peck. 8. Kirk Douglas. 9. George C. Scott. 10. Glenn Ford. 11. Karl Malden. 12. Audie Murphy. 13. Gary Cooper. 14. James Mason. 15. Karl Michael Vogler. 16. Wolfgang Preiss. 17. Werner Hinz. 18. Christopher Plummer. 19. James Mason. 20. Errol Flynn. 21. Robert Shaw. 22. Richard Mulligan. 23. Spencer Tracy. 24. Alec Baldwin. 25. Ralph Fiennes.

Acknowledgments

~

The author would like to thank the following individuals for their assistance, encouragement, and patience: God, my wife, Mary, Dan and Sherry Rausch, Norman and Marion Leistikow, John White, Steve Spignesi, Richard Ember, Michael Dequina, F. X. Feeney, Mike White, George Beahm, Fred Rosenberg, Josh Barnett, Cherie Fitzwater, Ronald Riley, Henry Nash, Peter Modesitt, Cyndee and Sam Timmerman, Aron Taylor, Mark Gardner, Sean Westhoff, Chris Watson, Ryan Kasson, Ryan Robertson, John Chapman, Kerri Hoisington, Ryan Hixon, J. R. Bookwalter, Keith Gordon, Ethan Hawke, and Jake Jackson. I would also like to thank my three beautiful daughters, Jordan, Jaiden, and Jalyn—a.k.a. "the Unholy Trinity"—for occasionally tearing up the house, fighting with one another, and pestering the cat in a manner quiet enough so as not to disturb me while working on this project.

About the Author

~

Andrew J. Rausch is the author of *Hollywood's All-Time Greatest Stars: A Quiz Book* (Citadel Press) and *The 100 Greatest American Films: A Quiz Book* (Citadel Press). He writes about movies for publications, including *Film Threat, Ain't It Cool News, Bright Lights Film Journal, Creative Screenwriting,* and *Shock Cinema.* He has worked on numerous B movies in various capacities, including executive producer, script supervisor, composer, and actor. He lives in Parsons, Kansas.

The author of the Foreward, **Keith Gordon,** is an accomplished screenwriter/director whose credits include *The Chocolate War* (1988), *Wild Palms* (1993), *Waking the Dead* (2000), and *The Singing Detective* (2003), as well as *A Midnight Clear* (1992) and *Mother Night* (1996), which are covered in this volume. In addition, Gordon is also a respected actor who has appeared in many films, including *Jaws 2* (1978), *All That Jazz* (1979), *Dressed to Kill* (1980), and *Christine* (1983).